MORE POWER SEWING

Masters Techniques for the 21st Century

Sandra Betzina Webster

author of *Fear of Sewing*
and *Power Sewing*

REVISED EDITION

Practicality Press
New York

This book is the result of more than four years of experiments and discussions with masters in the field of sewing. Many names are mentioned; many others preferred anonymity. For all named or unnamed who made this book possible, I thank you.

I am also grateful for four children and a husband who acknowledge and support my obsession to turn everything I learn in this field into the printed word.

Practicality Press
An imprint of Multi Media Communicators, Inc.
575 Madison Ave., Suite 1006
New York, NY 10022

Illustrations by Tina Cash-Walsh, Amy Maeda and Melanie Graysmith.
Photography by Barbara Thompson.

ISBN 1-880630-14-1

Library of Congress Catalog Card Number: 93-084530

Printed in the United States of America

Table of Contents

BEHIND THE JACKET SCENE

When to Underline

Is it necessary to underline a garment that will be lined? In some instances, yes. A lining's purpose is to reduce wrinkles while giving a finished appearance to the inside of the garment. The purpose of underlining is to support weak fabric or prevent interfacing and seam allowances from showing through.

Thus, white, off-white, and most pastels need to be underlined. If you are making a white jacket and plan to wear it over a colored or black shirt, you'll need underlining to prevent colors from showing through. If you can't decide whether to underline or not, cut out the garment. Sew a seam sample in a scrap. Press the seam open and superimpose the seam sample on your intended lining fabric. Are the seams visible? Next, superimpose seam sample with one layer of lining behind it onto contrasting fabric. If the seam allowances are visible in either instance, you'll need underlining.

Cotton batiste and pima cotton make the best underlinings because they are soft and pliable. Stores that carry quilting and/or heirloom sewing supplies always stock a good selection.

A wool crepe jacket should always be underlined because it is porous. If you can't find batiste or pima cotton underlining in a suitable color, lining fabric also works.

Underlining is a simple procedure. Cut the underlining pieces exactly the same size as outer fabric pieces. Place the underlining piece against the wrong side of the garment piece. Hand baste them together with long stitches. The common method of using dots of glue in seam allowances to glue underlining to garment is faster, but makes seam allowances stiff and more visible from the outside.

Do not machine sew underlining to garment before seaming. This extra machine stitching will cause fabric to draw up slightly, creating puckers in the seam that cannot be pressed out. Hand baste underlining fabric to garment pieces. Pin garment for construction and sew underlining and garment piece as one.

Facing
Hong Kong

■ To finish raw edges on front facings between the hem and lining on a jacket, use a strip of lining to make a Hong Kong finish. This finish is also an appropriate finish for jacket sleeves which feature a vent.

Silk Jacket

A silk jacket is one of the most versatile pieces you will ever own. Not only can you wear it all year, but if you underline the way I suggest, the jacket will resist wrinkles and retain its crisp appearance.

Without underlining, a silk jacket will lack "behind the scenes" support, creating the appearance of a silk blouse. With slightly more effort, you can move your garment out of the blouse category into the jacket class.

After you cut out the jacket from the fashion fabric, cut out all of the main pieces except the sleeve from flannelette. You are probably most familiar with flannelette used in baby's receiving blankets and pajamas.

Preshrink the flannelette before cutting by running it through the washer and dryer. Don't forget this step. Flannelette definitely shrinks. You have now cut flannelette for the front, side front, back, and side back pieces.

For additional support, fuse a layer of fusible knit tricot interfacing to the wrong side (non-fuzzy) of the flannelette on the front and side front pieces. Back and side back do not need extra support, therefore they are not interfaced. If all main pieces were underlined with flannelette and interfaced, the jacket would be too warm.

Since we are using the flannelette as underlining to give the silk support, the next step is to hand baste the flannelette to the wrong side of the main pattern pieces. Place the fuzzy side of the flannelette against the wrong side of the silk on front, side front, side back, and back. The front and side front have an additional layer of interfacing fused to the flannelette. After placing the fuzzy side of the flannelette against the wrong side of the silk on these pieces, you can see the fusible interfacing. While some sewers prefer gluing underlining to hand basting within the seam allowances, hand basting is preferable for keeping the seam allowances soft.

Facings, upper and undercollar, while not underlined with flannelette, need interfacing to give body. Fusibles are not recommended for application on silk because they leave a bubbly appearance after dry cleaning. Interface these pieces with a non-fusible medium-weight interfacing such as Armo Soft or Stay Shape. Jacket construction can now proceed as usual.

Flannelette is not used to underline the sleeve since this additional layer will make the jacket too warm in summer. Sleeve is completed with sleeve lining only.

Before hemming, trim flannelette out of hems. Line with China silk, "Ambiance" (Bemberg rayon) or silk crepe de chine.

This jacket is cared for by dry cleaning, not hand washing.

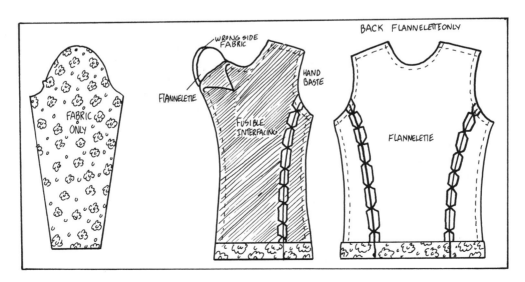

Jacket Support Secrets

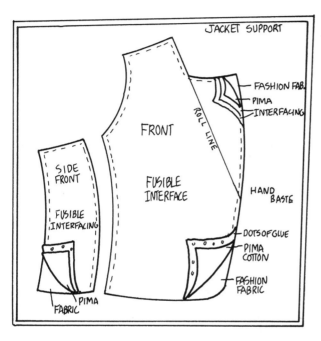

Do the lapels on your jackets lack the crispness found in their ready-to-wear counterparts? Perhaps you are using the wrong interfacing. If you were able to peek inside of an expensive ready-to-wear jacket, this is what you would find:

The entire front of the jacket is underlined with fusible knitted tricot interfacing or a similar weight fusible product. If jacket front has two pieces—a front and side front, both are interfaced. This interfacing is used to underline the front of a lightweight jacket such as raw silk or linen. Whisper Weft or a similar fusible product is used for a medium-weight jacket such as flannel or wool tweed. Using fusible interfacing as an underlining on the jacket front gives support to pockets and buttonholes as well as to the entire jacket front. It also prevents the slight vertical wrinkle which extends from shoulder to armhole parallel to armhole seam seen on most home-sewn creations.

Whisper Weft on the facing, upper and under collar, is a popular choice for most jackets. This ensures crisp lapels as well as cushioning lapel and upper collar from seam impressions in the pressing stage. If you

desire a very crisp looking man-tailored jacket, Suit Shape on the facing, upper and under collar, will give you these results, while still using fusible knitted tricot as front underlining.

Whenever using fusibles, always experiment on your fashion fabric to make sure no bubbles appear or interfacing "see-through" occurs. If the fabric is not porous, such as gabardine, you are not going to get a permanent bond. Therefore, if for any reason you cannot use a fusible directly on your fabric, either use a sew-in interfacing or cut an underlining for fronts and facings, fusing to the underlining instead. Pima cotton and batiste are the most popular underlining fabrics because they are soft and do not impose themselves on the outward appearance of the garment. While desirable, they are sometimes difficult to find. Fabric stores which specialize in quilting or heirloom sewing supplies always have a good supply of batiste and pima on hand. Preshrink these fabrics before using as underlinings, then fuse with an interfacing based on the results you desire in the finished garment (described earlier).

Is there ever an instance where an entire garment would be fused? Yes. If you were making a jacket from a loose weave, such as a hand woven or raw silk, a layer of fusible knitted tricot would make the fabric stronger, less likely to develop "pulls" in the thread. Another instance for total jacket fusing would be to give strength to a soft fabric (such as rayon crepe), yielding a more tailored result.

Press-on interfacings are a tremendous timesaver. Press-ons are used in the ready-to-wear industry primarily for this reason. If you have the time and the inclination, non-press-on products such as hair canvas can be substituted. Keep in mind that hair canvas cannot be included in the seam allowances. You may prefer to use press-on products because they tend to give a softer, tailored feeling, popular in today's fashion for women.

For extra lapel crispness, cut a triangular piece of Whisper Weft with the grainline parallel to the roll line. Place the triangular piece of interfacing against the fusing on the jacket front. This will provide the additional layer of interfacing on the lapel used in 90% of better ready-to-wear jackets.

Lapel Shaping

Regardless of what type of interfacing you use for tailoring, machine pad stitching in the lapel area can develop a memory for the lapel which adds to the professional look. In the lapel area, sew rows of machine stitching ¼ inch apart, parallel to the roll line. Not stitching by machine in the last ¾ inch of the lapel point will prevent stretching the point of the lapel. Machine stitching shows through to the back of the lapel, but will not be visible when facing is attached and lapel turns back.

Taping the roll line accomplishes two things: it prevents the bias fold on the lapel from stretching during pressing and it brings the lapel closer to the body in the slight hollow between the shoulder and the bust.

Lay a piece of twill tape along the roll line, on the side away from the lapel. Twill tape is stretched only in the middle third of the roll line. Starting at the top of the roll line near the neck, sew the twill tape to the roll line with no stretching for the first third. Using a fabric marker or chalk, draw a line through the twill tape and onto the jacket at the bottom of the second third of the roll line. Lift the twill tape and shift it down ¼ inch, so that the mark on the twill tape is ¼ inch lower than the mark on the jacket. Now you will notice extra fullness in the lapel under the twill tape. The feed dog will assist in easing this portion of the jacket to the twill tape as you sew the twill tape to the second third. The last third of the lapel is not eased. Sew the last third of the lapel to the twill tape. Stop machine stitching the tape to the lapel two inches above the top button on the roll line. Finish the last two inches by hand. Although most of the tape can be applied by machine, hand sew the tape for the last two inches above the top button to prevent visible machine stitching when the lapel rolls back.

Place interfaced lapel over a tailor's ham. Begin pressing with the iron parallel to the roll line. Press out toward the point of the lapel, rolling and shaping the lapel as you go. Press the remainder of the interfacing on the jacket front on a flat surface.

To eliminate the slightly curved seam often found in the short seam of the lapel points, try this technique: When joining the lapel to the jacket, after you turn the corner on the point of the lapel, begin to decrease the seam allowance to ½ inch, tapering back to a 5/8 inch seam allowance when you stop at the dot marking the join of the collar. If you suspect that the lapel may stretch slightly (loosely woven fabric) as you sew this seam, sew over ¼ inch strip of twill tape which begins and ends ½ inch short of the ends of this short seam to eliminate bulk. Reducing this short seam slightly in the center counteracts the force of gravity which makes the seam sink slightly in the middle of the short edge on the finished lapel.

If the lapel point on the facing is over an inch longer than the point of the collar, the lapel is peaked and needs the additional support of twill tape. Insert twill tape after turning the corner on the lapel while joining the jacket and the facing. In addition to twill tape, this seam should always be sewn in a gradual decrease from 5/8 to ½ inch in the center of the seam joining facing to jacket front from lapel point to dot indicating joint of collar to jacket.

These tips, combined with step-by-step pressing, will yield tailored results and praise from even the most critical eye.

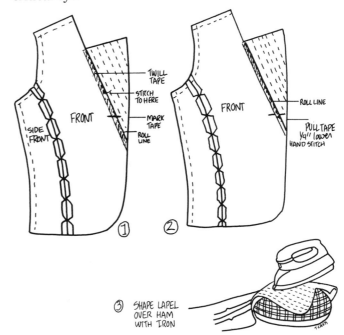

① ②

③ SHAPE LAPEL OVER HAM WITH IRON

Unlined Jacket

If you live in a hot climate or vacation in one, an unlined jacket can be a good friend. If you have time to make only one, consider making an unlined jacket in black or off-white linen. Linen comes in many weights. Make sure you purchase jacket weight, not blouse weight. By purchasing an additional half yard, the fronts can be cut double, eliminating the need for a facing and providing a clean finish to the inside of the jacket front, covering inside pocket construction.

Fuse jacket front and side front with fusible knitted tricot. Cut Whisper Weft in the shape of the facing pattern. Apply Whisper Weft to the second set of jacket fronts which will be used as the front jacket lining.

Unless the fabric is very lightweight, side seams will be pressed open. The side seam allowance which faces the front will be hidden by the second jacket front.

Since the back of the jacket will remain unlined, decide on an attractive seam finish. My first preferences are flashy seam finish (page 64) or the Hong Kong finish (see *Power Sewing*, page 197). Contrasting color in a seam finish is an attractive part of the design. This seam finish will be used on both sides of the seam in center back, side back, and one half of the side seam. Use the same treatment to finish armholes and hem.

The order for unlined jacket construction is as follows: Join front, side front, side back, back and shoulder seams. Press seams open. Join second jacket front to front edges. Complete collar. Attach second jacket front (acting as facing) to side seam, covering front side seam allowance.

Finish center back, side back, back half of side seams. Set in sleeves. Finish armhole with an attractive seam finish. Press up jacket and sleeve hems. Trim seam allowances out of hems. Finish hem edges with attractive seam finish. Press well. Hand sew covered shoulderpad into armhole.

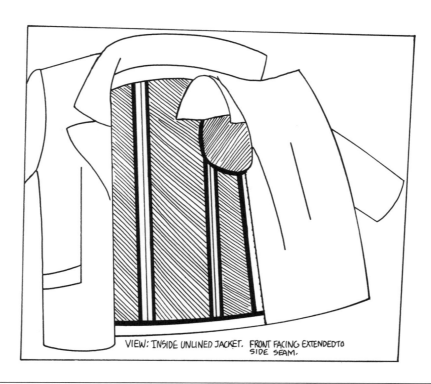

VIEW: INSIDE UNLINED JACKET. FRONT FACING EXTENDED TO SIDE SEAM.

Demonstrated on *Power Sewing* Video #7: *Hassle-Free Designer Jackets.*

Padstitch

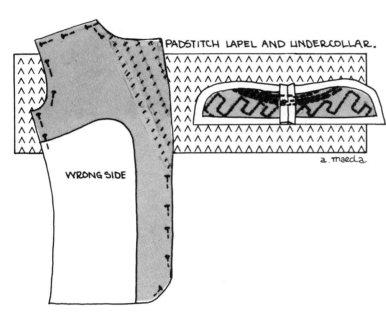

PADSTITCH LAPEL AND UNDERCOLLAR.

WRONG SIDE

a. maeda

Once a year you owe it to yourself to make an outfit whose life will extend far beyond a season or two. Think through the needs of your wardrobe carefully, and decide what piece is worth the extra amount of time and attention—perhaps a fall coat or a medium-weight blazer.

If you enjoy handwork and don't mind spending a little extra construction time, padstitching will give your lapels a memory, as well as a contour that will encourage a smooth fit over the chest area. Padstitches are small diagonal basting stitches, worked in rows, that attach the interfacing to the garment in the lapel and collar area.

On the wrong side of the garment, pin the lapel interfacing—usually a hair canvas—at the shoulder, armhole, neckline and front edge, from the top buttonhole to the hem. For sharper edges, use the technique in *Power Sewing*, page 71, "Working with Hair Canvas." Leave the lapel area unpinned, facing matching garment thread, attach the interfacing and the garment fabric at the roll line with small diagonal basting stitches. A diagonal stitch sewn at right angles to the edge of the garment will keep the interfacing from shifting throughout the life of the garment.

Roll the lapel over your hand as you work, creating a lapel roll, and molding the lapel as you sew. Try to catch only a thread or two of the garment fabric as you padstitch. Padstitch in rows $3/8$ inches apart, making each stitch $1/4$ to $3/8$ inch from the last. Always keep each new row of padstitching parallel to the roll line, which is where you started.

Hand padstitching the interfacing to the undercollar is the most effective technique for preshaping the collar. After pinning the interfacing to the undercollar, mark the roll line. Padstitching is not necessary in the seam allowances. To eliminate bulk, trim the interfacing $3/4$ to $7/8$ inch away from the seam line, depending on the weight of the fabric. Trim interfacing further away from the seam in heavier fabric as the trimmed seam allowance will add bulk enough.

Make the first row of padstitches along the roll line. Working toward the neck, make rows parallel to the roll line. To padstitch the remainder of the collar, begin at center back. Rolling the collar over your hand, padstitch diagonally, using the grain on the hair canvas or the garment fabric as a guide. The grainlines will be the same. Working in rows $3/4$ inch apart and with stitches $1/4$ inch apart, continue to padstitch the undercollar, working from the center back out to the collar ends. Padstitch each half separately. This method is taught in the tailoring class at The Sewing Workshop in San Francisco.

■ Roberta Carr in her video "Couture Techniques" gives excellent step-by-step, close-up instructions for padstitching. *(See Sources).

Chest Shield

What a disappointment to complete a coat or jacket and notice the shadow of shoulder pads making their presence obvious. The only insurance against this type of disappointment is a custom shield between the garment fabric and the pad. The shield serves two purposes: To make the shoulder pads invisible and to fill in the slight hollow between the shoulder and the chest on the jacket front. Both men and women's jackets require a shield.

If you have access to a tailoring supply house such as Bay Area Tailor Supply (see Sources), the pre-cut chest piece for a man's jacket front has the shield already in place. A pre-cut chest piece for a man's jacket can be adapted for a woman's jacket by merely cutting the extra padding included in the front shield above the bust.

To make your own shield pattern, cut a shield piece from the jacket front following the shoulder, armhole and roll line markings. The chest piece will extend from 2 inches underarm, around the armhole, over the shoulder, up to the roll line, then slope up over the bust and down to connect with the 2 inch extension underarm. Eliminate shield from all seam allowances to cut down on bulk.

Depending on the weight of the outer fabric, the shield can be cut of polyester fleece, pellon, or Suit Shape.

To help the jacket maintain its shape after wearings as well as give the jacket front crispness, underline the entire jacket front with a lightweight fusible such as knitted tricot interfacing, or a nonfusible preshrunk lightweight cotton such as cotton batiste. Join the shield to the front underlining so that the shield will be the layer between the lining and the underlining. A shoulder pad sewn in after the underlining will be cushioned by the shield. Therefore, the shield will soften the line of the shoulder pad.

To cushion the jacket back from shoulder pad imprint as well as prevent the back from stretching across the shoulders, underline the upper jacket back with a nonfusible interfacing such as Stay Shape. Use pattern neck and armholes as a guide, cutting down 2 inches underarm. Arch up toward the center back and down again to the opposite armhole. An extra layer of fusible weft, hair canvas or lambswool is then applied to upper back underlining. Using shoulder and armhole as a guide, cut back shield $1\frac{1}{8}$ inch smaller than shoulder and armhole. Pad stitch back shield to upper back underlining. All structural work in jacket is concealed by the lining.

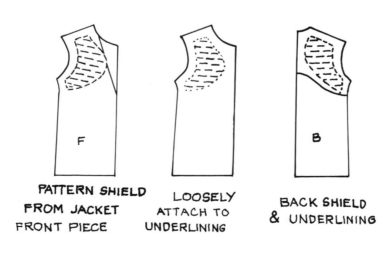

PATTERN SHIELD FROM JACKET FRONT PIECE

LOOSELY ATTACH TO UNDERLINING

BACK SHIELD & UNDERLINING

M. GRAYSMITH ©

Lapel Perfect

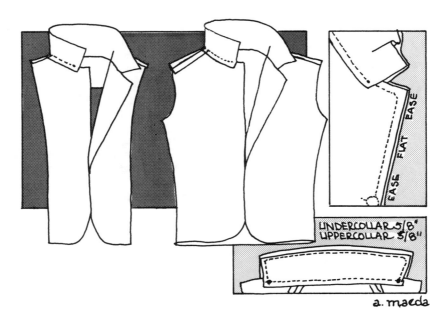

UNDERCOLLAR 5/8"
UPPERCOLLAR 5/8"

EASE FLAT EASE

a. maeda

Probably the most time-consuming aspect of making a jacket is lapel construction. For most people, the process provides aggravation and often yields less than perfect results.

Accuracy in both marking and sewing is critical to a perfect lapel. Make sure that pattern markings on all pieces are clearly visible.

Cut a back neck facing even if this piece is eliminated from the pattern. Use your jacket back pattern piece to get the correct shape at neck and shoulder. Cut the facing to match the width of the front facing. Sew shoulder seams in jacket and facings—exact 5/8 inch seam allowance are mandatory. If this is not done, the collar and neckline will not fit precisely. Staystitch necklines of jacket and facings at ⅝ inch. Clip necklines at 1 inch intervals.

With right sides together, pin upper collar to acket facing, matching markings. Sew in one coninuous seam, from one large dot to the next.

Then with right sides together, pin undercollar to jacket, matching markings. Sew undercollar to jacket, again from one large dot to the next in a continuous seam. Use small reinforcing stitches 1 inch before each

dot marking, stopping stitching precisely at the dot marking. Do not backstitch. Pin front facings to jacket front. Ease the facing to the jacket for 5 inches above the top button, sew the remainder of the seam flat, then ease for the last 2 inches again.

The ease near the roll line enables the lapel to turn out easily and the ease at the very corner enables the corner to lie flat.

Handwalk two stitches diagonally when turning the corner at the top of the lapel. Switch to small stitches ½ inch from the dot. Stop exactly at the large dot— the place where the collar joins the jacket.

Now it is time to close the collar. With right sides together, match up outer and undercollar, matching dots exactly. Start sewing at center back of collar. Handwalk two small stitches diagonally at corners to insure a sharp point. Sew from center back to large dot. Stop exactly at the dot, never sewing on more than two fabric thicknesses at one time. Do not backstitch, this puts too much thread in the seam and it will not press properly. Switch to small reinforcing stitches 1 inch before the place you want to stop. Proceed with other half of the collar.

Shawl Collars

While the simplicity and feminine curves of the shawl collar are appealing, a few tips are needed for professional results to prevent a pouffy appearance and a collar which refuses to flatten out along the contours of the coat or jacket.

For starters, the upper collar must be ⅛ to ¼ inch larger than the undercollar to enable it to "wrap around" the undercollar (turn of the cloth principle). Check upper and undercollar pattern pieces. If they are the same size, trim off ⅛ inch on light and medium weight fabrics and ¼ inch from heavy weight fabrics from the undercollar outside edge (not the neck edge).

Cut an underlining for the upper shawl collar in cotton organdy or cotton batiste. Cut fusible or nonfusible interfacing for the top collar. Hymo interfacing is too heavy for shawl collars. Acro makes a good choice for medium weight fabrics, Whisper Weft a good choice for lightweight fabrics. Fuse or hand sew interlacing to undercollar underlining. Join underlining to upper collar. Underlining the upper collar softens seam edges and prevents any unwanted effects of fusible interfacing which will not stay fused.

Interface the undercollar with the same interfacing used on the upper collar. Underlining the undercollar is unnecessary.

Consider piping the outside edge of the shawl collar. Piping helps the undercollar roll under and stay there. Edgestitching is helpful on most fabrics, but piping is an excellent choice for a fabric which does not press well such as gaberdine. Topstitching is another option for difficult fabrics.

After collar application is complete and seams trimmed, hand baste shawl collar into position with silk thread. Silk thread provides elasticity and will not leave press marks. Press and pound with tailor's clapper. If the upper and undercollar do not seem to be working together as a unit, spot fuse every 6 inches with ½ inch pieces of fusible web along the seam joining the facing to the lining.

Stab stitch upper collar to undercollar along the neck seam with double thread run through beeswax for strength.

A contrasting fabric shawl collar is often an attractive option. Construct in the same way. After pressing, you may find that you need to release the seam slightly where the shawl collar joins the hem. Since fabrics relax in different ways, one fabric may relax more than another. On a project in wool crepe with a moire taffeta shawl collar, the wool crepe relaxed on the jacket. The taffeta did not relax on the collar. The problem was solved by releasing ⅛ to ¼ inch from the taffeta seam allowance at the hem.

Shawl Collars

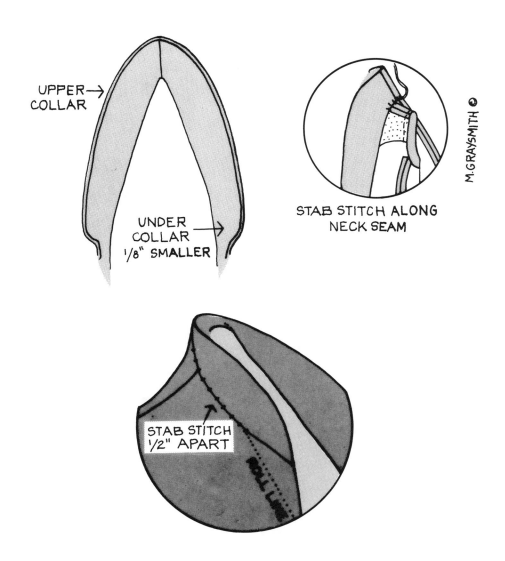

UPPER COLLAR →

UNDER COLLAR 1/8" SMALLER →

STAB STITCH ALONG NECK SEAM

M.GRAYSMITH ©

STAB STITCH 1/2" APART

ROLL LINE

■ Establish a roll line on garment before joining upper and under shawl collars. Stretch twill tape slightly (1/2 inch between shoulder and beginning of roll line) when applied. (See chapter "Lapel Shaping with Fusibles.") This step is mandatory if you want to avoid shawl collar gaposis.

Grade/Press/Stab Stitch Lapels

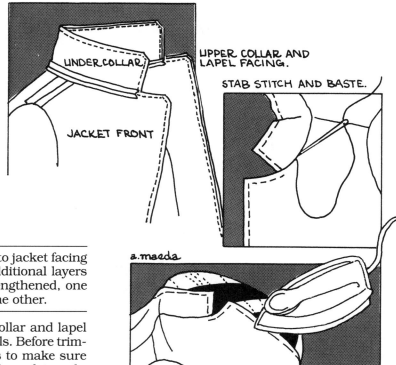

UNDERCOLLAR

UPPER COLLAR AND LAPEL FACING.

STAB STITCH AND BASTE.

JACKET FRONT

a.maeda

■ Lengthen stitch when joining facing to jacket facing or coat front to compensate for the additional layers of interfacing. If stitch length is not lengthened, one front of the coat will be shorter than the other.

Grading and pressing seams on the collar and lapel give the final touch yielding perfect lapels. Before trimming, check stitching at all key points to make sure stitching does not extend or fall short of large dot markings.

Press all seams open and stagger seam trimming, "grading" at $\frac{1}{4}$ and $\frac{1}{8}$ inch. The wider seam allowance lies closest to the outside of the garment, cushioning the shorter seam allowance. Trim corners closely and at an angle. Because you have sewn the collar in key areas with small stitches, close trimming should not cause alarm.

Turn collar and facings right side out—be sure to use a point turner rather than scissors. Place open seam together at neckline. Use a stab stitch with double thread run through beeswax to anchor the two seams together. Baste collar and lapel in desired finished position with silk thread, which is left in until after a professional pressing. Silk thread has elasticity and will not make an imprint during pressing.

Excess bulk has been eliminated in the lapel because at no time were more than two thicknesses sewn together, prohibiting trimming and movement. Because the seam is not sewn continuously where the four seams join, a small $\frac{1}{8}$ inch unsewn spot will manifest itself at this juncture. Do not close this small opening, it allows for movement in pressing.

Press and pound with a tailor's clapper. Mold and steam press lapel over tailor's ham. To eliminate stretching, let lapel dry completely before lifting off pressing surface.

Sleeve Head

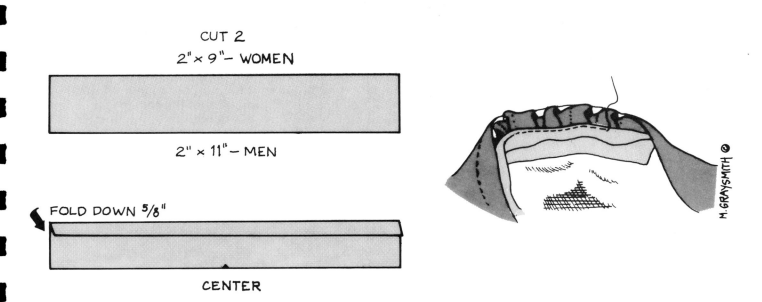

CUT 2
2" × 9" – WOMEN

2" × 11" – MEN

FOLD DOWN ⅝"

CENTER

M. GRAYSMITH ©

For a professional looking sleeve cap on coats and jackets, a sleeve head is mandatory. A sleeve head is an added layer of interfacing which lies between the sleeve and shoulder seam allowance and the sleeve cap itself. It acts as a cushioning agent to soften the hard edge of the seam allowance, rendering it invisible.

Traditionally lambswool was used exclusively for sleeve heads. Due to its expense, many manufacturers now substitute polyester fleece. You may use lambswool, polyester fleece, and in a pinch, cotton velour. Sleeve head strips must be cut on the grain line with the most give: bias for lambswool, crosswise for cotton velour, and any direction for polyester fleece, since it has no grain. If you have access to a tailoring supply house, pre-cut sleeve heads are available.

The sleeve head is applied after the sleeve itself has been inserted. Cut two strips 2 by 9 inches for women, and 2 by 11 inches for men. Along one lengthwise edge, fold down ⅝ inch. Press. Fold header strip in half and mark the center with a snip. Working with the sleeve and garment seam allowance pulled toward the garment, match up the center of the sleeve head with the shoulder seam on the jacket. Place the fold of the header strip ¼ inch toward the garment seam allowance, away from the sleeve and garment sewn seam. The smooth side of the header is against the garment. The ⅝ inch lengthwise fold faces away from the garment. The lengthwise fold on the header is moved ¼ inch toward the cut seam allowance to slightly grade the ⅝ inch edges. Sleeve header strips can be sewn by hand to the seam allowance or machine sewn through all thicknesses ½ inch from the cut seam edge or ⅛ inch toward the seam allowance from the original sleeve and garment seam.

The sleeve head is sewn from front notch across shoulder seam to back notch. It is not included in the underarm seam. Cut off any excess length in the sleeve head beyond the notches.

Sculptured Sleeve Cap

If you closely examine the sleeve seam at the top of the shoulder on jackets of European designers, you will detect not only the presence of a sleeve head to soften the hard edge of the seam allowance, but the presence of padding between the seam allowance and the sleeve cap. This layer of padding lifts the sleeve cap slightly, giving it a slightly rounded sculptured appearance, giving more definition to the shoulder silhouette. To create this effect do the following:

After inserting the sleeve, trim out small triangles in the seam allowance of the sleeve only, allowing it to lie flat without excess when the sleeve and garment seam are pressed toward the sleeve cap. Apply sleeve head.

Depending on how much lift you prefer, use either $1/2$ inch soft, fat upholstery cording or a 1 inch strip of polyester fleece folded in half lengthwise. Place the cording or folded strip between the seam allowance and the sleeve header, which lies next to the sleeve cap. Using beeswaxed thread, attach padding strip to seam allowance. This area is padded from the front notch, across the shoulder to the back notch.

After you turn the sleeve and garment right side out, you will see that the cap is now lifted slightly and well padded. Try it—I think you will like the results!

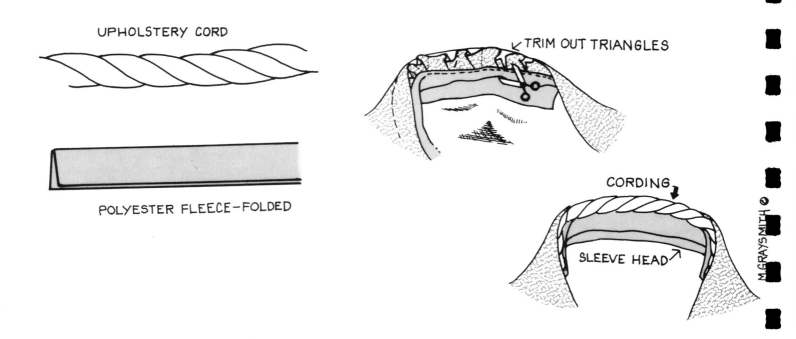

UPHOLSTERY CORD

POLYESTER FLEECE—FOLDED

TRIM OUT TRIANGLES

CORDING

SLEEVE HEAD

M.GRAYSMITH ©

TAMING THE SLEEVE

If sleeves in a jacket often present problems:

■ Cut sleeve pattern from scrap fabric. Insert. Perfect.

■ Substitute sleeve you like from another pattern. As long as sleeve style and size are the same, sleeves can be interchanged.

■ Allow 1 inch seam allowances when cutting out sleeve. Fabric can be released where needed.

■ If fabric is firm and will not be adverse to the eye, a sleeve cut on the bias is always more comfortable

Comfortable Sleeve Width in Jackets

If your wardrobe is full of a variety of sleeve styles—set-in, off-shoulder, and dolman—careful consideration must be given when choosing jacket style. If you want the option of wearing this jacket with everything, choose a style with low armholes and ample sleeve fullness to accommodate larger sleeve styles.

To determine arm girth, bend your arm slightly and measure the fullest part of the arm, about 2 inches down from the armpit. For a very fitted sleeve or blouse sleeve, minimum of $1\frac{1}{2}$ inch ease is needed for movement. For a dress sleeve, minimum of 2 inches is needed. For a set-in jacket or coat sleeve, minimum ease of $3\frac{1}{2}$ inches unlined to $4\frac{1}{2}$ inches lined is needed to allow traditional blouses and non-bulky sweaters to be worn inside. For set-in sleeve overcoat, 4 to 5 inches is needed. For low armhole, full-sleeved jacket to go over everything, minimum of 7 to 8 inches is needed to allow the options mentioned above. Use these measurements as guidelines for choosing jacket patterns.

Sleeve alterations may be made in several fashions. If your arm is full in the cap as well as the forearm, slit the pattern vertically from cap to hem. If addition is not needed in forearm, taper the sleeve at the sides from the elbow to the wrist (Illustration 1). If the upper arm is full from the armpit to the elbow, make additions at the seam sides tapering to zero by the elbow. For less bulk under the arm, lower underarm by $\frac{1}{2}$ inch when making sleeve width addition.

If you have larger arms in proportion to the bodice, you may have some difficulty easing in the sleeve. Do not limit the ease to the sleeve cap between notches. Run the easeline the entire distance of the upper sleeve curve (Illustration 2). This method gives comfort for fullness in the underside of the arm as well as allowing fuller sleeve to fit into smaller armhole.

If you have large bones, resulting in fuller forearm and wider wrist, measure the forearm at its widest place. Adding minimum of $1\frac{1}{2}$ inch ease, compare the lower sleeve width to your measurement plus ease. Make additions from 1 inch above the elbow to the wrist. Don't forget to alter the cuff as well (Illustration 3).

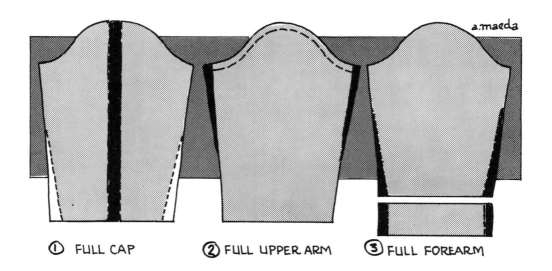

① FULL CAP ② FULL UPPER ARM ③ FULL FOREARM

a.maeda

Determining Correct Sleeve Length

If your sleeve has any detailing such as a vent or cuff, determining the correct sleeve length before you cut is mandatory. Sleeve length measurement is taken with the arm at a right angle. Start with the tape measure at the joint of the arm and the shoulder. If you have difficulty determining this point, decide on the placement of a sleeve seam which is most flattering by standing in front of the mirror. From the shoulder point, bring the tape measure down to the elbow, around the elbow, and down the forearm to the top of the wrist bone (Illustration 1). The finished sleeve will hang to the bottom of the wrist bone when the arm is in a relaxed position. Make notation of the distance from shoulder to elbow as well.

The sleeve length measurement you have taken should correspond to the sleeve length on the pattern—measuring from the seamline at the sleeve cap to the finished sleeve length. Remember this measurement does not include sleeve hem (Illustration 2). If these two measurements differ, the sleeve length must be altered.

A "lengthen-shorten" sleeveline is ordinarily indicated on the pattern. If the sleeve is a straight sleeve without shaping and darts, the full sleeve length alteration may be made at this point.

If the sleeve is a shaped sleeve, featuring a dart or an easeline at the elbow, the sleeve must be altered above or below the elbow for proper fit. Measure the distance from the seamline at the sleeve cap to the elbow placement which will be in alignment with the elbow dart or in the center of an ease indication. Compare this measurement to your measurement from shoulder sleeve placement to elbow. The difference between these two measurements determines the alteration needed above the elbow, even if an alteration line is not indicated on the pattern (Illustration 3). For proper fit, an individual may need to lengthen the sleeve above the elbow and shorten the sleeve below the elbow. If the sleeve features a cuff, don't forget to add the width of the cuff minus the seam allowances into your calculations (Illustration 4).

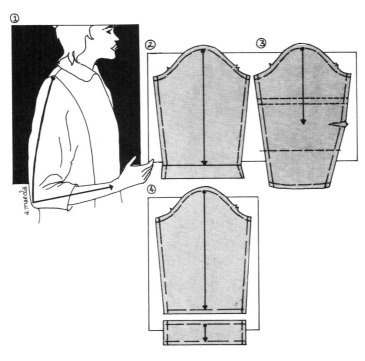

Too Much Sleeve Ease

Most sewers discover a sleeve has too much ease during the process of sewing the sleeve to the garment. Some fabrics ease better than others. Use this simple method for determining sleeve ease and sleeve ease will cease to be a problem.

Pin front and back bodice together at shoulder, enabling you to measure the entire armhole in one operation. For armhole measurement, place tape measure edge along the seamline of the garment armhole. For sleeve cap measurement, place tape measure edge along the seamline of the sleeve cap. The difference between the two measurements is called "sleeve ease," normally $1\frac{1}{2}$ inches. If the sleeve ease measures more than $1\frac{1}{2}$ inches or the fabric is difficult to ease, remove the excess ease from the pattern before cutting out the sleeve. Examples of difficult to ease fabrics include: wool gabardine, genuine and fake suedes, and leathers among others. For difficult-to-ease fabrics, allow no more than 1 inch sleeve ease, $\frac{1}{2}$ inch for a fabric like Ultrasuede®.

To remove excess sleeve ease from the pattern, draw a horizontal line across the sleeve pattern connecting the points where the sleeve cap joins the underarm. Cut pattern apart along this horizontal line. Draw one vertical line from the center of the sleeve cap to the horizontal line where the pattern was cut apart. Draw two more lines $1\frac{1}{2}$ inches on either side of the first vertical line angling the lines in to connect at the same point where the first vertical line intersects with the horizontal line where the pattern was cut apart. Make three slashes in the pattern from the sleeve cap to within 1/8 inch of the horizontal line cutting the pattern.

Divide the total amount you wish to reduce sleeve ease by three. Overlap each slash along the cap the amount of $\frac{1}{3}$ reduced ease.

Each overlap must not be more than $\frac{1}{4}$ inch. For every $\frac{1}{4}$ inch ease to be reduced, a slash is necessary. If sleeve ease must be reduced more than $\frac{3}{4}$ inches, additional slashes in the cap will be necessary. Tape overlapped slashes into position. Round out sleeve cap to smooth. Tape bottom part of sleeve back to sleeve cap along horizontal cutting line

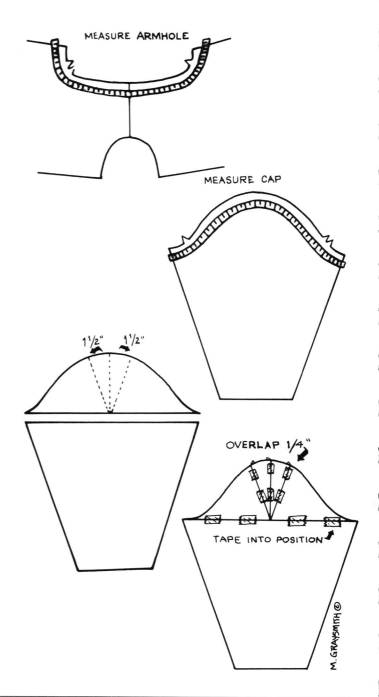

MEASURE ARMHOLE

MEASURE CAP

$1\frac{1}{2}$" $1\frac{1}{2}$"

OVERLAP 1/4"

TAPE INTO POSITION

M. GRAYSMITH ©

Rotating the Sleeve

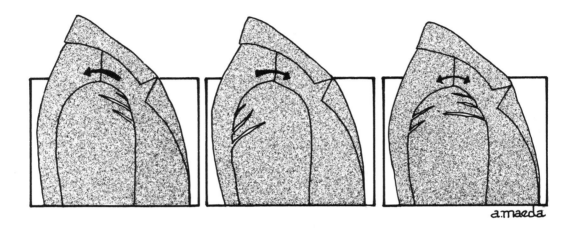

a.maeda

If perfectly smooth jacket sleeve seems the exception, try rotating the sleeve cap clockwise and counter-clockwise for smoother fit. Sleeve wrinkles can be a result of poor posture or uneven arm fulless. Both problems can be corrected by slight rotation.

Meticulously mark the shoulder placement dots on sleeves during the marking process. Run an easeline between notches over the cap of the sleeve. Fit sleeve gently over tailor's ham. Steam press sleeve cap slightly to flatten ease before joining sleeve to the jacket.

Sew long sleeve seams. Pin sleeve into jacket arm-hole opening, matching notches, shoulder and under-arm seam markings. Sew sleeve from front notch to back notch in underarm area only. Leave sleeve cap pinned. If your fabric is rather structured, it may be necessary to baste sleeve cap into opening for the try-on process. Trying on the garment in the "pin in" stage saves some time, but more importantly it increases accuracy.

Examine jacket critically in mirror. If sleeve does not hang perfectly, locate the problem. If sleeve creases slightly in front, rotate the sleeve cap $1/4$ to $1/2$ inch toward the back. Begin with $1/4$ inch rotation, rotate further if small rotation does not eliminate the problem.

If the sleeve creases slightly in back, rotate the sleeve cap to the front. Begin with $1/4$ inch rotation, increasing to eliminate the problem.

If sleeve creases are not in front or back but horizontal in cap, sleeve cap is too tall and too narrow. Trim off $1/4$ inch from the head of the sleeve cap, flattening cap slightly. Add $1/4$ inch to sides of sleeve cap ending addition by notches. Smooth out new cap lines. A slightly shorter, wider sleeve cap will result in a sleeve which fits easily in original armhole and eliminates horizontal wrinkles.

■ For difficult to ease fabrics, stretch a 1 1/2 inch strip of mohair wool over sleeve cap for easing. When strip releases, ease is pulled into cap. Leave strip in seam to pad sleeve cap.

Narrow Hip By Narrowing Sleeve

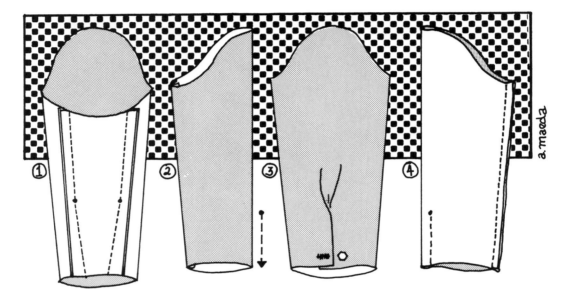

Paring down the width of a jacket sleeve by 1 inch can actually take 2 inches off your hips, one on each side. In its relaxed position, the sleeve ends at the widest part of the hip, apparently adding width to the body at the place most women need it least.

The finished width of the average jacket sleeve is 12½ inches. After measuring jackets in ready-to-wear and experimenting with jackets from patterns, I find an 11 to 11½ inch width is more flattering. The narrower sleeve width is still easy to slip on and off with the added bonus of narrowing the silhouette.

Before you routinely taper, measure both pieces of the two-piece sleeve within the seam allowances. If the sleeve measures 12½ inches and 11½ inches is desired, a total of 1 inch must be removed. In a two-piece sleeve, simply sew ⅞ inch seam allowance on sleeve seams at sleeve bottom, tapering back to the original ⅝ inch seam allowance at the elbow. In one-piece sleeve, sew 1⅛ inch seam allowance at sleeve bottom, tapering back to the original of ⅝ inch right above the elbow.

Since the forearm is one of the most attractive parts of a woman's body, dress and blouse sleeves should be narrowed at the hem to allow the sleeve to be pushed up and stay up.

Two treatments are particularly attractive. For the first, hem the sleeve and press a crease in the side of the sleeve by laying the underarm seam to one edge. Press crease in the side of the sleeve for 4 inches. Make buttonhole near the edge of the crease. Try on the sleeve to determine how far toward the sleeve back the button must be sewn to make the sleeve snug at the forearm (Illustration 3). If you hate buttonholes, eliminate the buttonhole and use a button to anchor the pleat into position.

Another technique to tighten up the sleeve is to turn the sleeve wrong side out. With underarm seam to one side, press a 4 inch crease at the opposite outside edge. Pin out a 1 inch tuck, total 2 inches parallel to the crease. Try sleeve on. Push sleeve up on forearm. Determine whether larger or smaller pleat must be sewn for the sleeve to be snug at forearm. Sew pleat length of 4 inches with right side together (Illustration 4). Press pleat toward front of sleeve on wrong side. Hem.

Sleeve Facing Contrast

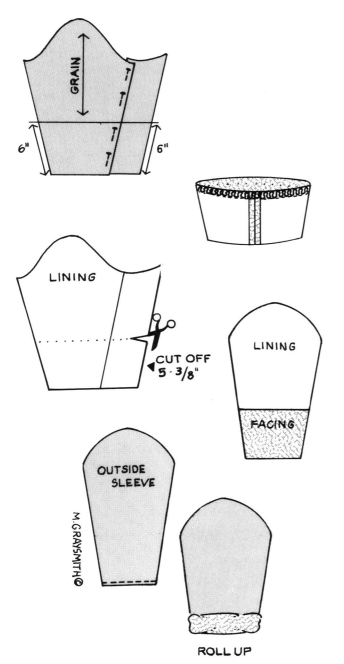

Since beauty experts advise us that the forearm is the last to go in the aging process, why hide this beautiful part of the female body? In addition to revealing the forearm by rolling up sleeves on a jacket, you can reveal your creativity as well by using compatible contrasting fabric for the sleeve facing.

If you plan to roll up sleeves on a jacket without revealing the sleeve lining. a jacket sleeve facing must be used. To make a pattern for the sleeve facing, fold up the sleeve hem so that the length of the sleeve extends 5/8 inch past the finished sleeve length. If you are using a two piece sleeve, overlap seam lines on the seam closest to the front of the sleeve. Cut a 6 inch sleeve facing to reflect the lower 6 inches of the entire sleeve.

If you want to turn back sleeve to match the jacket, use a 6 inch piece of jacket fabric. Subtle striped or paisley lining fabric is often used as a sleeve facing to give the jacket a little zip.

Whatever fabric you decide to use for a sleeve facing, interfacing is advisable to give crispness to the sleeve rollback. Use the same grainline for the sleeve facing as used on the sleeve itself.

Join sides of the sleeve facing to form a circle. To allow for turn of the cloth principle, sew straight edges of sleeve facing with a generous $\frac{5}{8}$ inch (not quite $\frac{3}{4}$ inch) seam. Overlock or seam finish wide end of the sleeve facing if the jacket is unlined. If the jacket is lined, join facing inseam to sleeve lining which has been cut $5\frac{5}{8}$ inches shorter than the original seamline. Provision in length has been made for the seam.

With right sides together, join sleeve and sleeve facing at the bottom of the sleeve. Press, trim seam allowance. Turn facing to inside of the sleeve. Hand tack in place at seam lines if sleeve is lined or around the entire circumference if sleeve is unlined.

Press and pound edge flat. Turn to right side with one or two rolls.

Sleeve Fitting for the Larger Figure

As a woman's body gets larger, size 14 and over, the figure becomes more difficult to fit. Upper chest and shoulder areas do not grow in proportion to the bust, arms, and abdomen. Most domestic patterns are cut too wide across the upper bust area. To compensate for this, according to large size fitting specialist Gale Hazen, of The Sewing Place in San Jose, California, purchase pattern one or two sizes smaller than the full bust measurement indicates. To allow for the necessary width needed at bust, waist, and hip, make adjust-

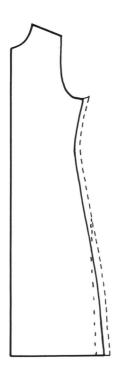

pattern envelope indicated for the size you purchased. This total alteration is divided by 4 to arrive at the alteration needed at each side seam. If more of your fullness is in front, add more proportionally to the front pattern pieces; try a two to one ratio front and back.

A similar addition must be made to armhole facings or sleeves. If the sleeve addition is added straight out at the sides of the sleeve, the result is too much full-

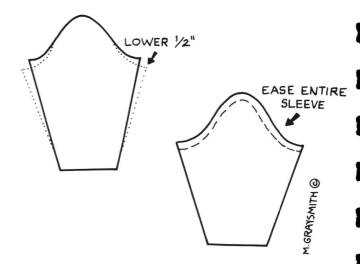

ness right under the arm. For a better fit, lower armhole ½ inch as sleeve width is extended. The result is comfortable with a less bulky appearance. For many figures, sleeve additions may be tapered to the original by the elbow since forearms are slim in comparison.

If the arm is quite large in comparison to the rest of the body, cut the sleeve on the bias when fabric allows and do not limit ease to between the notches. Ease sleeve from seam to seam.

ments at side seams from underarm to hem. If hips are narrow in comparison, hip addition may be tapered in slightly to give a slightly pegged appearance (very slimming on the large figure).

To determine alterations needed at side seams, compare your measurement to the measurement on the

---

■ Rolled up or pushed up sleeves are everyone's good friend, especially the large sized woman.

Altering the Kimono Sleeve

Changing the size of the kimono sleeve need not be intimidating if you remember to change the placement of the dot-placement marking for the joint of the sleeve and the body of the kimono. Determine the amount to be added or subtracted for an attractive kimono sleeve. This amount should correspond to the amount you normally alter a traditional sleeve. If you have large arms and add 1 inch to a traditional sleeve, 1 inch will be added to the kimono sleeve, $\frac{1}{2}$ inch at each side or the underarm seam. This requires you to drop the sleeve placement dot $\frac{1}{2}$ inch on the body of the kimono as well (Illustration 1). New dot placement allows the kimono body and sleeve to match up precisely without changing the size of the body of the kimono. If the forearm is slim, additions can be tapered down to zero at the sleeve bottom.

For small arms, the alteration can be reversed. To take $1\frac{1}{2}$ inch of fullness from a kimono sleeve, $\frac{3}{4}$ inch will be cut away from each side of the kimono underarm sleeve seam. Move the body placement dot $\frac{3}{4}$ inch in towards the sleeve body. On the kimono body move the sleeve placement dot up $\frac{3}{4}$ inch (Illustration 2).

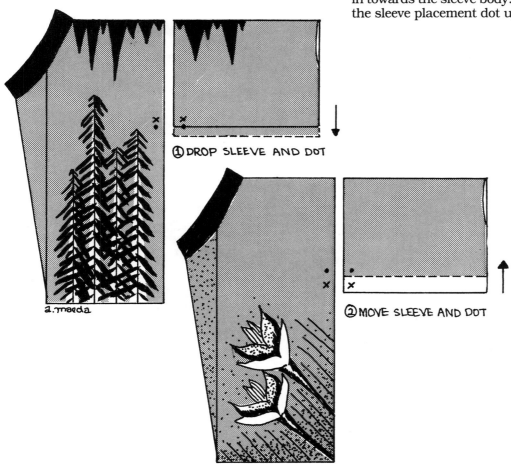

① DROP SLEEVE AND DOT

② MOVE SLEEVE AND DOT

a. maeda

Changing Set-in Sleeve to Dolman

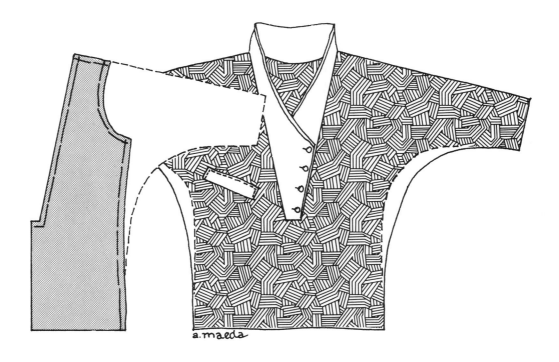

a. maeda

If you prefer the smooth shoulder line and easy fit of the dolman sleeve but the pattern detailing that you love features a set-in sleeve, consider changing the sleeve.

Buy, or pull from your own pattern files, a pattern with a dolman sleeve that can be used as an overlay. Join pattern, butcher paper or newspaper together with tape or glue to form a piece large enough to copy the new pattern on to.

Lay the bodice pattern you want to change onto the paper. That will be the bodice piece to which a set-in sleeve would have been applied. Using the dolman sleeve pattern as an overlay, line up shoulder seams and center fronts.

Depending on the style of the necklines, the necklines may or may not line up. Don't drive yourself crazy over ¼ inch. Dolman sleeves are much more forgiving than set-in. Assuming you prefer everything about the

set-in sleeve pattern except for the sleeve, trace the pattern shape onto the paper except for the shoulder and underarm seam.

From the overlaid dolman sleeve pattern, trace the longer shoulder and sleeve seam and the underarm seam onto the paper. The new paper pattern should now reflect a combination of the two patterns. Treat front and back pattern pieces in the same manner, lining up shoulder and center front or center back seams.

Complete shoulder seams and neck detailing. Machine baste underarm seam. Try on garment for fitting. If you plan to wear a belt, belt the top or dress. Study the silhouette carefully in the mirror. Would the style be more flattering if you deepened the underarm seam? If so, gradually taper in underarm seam to a depth of 1 to 2 inches.

Overlock or clip trimmed seam to prevent wrinkles at the underarm area.

Inside Jacket Finish

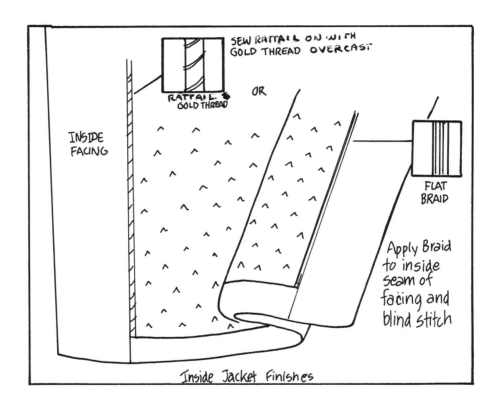

Inside Jacket Finishes

Well Shaped Shoulderpad Secrets

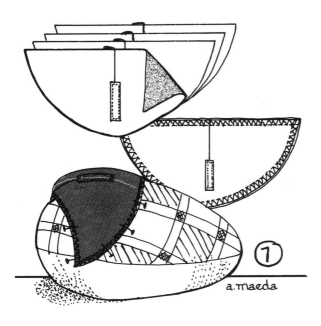

a. maeda

A few years ago, I bought a Krizia sweater that came with the most wonderful shoulderpads that slipped in and out with velcro. These pads were unique and totally invisible under any garment. I started wearing them with everything I owned. My daughter came home from college, borrowed the shoulderpads and then refused to give them back. After studying them, I realized it was not their shape but the way they were covered which gave them their contour and invisibility. Cover a pair of shoulderpads with this method and they will become your favorite accessory. To protect the shape of shoulderpads in a lined garment through dry cleaning, cover with fusible knit before inserting in garment.

Find a set of pads whose shape you especially like. Try a variety on under garments and see which shapes will be the most versatile and comfortable. Because these polyester pads are shape pressed by machine, a hard edge is formed around the pad. Cut off ¼ to ½ inch around the edge. The secret to their invisibility lies in the pad cover which is knitted tricot press-on interfacing. Since the greatest stretch in the interfacing is crosswise, lay the pad on the interfacing with the long dimension of the pad on the crosswise grain of the interfacing.

Allowing 1¼ inch seam allowances all around, cut four thicknesses of interfacing, two for each pad. Through one thickness only, make a ½ inch wide dart in the middle of the straightest side. Sew the ½ inch dart (taking out a total of 1 inch of fabric) toward the opposite side, tapering the dart to zero by 2½ inches. The wrong side of the dart is formed on the glue side of the interfacing. Cut open dart. Cut a piece of velcro 3 inches long for each pad. On the right side of two of the four pieces, place a 3 inch piece of velcro in line extending the line of the dart. Use the sticky side of the velcro. The velcro starts where the dart ends. Sew velcro in place through one thickness of interfacing.

Place velcro cover glue side down against raised side of the pad. Place pad on ham. Pin in place. Shape cover of pad over the top of the pad. Steam well and press cover onto pad over ham. Using a second piece of interfacing without velcro, place glue side against hollow side of pad. Using steam iron, press interfacing to form shape of underside of pad. The pad is now sandwiched between two layers of interfacing and well shaped (Illustration 1).

Overlock or zigzag through all three layers—the two interfacings and pad together—around the outside edge of the pad. Be sure to catch pad in the stitching.

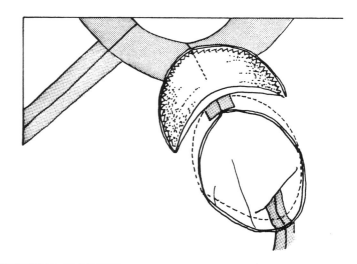

Well Shaped Shoulderpad Secrets

This stitching gives the pad its shaped memory. If excess was not cut off in the overlock process, cut excess away from stitching. Place finished pad over ham. Pin into shaped position. Steam press well again. Allow steam to dry before removing pad. Sew opposite pieces of velcro (smooth side) to the shoulder seams of all garments (Illustration 2). This step can be eliminated on sweaters.

For the giant 1 inch thick dolman type pad, cover differently. Cut a circle of one dart 4 inches long and 5 inches wide, centering dart placement between crosswise and lengthwise grains. Sew dart in interfacing. Center dart on top of pad as illustrated (Illustration 3). Press interfacing onto top of pad shaping over tailor's ham with iron. Fold back pad cover into position. Press and shape. Overlock or zigzag edged including pad in stitching. Position on garment with dart at shoulder seam. Extend pad ½ inch past seam into armhole at cap.

If you live in an area with a poor assortment of shoulderpads, you might want to order a bag of pads with eight sets of assorted shapes from The Sewing Workshop (see Sources).

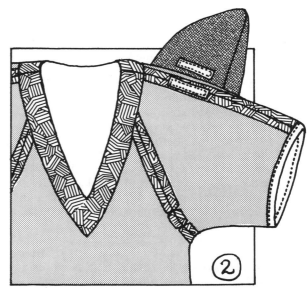

a.maeda

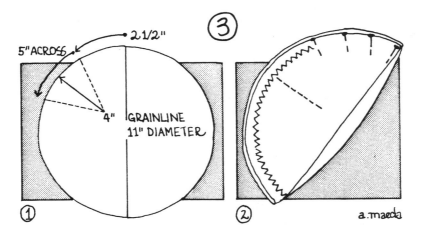

③

2 1/2"
5" ACROSS
4" GRAINLINE
11" DIAMETER
①   ②   a.maeda

■ Camouflage extreme sloping shoulders by inserting two sets of shoulderpads in jacket.

Hidden Shaping in Yoke

Cut bodice yoke double. Cut one layer of polyester fleece from yoke pattern. Mark shoulder placement from pattern onto polyester fleece. Three more smaller layers will be used on each shoulder to build up shoulder contours. Cut 2 shapes of polyester fleece 1 inch from neckline toward shoulder and $\frac{1}{8}$ inch from back yoke seam, front yoke seam, and armhole seam. Make 2 more layers $\frac{3}{4}$ inch smaller on all sides except armhole. Make another 2 layers $\frac{3}{4}$ inch smaller on all sides except armhole than the last 2. Layer fleece shapes onto yoke fleece layer centering at shoulder seam, graduating from larger to smaller. With waxed thread, stab stitch all fleece layers together loosely along shoulder markings on fleece. Do not pull thread tight crushing layers at shoulder. Cut one layer of fusible knit interfacing from yoke pattern. Place glue side of interfacing against stacked shoulder shapes. Fuse interfacing to polyester fleece. Fused interfacing will assist stab stitch in keeping shoulder shapes in place.

Sandwich bodice back between 2 fashion fabric cut yokes. Sew back yoke seam. Against the wrong side of the outer yoke, place fleece side of padded yoke. Join fleece to yoke at back yoke seam by sewing through original seam line joining yokes to bodice back. Before sewing seam, check placement of shoulder padded fleece. From the right side of the shirt, graduated shoulder shapes go toward the shoulder from large to small. Lengthen stitch slightly when sewing through fleece to avoid creating an indentation at the seam.

Trim fleece from back yoke seam allowance. Press yokes up—fleece is sandwiched between yokes. Topstitch back yoke seam.

Place right side of front bodice against right side of outer yoke plus fleece layer. Sew front yoke seam joining bodice to yoke and fleece layer, sewing with bodice side up. Trim fleece from seam.

Join under front yoke to front yoke seam with slip stitch or by turning the seam back on itself and machine sewing. Press. Topstitch front yoke seams. This method permits the garment to hang beautifully on a hanger as well as on the body.

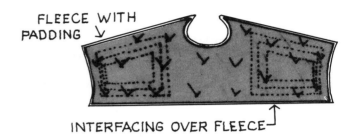

FLEECE WITH PADDING ↓

INTERFACING OVER FLEECE ↵

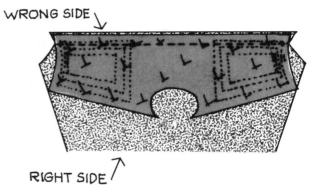

WRONG SIDE ↓

RIGHT SIDE ↗

M. GRAYSMITH ©

Silk crepe de chine jacket, made from a Burda pattern, is underlined everywhere except sleeves in flannelette (see page 7). On jacket front, side fronts and facings, additional support is given to the flannelette with fusible tricot knit. Back and sleeves are not interfaced. Jacket is fully lined with China silk.

Compatible fabric is used on shawl collar (see page 15) which is underlined with flannelette fused with fusible knit tricot. Additional crossgrain fabric strips in silk were used for the double piping (see pages 210-211).

2. Multicolored wool tweed provides an attractive canvas for this asymmetrical Issey Miyake pattern from Vogue (see pages 6 & 8 for interfacing decisions). Blouse is made from 4 lambsuede skins (see page 180 for technique). Turquoise buttons with sterling silver bevels come from Paco Despacio (see Sources for address).

1. Wool gabardine trenchcoat (see page 142 for gabardine tips) is made from a Shermaine Fouché pattern (see Sources for address). Since fusibles will not give long term adhesion on gabardine, a medium weight sew-in, such as Stay Shape, is preferable. Handwoven scarf from Tim Veness.

Unlined linen jacquard jacket *is made from a Burda pattern. Although jacket is unlined, jacket fronts are cut double to help lapel stay in place and give a clean finsh to the inside of the jacket behind the pocket (see page 10). Second front is attached by hand to side seam. Jacket support (see pages 6-7) comes from fusible knit tricot interfacing behind front and side fronts, and Whisper Weft, in the shape of the front facing, fused to the second jacket front finishing the inside of the jacket. Jacket seams in back of jacket and hem are finished with a flashy seam finish (see pages 64-65). Antique buttons are a nice surprise.*

*Off **white barathea wool** is underlined with cotton batiste to prevent seam shadowing common on white fabrics. Fusible knit tricot interfacing is fused to cotton batiste underlining on entire jacket fronts (see page 8). Whisper Weft is fused to cotton batiste underlining on front facing. Purchased rayon twill piping outlines jacket front. Buttonhole pockets (see **Power Sewing** page 180 for technique), antique ivory buttons and charms transform a simple silhouette into memorable wearable art.*

INTERFACING SUCCESS

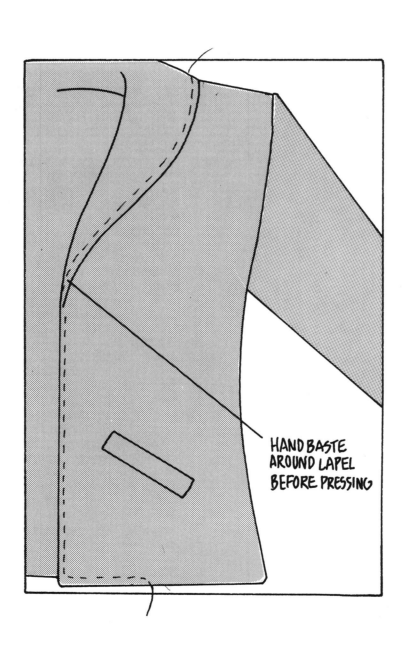

HAND BASTE AROUND LAPEL BEFORE PRESSING

Problems
with Fusibles

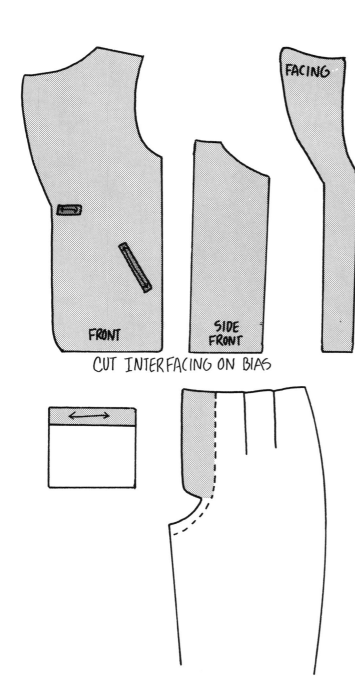

CUT INTERFACING ON BIAS

One bad experience with fusible interfacing on a favorite fabric is enough to turn a sewer off fusibles forever. Certain fabrics are simply not compatible with fusibles. For starters, if your ironing board has a teflon cover, your success with fusibles will be erratic. The teflon nonporous surface will not absorb steam, simply bouncing it back. Unless the garment fabric is capable of absorbing all of the steam, the steam bounces back from the teflon cover, through the fabric, against the interfacing. The result is air bubbles in the interfacing. By understanding the nonporous principle, you can then understand why fusibles do not work well on man-made suedes and leathers, gabardines and other tight weave or dense fabrics. Before you cut press-on interfacing from pattern pieces, experiment with a scrap of interfacing and with a scrap of garment fabric. Your chances of being unbiased about results are better before cutting time and interfacing are spent.

Should fusible interfacing be preshrunk? If you plan to hand wash and drip dry or dry clean the finished garment, preshrinking fusible interfacing is unnecessary. If you plan to put the finished garment through the dryer, preshrinking is mandatory. To preshrink interfacing, simply dip interfacing in a basin of medium to hot water. Squeeze out excess water. Hang over shower and let drip dry.

In my experience, drying clothes in a dryer prematurely ages them. Anything washable that you care about should be air dried to retain its freshness.

What grainline should be used when cutting interfacing? As a general rule, interfacing should be cut on the same grain as the piece to be interfaced. Of course, whenever there is a rule, you will find a notable exception. On pockets, the lengthwise grain of the interfacing goes across the pocket. When buttonholes are involved, cut an extra lengthwise grain of the interfacing in the same direction as the buttonhole. The strength of the grain will prevent the buttonhole from stretching. For example, if you plan to fuse a jacket facing with lengthwise grain of fusible to match the grain of the jacket, but you plan to put in a horizontal buttonhole in the jacket, add an extra strip of lengthwise grain fusible behind the buttonhole parallel to the buttonhole to prevent the buttonhole from stretching during use.

Problems with Fusibles

If you are making a shirt with vertical buttonholes, the strip of interfacing is cut with the lengthwise grain going up and down the shirt.

When it comes to pockets, fusibles end the problem of pocket stretch and sag. Always fuse a lengthwise strip of fusible interfacing behind welt pocket to help the pocket retain its shape. The lengthwise grain of the interfacing is parallel to the pocket opening. To prevent patch pockets on a jacket from sagging, interface the whole pocket with the lengthwise grain on the interfacing going across the pocket. To give body and prevent wrinkles, seam allowances and fly front extensions for zippers should be interfaced with lengthwise strips of interfacing.

Only by fusing a sample to scrap fabric can you see the results.

Results cannot be predicted in advance. My favorites are knitted tricot, Armo Weft, Armo Whisper Weft and Pellon Shirt Tailor.

For best results, use this method for fusing. Cover fabric and interfacing with a damp presscloth or spray presscloth with water. With a hot iron on a steam setting, hold iron in one place for 10 seconds. Do not push the iron around—this stretches the interfacing, causing it to become unglued in time.

Use a press and lift motion. Iron temperature may need to be lowered slightly for some fabrics. You can determine this from the sample. Most fabrics need a fairly hot iron for good adhesion. If the garment will be put in the dryer or dry cleaned—one last step is necessary for long lasting results. Repeat the press and lift motion with steam and a damp presscloth from the right side of the fabric.

■ If you don't have time to preshrink interfacing, cut interfacing on the bias to prevent fusible from drawing up garment piece.

■ Bridal tulle makes an excellent interfacing for collars, facings, and under buttonholes on lace garments. Tulle gives soft stability without interfering with the transparency in the lace.

■ Sponging is the industry term for shrinking with steam. Aside from shrinking the fabric, sponging is important to remove unwanted finishes needed for the loom process and raising the nap.

Interfacing Decisions

Choosing an interfacing can be confusing, especially with so many products on the market. Before you make a decision, ask yourself precisely what you want the interfacing to accomplish. Do you want the interfacing to give quiet support or create structure?

Structural support is often desirable in the jacket front to eliminate wrinkles between the armhole and center front as well as to give a more tailored crispness to the jacket. Interface the entire jacket front with fusible knitted tricot. If you want the body of a fusible, but are unwilling to risk fusing directly onto the fashion fabric, underline with cotton batiste or cotton voile, and fuse to the underlining. Interface the facing with Armo Weft fusible. Using a slightly firmer interfacing in the facing gives the lapel and jacket edges a sharper look.

How about interfacing as quiet support? For a soft collar, tab front, pocket flap or cuff, choose a soft interfacing such as Pellon's Sheer. This interfacing will not interfere with the overall look of the garment but will give a very slight crispness to keep the detailing from wrinkling. It will also control stretching in details during the construction process. Press-on interfacings are time-savers, but be certain they are compatible with your fabric before applying them to the garment.

Test a sample on a scrap of fabric. Critique the sample carefully, making certain that the fabric has not been transformed in any undesirable way such as puckering. Sew-in silk organza is a far better choice for silk and silk-like polyester for precisely this reason.

Interfacing can be helpful even when it is not called for in the pattern. A bias strip of interfacing placed on the hem allowance of sleeves and bottoms of jackets and coats gives a smooth line, assisting the garment in retaining its shape.

Finally, question whether the use of interfacing is necessary at all. If your sole purpose of using an interfacing is to keep the neckline from stretching, a far better solution would be to eliminate the interfacing and use stay tape instead.

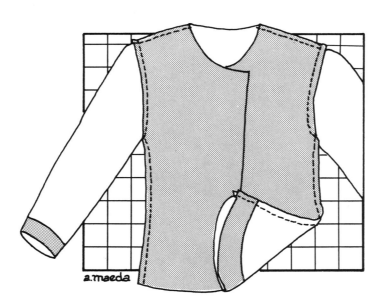

a.maeda

Interfacing Pant Hem

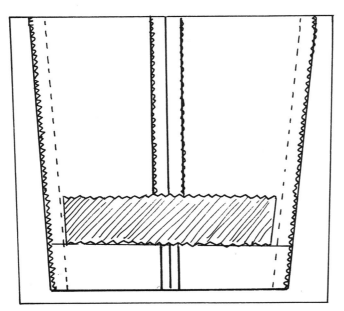
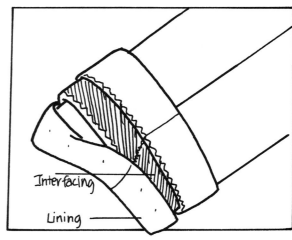

Interfacing

Lining

■ Rippling in pant hems can be avoided by interfacing the lower $2\frac{1}{2}$ inches of the pants. Sew inner leg seam. Allow for $1\frac{1}{2}$ to 2 inch pant hem. Press up pant hem allowance. Trim seam allowance to $\frac{1}{4}$ inch in hem portion. With pinking shears, cut a strip of lightweight fusible interfacing $2\frac{1}{2}$ inches wide. Position strip on pants with one long edge at hem crease, so that interfacing is fused on the pants, not on the hem allowance. Interfacing will not only give the hem body, but also cushion the pants from hem imprint. If pants are lined, attach bottom of lining to top of pant hem with a hang tack.

Choose Correct Necklines

a. maeda

Choosing the most flattering neckline has more to do with the shape of the face and length of the neck than mere personal preference. What looks great on somebody else is often a disappointment on you. Unfortunately, this fact is often discovered after the garment has been completed. Here are some guidelines to help avoid this mistake.

Pull hair back away from the face severely and look closely in the mirror. Categorize your face as oval, round, triangular or square. The round shaped face has full cheeks. The triangular face has a rather pointed chin. The square face has a square jaw. The oval face is perfectly proportioned. We all wish we had that one. Look at your neck carefully. Is the neck long, short, thin, or wide? (If you have difficulty putting yourself in a category, a teenager in the house can be trusted to be brutally honest.)

Scoop necks, turtlenecks and stand-up collars emphasize roundness in the face but will soften a triangular face. While flattering to most faces, V-necks should be avoided by the triangular face as the V-neck draws the face down and makes it appear longer and slimmer. A jewel neck is rarely flattering on anyone without changing the optical illusion with a scarf or a necklace. A square neck can be worn by all face shapes except the square, where it will overemphasize the jaw. The bateau or boat neck broadens the jaw while at the same time shortening the neck.

Knowledge of these facts can help you avoid unflattering necklines or help camouflage the effect with the use of accessories. An opera length necklace worn with an unflattering neckline can counterbalance a round face, minimize broad shoulders or minimize a full bust. A long necklace also lengthens the neck. A substantial chunky choker-style necklace can soften a triangular face worn with a V-neckline. Scarves knotted low—as well as contrasting lapels—can give illusions of length, break body width, and take away roundness in the face.

■ Wardrobe selection is made easier if you face all garments in the same direction.

NECKLINE
SUPPORT SECRETS

Wrap Blouse Success

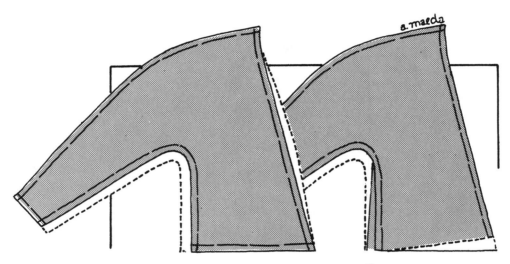

① ADD FULLNESS, SIDES AND CENTER. ② TRIM BOTTOM EDGE.

Trying on the wrap blouse in its final stage of construction can be a disappointing experience if the wrap reveals too much by not wrapping enough or gaps away from the body revealing even more.

Being quite familiar with this problem, here are some precautions and solutions to the wrap blouse "reveal-too-much syndrome." When cutting out the wrap initially, make sure the necessary pattern alterations for your figure are made on the pattern.

If your waist and hips are larger than those indicated on the pattern and no additions are made, the garment will not be able to sufficiently wrap around the larger waist. In addition, use 1 inch seam allowance at the side seams which can be released if additional wrap is desired. If the bust is full, fill in an additional $\frac{1}{4}$ inch at the front in the area of the bust (Illustration 1). Check the amount of blouson indicated on the pattern. More than an inch of blouson ends up causing the front wrap

to blouse open. Fold out excess of 1 inch blouson at the lengthen/shorten line.

Cut stay tape—using the pattern as a guide—the length of the diagonal seam. Ease the neck to fit the stay tape. Stay tape eliminates any stretch as you sew and as it is worn on the diagonal wrap seam. Continue with construction.

Most wrap styles wrap better if shoulderpads are inserted—they lift the shoulder a bit and allow the garment to hang better. In the final fitting, if the wrap is still unacceptable, two final options are available. If you want the wrap to lap over more, release the side seams a bit to give the front more fabric to overlap. If the problem is gaping, consider trimming off $\frac{1}{2}$ inch to 1 inch at the bottom edge tapering to the original cutting line at side seam (Illustration 2). This allows the diagonal seam to pull in closer to the body.

Off-Shoulder Necklines

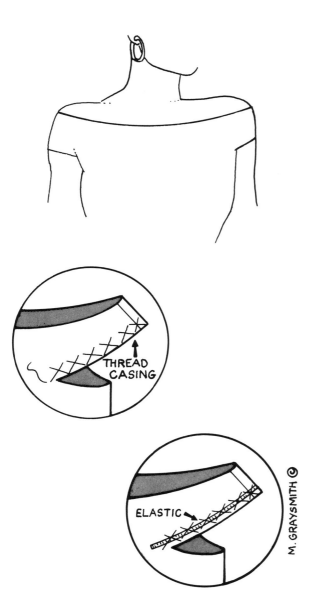

THREAD CASING

ELASTIC

M. GRAYSMITH ©

Meant for sipping champagne at elegant dinner parties, the off-shoulder garment while flattering and sexy can be a real problem keeping on the shoulder unless some precautions are taken. To begin with, forget about wearing the off-shoulder garment under any coat. A shawl or wrap is a must. Anything with an armhole will push up the shoulders and cause giant gaposis in the center front.

In the best of conditions, what's to keep the off-shoulder garment from simply "slipping off the shoulder" down to the elbows? Clever use of round elastic and a bit of hand stitching is the answer.

Along the top edge of the armhole 1/4 inch from the finished edge, make a thread casing with double beeswax thread or buttonhole twist if available. A thread casing is formed by a cross-stitch wide enough for elastic to pass through. With a bodkin, insert a strip of round elastic through the casing. Pin one end and pull elastic so that it is 1/2 to 1 inch shorter than the edge to which it is attached. While elastic is still pinned, try on the garment. Adjust elastic so that it is comfortable but snug on the shoulder. Anchor ends of elastic well on the inside of the dress. While the off-shoulder garment is on the hanger, the shoulder will appear to draw up slightly. On the body, the elastic stretches slightly over the shoulder to lie snug and smooth.

Neckline Control

Over the years certain masters have managed to control not only the drape of a neckline but the precise placement of the neckline as well.

On a strapless or low V-neckline, use a strip of feather boning sewed to the dress at the center of the bust to anchor the dress to the body when slipped behind the bra. Make a 4 inch long casing for a 3 inch strip of feather boning. Slip stitch ends. Sew one end of encased feather boning to lining or facing at the center front, ¼ inch below the top of the facing. The lower end is left free to slip behind the center front of the bra.

Another secret is the use of a suspended weight to control the drape of a neckline. A coin such as a nickel or drapery weight can be used for this purpose. Cut 6 inch strips of lining twice the width of the coin or weight plus 2 seam allowances. Fold strip in half lengthwise. Sew lengthwise side and one end at a shy ⅝ of an inch. Press seams open and trim. Turn right side out. Slip weight in opening and let fall to the bottom. Stitch above weight to prevent shifting. Turn in raw edges at the top of the strip and slip stitch. Sew top end of the weight to the inside of the dress at the bottom of the facing.

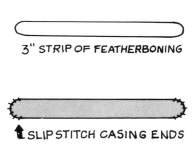

3" STRIP OF FEATHERBONING

SLIP STITCH CASING ENDS

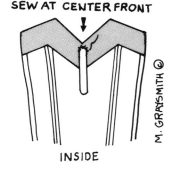

SEW AT CENTER FRONT

M. GRAYSMITH ©

INSIDE

Neckline Control

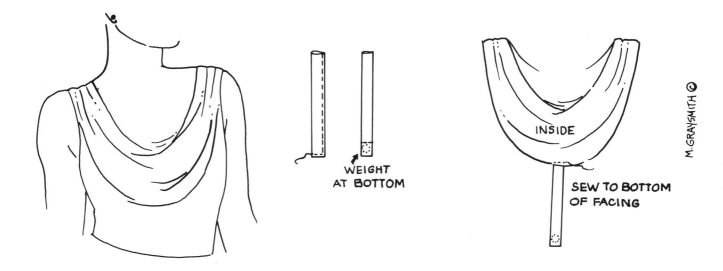

WEIGHT AT BOTTOM

INSIDE

SEW TO BOTTOM OF FACING

M.GRAYSMITH ©

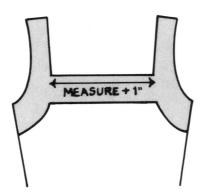

MEASURE + 1"

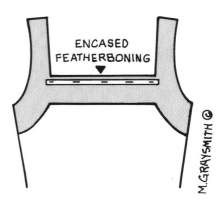

ENCASED FEATHERBONING

M.GRAYSMITH ©

The low square neckline can only be dramatic if the line is kept perfectly straight and smooth across the bust with or without movement. Measure the length of the horizontal front edge of the neckline. Cut narrow feather boning 1 inch longer an this measurement. Cover feather boning in a casing of lining fabric. Turn in ends of casing and slip stitch. Sew enclosed feather bone to the inside of the dress to lining or facing, just below the finished neckline.

Scoop Neck Insurance

Making a scoop neckline can be a hit-or-miss proposition. The scoop is often too wide, showing bra straps, or too low to permit other than occasional wearings.

Since shoulder width and bust height vary from individual to individual, it stands to reason that a scoop neck must be customized.

To determine a flattering scoop neck for you, put on your favorite bra and stand in front of the mirror. Tie a loose string in the shape of a jewel neckline. Mark on your shoulder what you consider to be a flattering distance from the jewel neck which adequately covers your bra strap. Mark the lowest point of the scoop desired in center front. From shoulder to center front, draw in the ideal scoop for your body. Draw a straight line marking the center of your body from the jewel neckline (indicated by the string) to center front of the scoop. Measure the length of this line. Now measure the distance halfway up the center front from the side of the scoop to the center front line drawn on your body. Measure distance from jewel neckline to inside of shoulder seam. You should now have three key measurements: the distance from standard jewel neckline to shoulder, the width of the scoop from center front, and the depth of the scoop from jewel neckline.

Now you have two choices: First, you can make a new custom scoop front pattern using the basic body sloper as a base since it features the jewel neckline. This scoop can then be used as an overlay on other patterns featuring a scoop neck. This method is the easiest and most time-saving. Second, you can keep these measurements and compare them to measurements taken on a scoop neck pattern. Fill in seamline as measurements dictate.

a.maeda

Scoop Neck Insurance

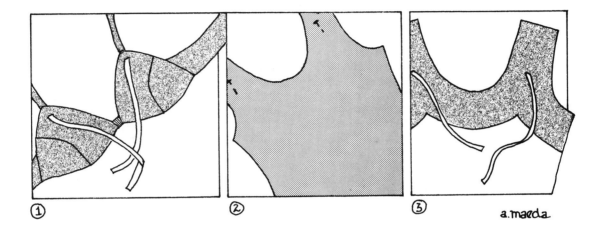

① ② ③ a.maeda

Scoop necklines are always more flattering if the facing is eliminated and a self fabric bias strip is substituted. Don't forget to use stay tape or a narrow strip of selvage at seamline to prevent neckline from stretching during the pressing process.

Credit to: Barbara Kelly.

If you love low, scooped necklines but hate the sight of underwear—visible with any small movement—this tip is for you. As a collector of books, I've found many treasures like this one from *Sewing Tips by World Famous Designers* (copyright 1967). Cut four 8 inch lengths of narrow satin ribbon, color matched to the dress fabric. Sew one end of each of two ribbons to the top of the bra at the highest point of the cup (Illustration 1). Try on the dress. On the outside of the dress, mark the corresponding place where the ribbon will be joined onto the inside of the dress with pins (Illustration 2). Remove dress. Transfer pin markings to the inside of the dress on the lining or facing. Sew last two remaining ribbons to the inside of the dress at the transferred markings (Illustration 3). Don't forget to turn under raw edges of ribbons before sewing.

After dress is complete, slip it on. Tie matching ribbons onto firm bows. Tuck bows and ribbon ends inside bra.

■ Use silk thread for hand basting. Silk thread has elasticity and will not show press marks.

Get a Handle on the Halter

As summer approaches, fashion turns to fun dresses, like the halter dress.

Not all halter tops are alike; some are more flattering and fit better than others. Try on several styles in ready-to-wear. Find the one which is most flattering to you. Study the cut of the armhole and the manner in which the armhole joins the collar. Pay attention to the choice of fabrics used in ready-to-wear, especially the weight if knits are used. Since numerous halter-style patterns are available, find two which resemble the ready-to-wear styles that flatter your figure.

Since precise fit is necessary for a halter top, make a pretest of both patterns. Pretest the halter top in a fabric weight similar to the fashion fabric. Although a very fine imported cotton or rayon knit is an excellent choice for gathered styles, a more fitted style requires a fabric with a bit more substance, such as a heavier-weight knit; medium-weight cotton or linen. Using a lightweight knit in the more fitted styles will result in an overly fitted look resembling that in bodywear.

Seam tape at the armholes, front and back, is mandatory for halter styles. Use the pattern as a guide for cutting the seam tape length. Ease the armhole to fit the seam tape. If the halter top is for an individual with a full bust, run an easeline on the front armhole for $1\frac{1}{2}$ inches on either side of the front notch (Illustration 1). In a fabric which is difficult to ease, pull in fabric slightly with a narrow $\frac{1}{4}$ inch strip of "invisible elastic." This is the area which will tend to pull away on the full-busted figure. Press the eased area before seam finishing. Seam tape is applied after the easing process is complete.

In some styles, consider eliminating the use of facings in favor of a bias wrap seam finish. Elimination of facings eliminates bulk, giving a clean finish which lies closer to the body (Illustration 2). If knit fabric is used, the finish strip is cut on the crosswise grain rather than true bias. Knit fabric has its greatest stretch with resiliency on the crossgrain.

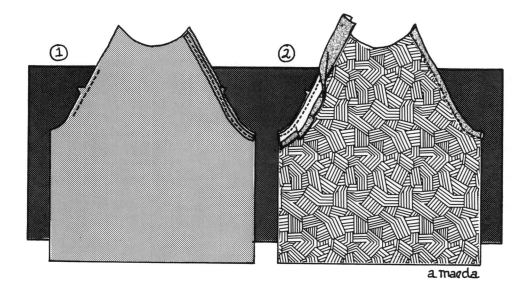

a. maeda

Neckline Recovery

SEE THRU ELASTIC

M. GRAYSMITH ©

Since most flattering necklines in knit garments need to stretch slightly to go over the head, stay tape cannot be used. If no stabilizer is used, many knits will stretch out slightly at the neck, losing the original flattering cut at the neckline. To stabilize the neck as well as provide some stretch, use a strip of $1/4$ inch invisible elastic at the neckline and shoulders. Check the notions department for this product or order from Clotilde's Mail Order House (see Sources). Do not stretch this transparent elastic as it is applied; merely apply as you would a strip of twill tape. Cut unstretched lengths of invisible elastic using the pattern pieces along the seamline as a guide. Since the unstretched elastic represents the actual seamline, it may be necessary to ease the fabric slightly to conform to the cut elastic if the knit fabric has stretched slightly during handling.

■ Allow plenty of ease in bias garments. Overfitting makes fabric wrinkle and draw across body.

■ If family members criticize or do not appreciate your work, stop sewing for them. Sew for yourself—you will have more fun!

Neckband Perfection

If you compared two men's tailored shirts side by side, the home sewn will differ significantly from the ready-to-wear version in the most visible area of the shirt—the neckband. Most home sewers are still fighting a seemingly losing battle against bulky unclean finished ends. Margaret Islander, owner of the Islander School of Fashion in Grants Pass, Oregon offers a tip which she calls the "burrito technique," which yields beautiful results.

For crisp collars and neckbands on man tailored shirts, interface both upper and undercollar and neckband. Fuse Pellon sheer weight on the under layers and Pellon sheer tailor on the outer layers. "The heavier interfacing always faces the public," says Islander. Cut interfacing out of corners before fusing. For fused interfacing which stays fused: Use a damp presscloth with a medium high iron setting over every square inch of the area to be fused for 10 seconds.

Compatible with her training in the garment industry, Islander uses $\frac{1}{4}$ inch seam allowances at the shirt neckline and on collar and neckband edges. Cut all seam allowances at the neckline down to $\frac{1}{4}$ inch before you begin the collar process and you will find application will go much smoother. Home sewers are the only sewers who use $\frac{5}{8}$ inch seam allowances at the neck. Switch over to the technique used by the professionals. In addition, Islander suggests using a sensible notch system $\frac{1}{8}$ inch snips to indicate centers on collars, yokes and bodices.

Join upper and under collar at outside edges. Handwalk one small stitch at corners to give the corner room to turn (2 stitches if collar is long and pointed). Trim, press, turn and press again. Topstitch collar. Machine baste neck edges of collar together. Remember you are now using $\frac{1}{4}$ inch seams. Join finished collar to the outer neckband, with the under collar against the outer neckband. Use only a $\frac{1}{8}$ inch seam here for basting. Set aside. Remember that you are using $\frac{1}{4}$ inch seam allowances on all other seams. Matching notches, join the inner neckband to the neck edge of the shirt, placing the right side of the inner band to the wrong side of the neckline edge. Sew with $\frac{1}{4}$ inch seam.

Place inner and outer neckbands together, sandwiching the collar in between. Tuck front edges of shirt

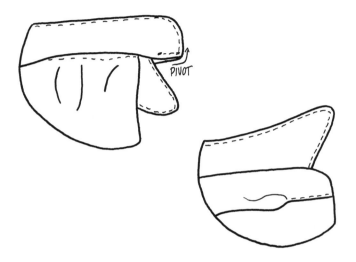

up inside the band pieces for about 2 inches. Now for the "burrito technique." Start sewing on the band about 1 inch to the end of the neckband, to the front edge of the shirt. Leave the needle in the fabric, pivot, sew the end of the band and around the top of the band (where the collar is basted) in a $\frac{1}{4}$ inch seam (Illustration). Continue seam around to the other end of the neckband and into the neckline seam 1 inch. On difficult stretchy fabrics, you might want to finish ends separately and meet seams at center back. Turn right side out and press ends.

The next step will close the bottom edge of the outer neckband onto the right side of the shirt. Using the now visible seam line as a guide, turn under exactly $\frac{1}{4}$ inch on the lower neckband seam. Place the folded edge right onto the seam line. Topstitch close to the edge, closing the seam. Continue the seam close to the edge all around the neckband. If you have been careful and used exactly $\frac{1}{4}$ inch seams in the neckline throughout, the neckband topstitching will look identical on both sides of the neckband.

Anyone who would like to turn out shirts like the professionals in $2\frac{1}{2}$ hours should view Margaret Islander's two excellent videos, *Shirts, Etc.* (see Sources).

PATTERN REFINEMENTS

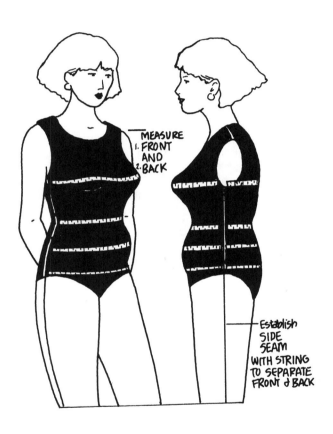

MEASURE
1. FRONT
AND
2. BACK

Establish
SIDE
SEAM
WITH STRING
TO SEPARATE
FRONT & BACK

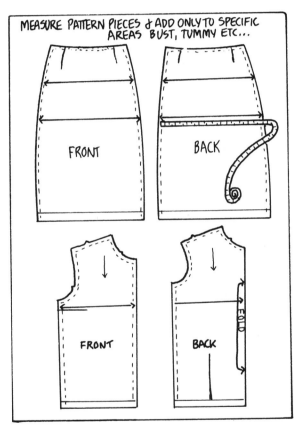

MEASURE PATTERN PIECES & ADD ONLY TO SPECIFIC AREAS BUST, TUMMY ETC...

FRONT

BACK

FRONT

BACK

FOLD

■ When seaming fabrics which have a tendency to relax, seam with a narrow zigzag (.5mm) and regular seam length (2mm). Seams will not draw up on the finished garment since the slight zigzag allows them to lie flat in the pressing.

Cause and Cure for Backriding Shoulder Seam

Garments may slip to the back at the shoulder because of incorrect shape and size of the armholes. As an insurance policy, check the pattern at these key points before cutting the bodice of the fashion fabric; depth of front and back armhole, length of front and back shoulder seam, and shoulder placement dot on sleeve piece.

By studying the body, you will observe that more fabric is needed in back rather than in front for ease and movement in the armhole. Therefore, the back armhole should be slightly deeper than the front armhole. Compare front and back armholes of your pattern. If the depth of the armhole is the same, cut off $\frac{1}{4}$ inch horizontally from the front shoulder, parallel to the original shoulder cutting line and add $\frac{1}{4}$ inch horizontally to the back shoulder parallel to the original shoulder cutting line. Next, check shoulder placement dot on sleeve by folding sleeve in half. If the shoul-

der seam placement dot is in the center of the sleeve, move dot toward the sleeve front by $\frac{1}{2}$ inch. This change on the sleeve puts the ease in the back of the sleeve where it is needed. Pin in sleeve. Try on. Adjust cap by slight rotation if it is not hanging perfectly straight.

Finally, check the length of the shoulder seam. If the shoulder seam front and back is the same length, trim $\frac{1}{8}$ inch from the front shoulder seam at the armhole. Taper subtraction smoothly to zero within the armhole. Add $\frac{1}{4}$ inch to back shoulder seam at armhole tapering to zero at armhole notch. Ease the back shoulder to front when sewing shoulder seam. A slightly eased back gives extra fullness where needed over the rounded shoulder.

Make these changes on your pattern before you cut out and you will never again have shoulder seams that slide to the back.

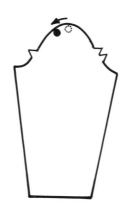

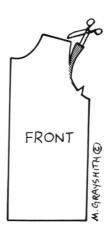

Vintage Garment Shoulder

If you prefer the high armhole and broad square shoulder of vintage garments, try this technique compliments of Shermaine Fouché.

On the bodice armhole front and back, add ½ inch height and ½ inch width to the shoulder seam. Taper shoulder addition to zero by the neckline seam. Taper armhole addition to zero by arm hole notch. This adjustment will accommodate a larger shoulderpad as well as giving a squarer, more pronounced shoulder line.

To allow freer movement when raising the arm as well as visually extending the distance from armhole to waist, giving the illusion of a slimmer silhouette, try the following: Raise underarm seam on front and back bodice by ½ inch. Taper addition to zero by armhole notches.

To compensate for armhole changes on the bodice, changes must be made on the sleeve as well. Raise underarm seam on sleeve ½ inch, tapering addition to zero by notches. On sleeve cap, add ½ inch from armhole shoulder dot at cap tapering to zero 1 inch from shoulder dot at sleeve back and tapering to zero at notch on sleeve front. If body dips in slightly between the shoulder and armhole, end ½ inch addition sooner on sleeve front and perhaps even scoop out sleeve slightly ⅛ inch at notch or cave-in.

If a two-piece sleeve is used, overlap one sleeve seam onto another to make position for sleeve adjustments easier. Reshaping the sleeve cap in this manner allows it to relate more to the shape of the arm. Pin sleeve into garment and try on. If sleeve is not hanging perfectly, rotate sleeve caps slightly to eliminate the problem.

Whenever you are experimenting with sleeves, cut one sleeve from scrap fabric first and pin it to garment. This simple step can save you hours of frustration.

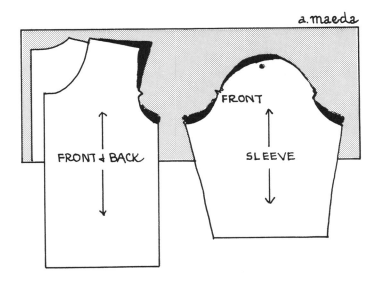

a. maeda

FRONT & BACK

FRONT

SLEEVE

Feminine Shoulder Curves

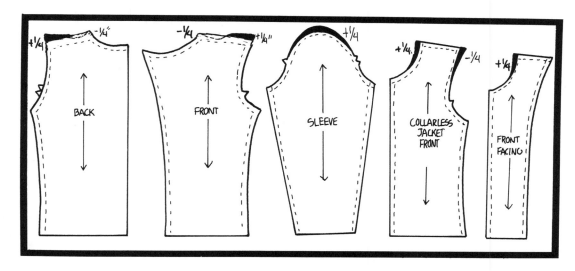

The prominent square shoulders of today's fashion cannot hold a candle to the well shaped, prominent shoulders seen in vintage jackets. The shoulders were not only broad but anatomically correct, dipping slightly at the clavicle, following the natural curve of the shoulder. To create the look found in vintage jackets, the straight shoulder seam will be replaced by a seam which resembles a gentle wave dipping and rising.

First, study the curve of your shoulder in the mirror. You will notice that the shoulder dips down slightly at the clavicle, approximately 1¼ inches from a jewel neckline seam. Locate this distance on your pattern and mark with a dot along the shoulder seam. Starting at this point on the shoulder seam, approximately 1¼ inches away from the jewel neckline seam, begin to lower the shoulder seam ¼ inch for a distance of approximately 1¼ to 2 inches, tapering smoothly back to the original seamline.

At this point, begin raising the shoulder seam ¼ to ⅜ inch for the remainder of the seam. Amount is determined by how pronounced you want the shoulder to be. Shoulder shaping is made on both front and back jacket pieces. To accommodate the height added to the shoulder on the body, height is also needed at the top of the sleeve. Add ¼ to ⅜ inch (whatever amount you

added for shoulder height) to the top of the sleeve. Taper smoothly into the front and back notches on the sleeve cap. You may decide to use a thicker shoulder-pad in the jacket.

The effect on the body is a slightly curved, more feminine shoulder. This shaping lies smoothly when it is customized to the curve of your natural shoulder line. Try a sample in scrap fabric to determine exact shaping.

If you examine a collarless vintage jacket, you will notice that the shoulder seam did not stop abruptly at the neck itself. To adapt this change to the pattern, add ¼ inch to the front neckline at the shoulder. Trim off ¼ inch from the front armhole at the shoulder. Blend changes well, smoothly into neckline and armhole as soon as possible. No changes are made on the back, or neckline will be too large.

Since armhole length on jacket front is still the same length after additions and subtractions, you will have no difficulty joining front and back shoulder seams in construction.

Reshape front facing slightly to mimic change made on neckline at shoulder.

Credit to: San Francisco couture designer Shermaine Fouché, who generously shared this knowledge.

Better Bodice Fit for Drop Shoulder & Raglan

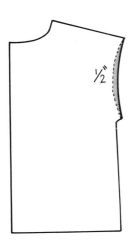
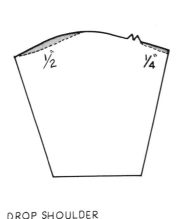

DROP SHOULDER

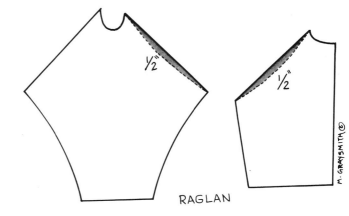

RAGLAN

Drop shoulder and raglan sleeve garments often have one problem in common: too much fabric above the armpit in the front. With some simple pattern changes suggested by designer Shermaine Fouché, instructor at The Sewing Workshop in San Francisco, both designs can be flattering and wrinkle free.

For drop shoulder garments, pattern changes are made on bodice front and sleeve only. On bodice front, divide armhole in half. This point marks the point of maximum alteration on the armhole. On bodice front armhole, trim off $\frac{1}{2}$ inch right about the bust, where the body is slightly concave, tapering smoothly to zero in both directions of the armhole.

The front of the sleeve must be shaped identically to the changes made on front bodice. Divide sleeve in half from shoulder seam dot to underarm seam. This point on the sleeve marks the maximum alteration. On sleeve front at armhole, trim off $\frac{1}{2}$ inch at front armhole center marking, tapering smoothly to zero in both directions on sleeve. These pattern changes on the drop shoulder garment will eliminate excess fab-

ric in bodice front. The drop shoulder sleeve has a flattened sleeve cap which will fit better in back with a simple alteration on the back of the sleeve. Shape the back of the sleeve slightly by cutting away $\frac{1}{4}$ inch between back notch and underarm seamline. Taper $\frac{1}{4}$ inch smoothly in both directions. No matching alteration is needed on back bodice.

A similar pattern change is made to eliminate bulk in the raglan sleeve garment. Most women's chests dip slightly about halfway between the neck and armhole. Unless a slight curve is built into this seam, the bodice will not lie flat. Divide raglan sleeve seam in half on bodice and sleeve fronts. These points mark the points of maximum alteration. On front seams of bodice and raglan sleeve front, trim $\frac{1}{2}$ inch at maximum alteration points. Taper $\frac{1}{2}$ inch subtraction from the original cutting line at the maximum alteration point smoothly to zero in both directions along front raglan seam lines on both pieces.

These slight pattern changes can make all the difference in how you feel in the finished product.

Reshaping the Seams

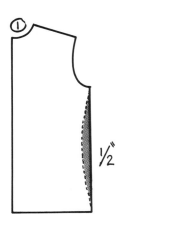

Subtle shaping at the side seams is needed in every garment you make. (Get in the habit of slipping in a bobbin of contrasting thread as you baste the side seams before fitting.) Slight shaping at the side seams mimics the body's curves, resulting in a less boxy, more flattering silhouette.

Even if a small waist is not one of your attributes, taper the side seam $\frac{1}{2}$ inch at the waist and the illusion of a waist results (Illustration 1). If you are short waisted, make yourself look longer waisted by tapering in $\frac{1}{2}$ inch slightly below ($\frac{1}{2}$ to $\frac{3}{4}$ inches) your natural waist.

Unless you are long waisted, the dolman style can make you look top heavy without some alteration at the underarm seam. Begin reshaping at the waist, basting $1\frac{1}{2}$ to $2\frac{1}{2}$ inches into the curve at the underarm on the dolman sleeve (Illustration 2). Since you haven't trimmed anything away, don't be afraid to do major reshaping. Taper the seam back to the original by the elbow or continue to taper to the wrist if you like a close fit around the forearm.

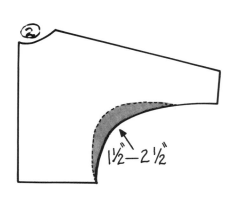

A full bodice is especially flattering if contrasted with a well fitted forearm. Many pattern sleeves are simply too full for the popular push-up sleeve. For a good fit around the wrist, the sleeve must measure 1 inch bigger than the wrist, giving 1 inch ease. If you plan to push the sleeves up, the sleeve should measure 1 inch larger than the forearm. Reshape the underarm sleeve by curving the underarm seam from the armhole to the elbow. Straighten out the last half of the seam to the wrist (Illustration 3). Don't be surprised if you end up taking out 2 inches or more from the sleeve. Since you are basting, you can afford to be daring. After you try on the garment for fit, determine the ideal sleeve width for you. Post it in a conspicuous place. You will make this alteration again and again.

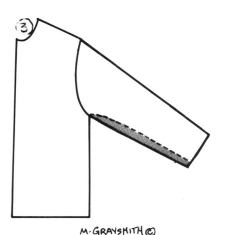

M. GRAYSMITH ©

■ Bias seams—Pop seam called *cracking* in areas which will be under stress when wearing, such as shoulders and underarm seams. After cracking, re-stitch. Stress areas are now reinforced.

Keeping Your Options Open

Even the best home sewer must cease being a dreamer when it comes to patterns. Let's face it, very few patterns "as is" turn out as well as we hoped or envisioned from looking at the pattern envelope. This does not mean that the final result cannot surpass our dreams, but realistically, pattern changes will have to be made to achieve the desired result.

Unless you are 5-feet-9-inches tall and weigh less than 125 pounds, very loose fitting styles—in the pattern size you normally buy—may dwarf the figure and look extremely unflattering. If the pattern is described as "very loose fitting," simply buy one size smaller than you normally buy and make the same adjustments you would on the correct size pattern. Do not assume that pattern additions for large hip and large waist can

be eliminated in a loose fitting garment. Elimination of these additions will actually draw attention to the problem. Fabric fullness will not be well distributed, and may pull slightly in the oversized area.

The following are pattern changes most often required to make a garment a success.

• Always check the finished length on the back of the pattern envelope. To maintain the shape of the garment, add or subtract length before you cut out. A skirt that's too short can ruin the whole silhouette.

• In a rectangular shaped skirt, a shaped version will be more flattering. If the skirt grainline is parallel to center front, center back, or side seams on a shaped skirt, change it. Make new grainline in center of panel by folding the skirt in half lengthwise. Fullness will be evenly distributed and more flattering. (See *Power Sewing*—"Changing Grainlines.")

• Add or eliminate kick pleats as desired.

• If you like a more fitted pant, use Burda; the European fit in pants is closer to the body. Check bottom width of pant legs. Taper inside and outside leg seams equal amounts to keep pants from twisting.

• Feel free to add, eliminate, or substitute pockets on all garments.

• Always check width of facings before cutting. Since the finished version tends to be skimpy, add $1/2$ to $3/4$ inch width to outside facing edge.

• On stand-up collars, compare collar width to your needs. Cut collar pattern in scrap fabric. Pin to neckline. Add or subtract stand-up collar height to suit you.

• For better wear and shaping, add a center back seam to coats and jackets.

• Allow wider seam allowances in cutting for special seam treatments.

ELIMINATE FULLNESS UNDER ARM

a. maeda

Keeping Your Options Open

• Plan for topstitching by having a double needle and thread on hand for special effects.

• Try on bodice right after you insert the first sleeve. Pin in the side seams. Slip in a shoulder pad if the style calls for one. Check the placement of the sleeve seam. If the seam appears a bit extended, try moving in the cap a half inch or so. Complete the narrowing process by the armhole notch. Changes in the sleeve seam are easy to this stage because the side seams are not sewn and machine stitches need only be removed from one sleeve. Complete sleeve insertion.

• Keep your options open. No matter how well you have altered the pattern for your particular figure, side seams should always be basted before trying on. Your particular body shape and the fabric determine how much styling ease is flattering. If seams are merely basted, you are more likely to make changes. If the garment has a front opening, make sure the center front markings match up exactly. Refit the side seams to suit yourself.

• Check the button placement before buttonholes are made. Re-space if necessary. Once you realize that it is possible to make numerous changes while the garment is in progress, you are on the road to fewer failures and more "perfect for you" styling. Consider pattern changes a part of the creative process and you will resent the pattern less and enjoy the results more.

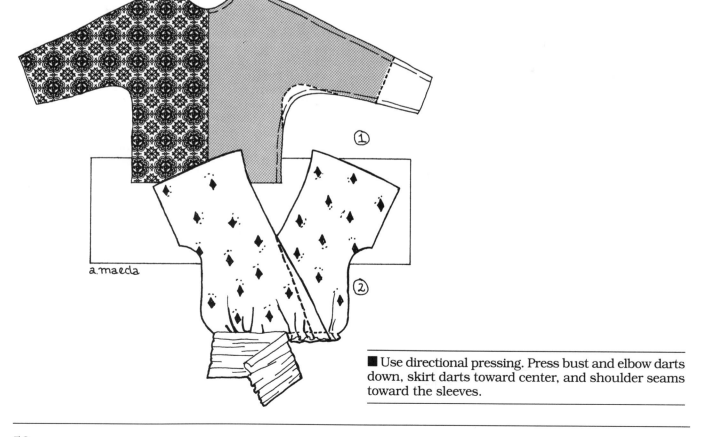

a.maeda

① ②

■ Use directional pressing. Press bust and elbow darts down, skirt darts toward center, and shoulder seams toward the sleeves.

Multisize and the European Cut

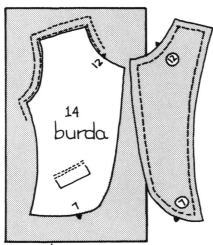

a.maeda

Multisized patterns are rapidly becoming the norm rather than the exception. If you find the numerous cutting lines confusing, perhaps these hints will be helpful. Pattern adjustments for the disproportionate figure are easy with multisized patterns.

Check the measurement chart connected with the sizes in the back of the pattern books. Most individuals fit into one size on top and one to two sizes larger on the bottom. For example, a size 10 may fit perfectly in the bust; for the hips a size 12 is needed. In a multisized pattern, use the size 10 cutting line for the upper bodice, neck, armhole, sleeve and bust area. Starting a little above the waist, begin using the size 12 cutting line for the lower half of the body. Connect the size 10 and size 12 cutting lines with a smooth gradual transition.

Before you actually begin to cut out the fabric, spend a few minutes with the pattern tissue itself. Using a colored broad tipped felt pen, trace over the size line you plan to use. This technique is valuable in multisized American patterns as well as multisized Burda patterns. If you are still confused by the multitude of lines, cut away the excess pattern tissue.

Despite the fact that the home sewer is always on the lookout for great patterns, Burda, the German pattern company, is often overlooked. Burda offers instructions in three languages including English. The European cut tends to be less bulky, curving more to the contours of the body.

Some of Burda's differences: Sleeve caps have a different shape. The shoulder line is always off center, giving more ease to the back of the sleeve for comfort and less ease to the front, eliminating puffiness. The shoulder line of the bodice is raised but the underarm has been raised as well, closer to the armpit. The cylinder of the armseye is the same, but by having the sleeve set higher under the arm, greater freedom of movement is allowed without the entire bodice pulling up from the waist when the arm is lifted. In addition to comfort, a higher armhole gives a longer look in the bodice with slimming results.

Burda patterns are multisized with up to six sizes in each pattern. Multisize can work to your advantage, since it gives you the option of using whichever size corresponds to your body measurements in different areas.

Lines printed on Burda patterns are sewing lines, not cutting lines—seams and hem allowances are not included in the pattern. Why? Europeans prefer to adjust to the working part of the pattern, adding seam and hem allowances after the alteration process.

Multisize and the European Cut

Although the absence of seam allowances seems strange at first, adding seam and hem allowances is easy—especially with the aid of a rotary cutter with arm. Run the arm along the edge of the pattern. The rotary cutter cuts ⅝ inch away from the arm, adding the seam allowances as you trace around the edge of the pattern.

If you prefer scissors—or haven't invested in a rotary cutter yet—a Burda double tracing wheel with chalk attachment is also available which makes the cutting line with chalk as you trace around the pattern. If you have been sewing a long time, simply add on an estimated ⅝ inch seam allowance as you cut out the garment.

Numbered notches eliminate confusion during construction. For fabric marking, try using adhesive dots at the notch placement on the fabric. Write the corresponding notch number on the dots.

I have found through personal experience that Burda tends to run a bit full in the shoulders so you might want to use the smaller size in the shoulder areas on a loose-fitting jacket. Secondly, although I prefer the European cut of the pants to its American counterpart, the crotch tends to run a bit short. This can easily be taken into consideration by adding ¾ crotch length to the pants in your size.

Finally, don't try to second-guess a Burda pattern by using a size smaller/larger, etc. Simply use the size which corresponds to your measurements. My experience has been that the ease allowance is perfect for the style. If Burda is not available in your area, call toll free 1-800-241-6887 to find the nearest source.

■ If you can't find Burda in your area, write to Burda Patterns Inc., P.O. Box 670628, Marietta, GA 30066, and request nearest store where available or a small home catalogue. Burda also puts out a good booklet on "Fitting Tips" with their patterns. To get one, put two letter stamps on a legal-sized envelope.

■ Decide at the beginning of the season what additions are needed in your wardrobe. Number by priority so you can start sewing on the most needed items first.

MANDATORY MACHINE KNOWLEDGE

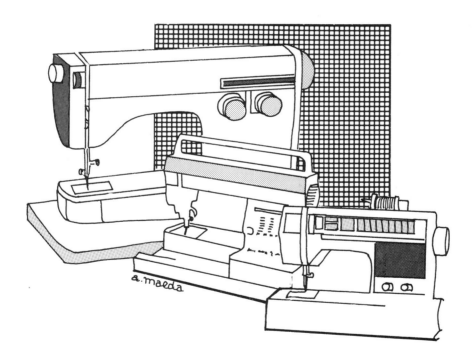

a. maeda

■ If you are approaching 50 and thinking of buying a new sewing machine, make sure the model has a needle threader. Trust me—sooner or later you will need it.

Stitch Length Understanding

According to former sewing machine repair woman Gale Hazen, pattern instructions could be a little more explicit in stitch length for various tasks. Here are some tips which will be helpful.

On machines which number zero to four (on older machines #1 corresponds to 18 to 20 stitches per inch, and #4 corresponds to 6 stitches per inch), follow these directions: To stitch, use stitch length 2 for fine or soft fabrics, length 2½ on medium to heavy fabrics, and length 3 for heavy to thick fabrics to prevent pucker.

To baste, use stitch length 4 and reduce upper tension if fabric is puckering, pulls out easily or knots are visible on the bottom.

To gather, use stitch length 4 but increase upper tension to slightly pre-gather and create gathers which are easy to adjust.

To ease, use stitch length 3 to prevent tiny pleats in the ease.

Reduce upper tension if you may need to pull the bottom thread slightly for increased ease. To reinforce, use stitch length 1.5 for increased strength in areas of stretch such as collar points, seams in a corner, and lapel joints.

To stay stitch, use stitch length 2 through a single layer to prevent stretching. To give stretch to a seam on knits or give to bias seams, use stitch length 1½ and the zigzag width of 1.

■ To keep seams from shortening when joining facing to a coat or jacket, lengthen the stitch. Since interfacing is involved, you are sewing through more layers. If the stitch is too short, it draws up the seam, shortening it. Lengthening stitch is also important when piping is involved. Additional fabric layers require a longer stitch to penetrate depth without affecting length.

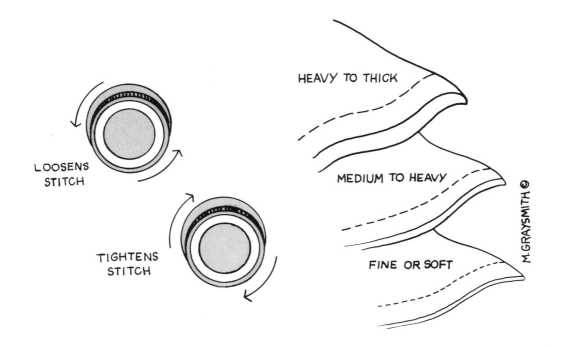

LOOSENS STITCH

TIGHTENS STITCH

HEAVY TO THICK

MEDIUM TO HEAVY

FINE OR SOFT

M. GRAYSMITH ©

Puckered Seams

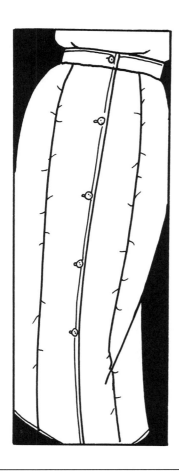

■ Puckered seams on wool result when the fabric is not allowed to dry completely on the surface.

The beginner is not the only seamstress troubled by puckered seams. Incorrect handling of a new fabric or an incorrect needle can baffle even the experienced. If you own a serger, and overlock the raw edges before you sew, be careful not to stretch the fabric as you are overlocking. If the fabric is weak, feed the fabric into the serger needle gently, preventing the fabric from hanging off the throat plate in front.

Before you begin sewing garment seams, experiment with a fabric sample to determine correct needle size and stitch length.

Puckered seams are often the result of needle and fabric incompatibility. A fine fabric will draw up in a slight pucker when sewn with a heavy needle. A dense fabric sewn with a fine needle will break the top thread at regular intervals.

Correct stitch length is equally important to determine on the fabric sample. Fine fabrics call for a shorter stitch length; however, a stitch length which is too short will result in overworked seams which will not press flat. Bulky fabrics call for longer stitch lengths to allow each stitch to go through both fabric layers.

Machine technique can create puckers if the handling of fabric is incorrect. Never stretch the fabric by pulling too hard from the front, back, or both. A stretched fabric will result in a wavy seam with too many stitches.

If you work out pucker problems on a sample, you won't be plagued by puckered seams which reappear several hours after pressing. Don't be fooled into thinking that pressing can solve your problems. Pressing is only a temporary solution. Correct steam, iron temperature, and pressure should also be determined on a fabric swatch so that shiny fabric and seam imprints can be eliminated from the final garment.

For some reason, puckered seams are more common in man-made than natural fibers. If you are using a man-made fiber, cut a lengthwise test strip off the fabric before cutting out the garment. Sew a test strip. changing the variables above.

Examine your strip carefully. If seam puckering cannot be eliminated, consider changing the grainline on your pattern pieces and cutting your garment on the crosswise or bias grain. The fabric is more relaxed on the bias and crosswise grains and puckering can be eliminated.

To avoid puckering in a topstitched seam, always press the seam well before topstitching. Hold the fabric taut from front to back while stitching. Final press.

Presserfeet

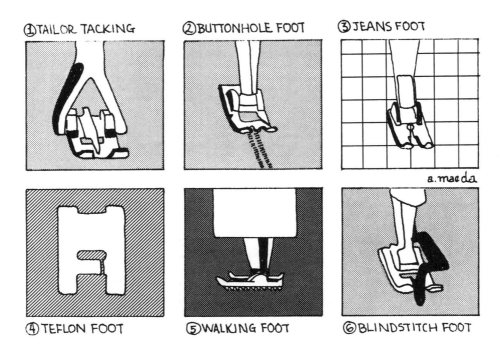

① TAILOR TACKING   ② BUTTONHOLE FOOT   ③ JEANS FOOT

a. maeda

④ TEFLON FOOT   ⑤ WALKING FOOT   ⑥ BLINDSTITCH FOOT

Most sewers never think to change the presserfoot except when they need a zipper foot to put in a zipper. If it were possible to put in a good zipper without it, most sewers would never change the foot at all.

Specialized presser feet can greatly simplify a sewing task. Tailor's tacks can be made in a jiffy on the machine by merely switching to the tailor tacking foot (Illustration 1). Buttonholes will not be nearly as professional if you fail to use the button-hole foot. This foot features ridges which create a channel for the raised sides of the buttonhole as you sew, keeping the buttonhole opening standard with each one (Illustration 2).

If you sew a lot of heavy fabric such as denim, try the combination of the jeans foot with the Schmetz H-J jeans needle (Illustration 3). This combo eliminates irregular stitching over bulky areas. For leather, suede and vinyl, use the Teflon foot which slides smoothly over potentially sticky surfaces (Illustration 4). For handwovens, velvet, velour, or any fabric which requires exact matching such as plaids and stripes, use the walking foot (Illustration 5). The walking foot, sometimes called the "even-feed foot," gives a feed dog effect to the presserfoot, preventing shifting and stretching of the upper fabric.

For perfect topstitching, try the blind stitch foot, riding the ridge along the edge of the fabric (Illustration 6). This foot is also perfect for sewing creases. For a wealth of information on presserfeet send for Betty Dodson's "Feet Smart," a booklet available from Update Newsletters (see Sources).

Topstitching Know-How

■ Press garment well before topstitching. Loosen top thread tension.

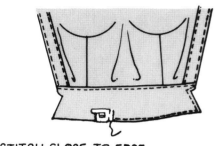

STITCH CLOSE TO EDGE

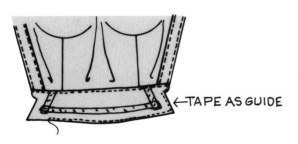

←TAPE AS GUIDE

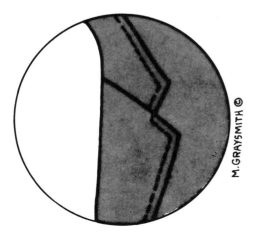

M.GRAYSMITH ©

If you will closely examine the topstitching on a designer shirt, you will usually find two rows of topstitching—one row very close ($\frac{1}{16}$ to $\frac{1}{8}$ of an inch) from the finished seam edge and another row parallel, $\frac{1}{4}$ inch from the first. Topstitching thread is not used. The garment is topstitched with the same thread which constructed the garment. In this case, topstitching provides subtle detailing but more importantly, prevents seams from rolling in, insuring a sharp flat finished edge which will remain the same throughout the life of the garment. To achieve topstitching so close to the edge, the edgefoot is the answer. The edge foot holds the fabric in place and will allow you to stitch quite close to the edge when the fabric is positioned against the knife on the foot (Illustration 1). If parallel topstitching is difficult for you, try the double needle or use well positioned Scotch tape as guide. Do not sew through the tape (Illustration 2).

If you want the topstitching to become a focal point drawing attention to design features, topstitching thread is needed. To eliminate skipped stitches and thread breakage when using this thread, a topstitching needle designated with the letter N is needed. While the needle is not larger in diameter than a regular needle of the same size, the eye opening is longer allowing the thicker thread to pass through easily without tugging or fraying. While some machines can tolerate the thick thread on the bobbin as well by loosening the tension, some cannot. Beautiful topstitching is possible by using topstitching thread on the top and regular thread in the bobbin. Select a topstitching needle compatible with fabric weight. If your fabric is heavy or dense, Schmetz 90/14N will work well. If your fabric is lighter weight, Schmetz 80/12 N is a better choice to eliminate poking larger holes for stitching than necessary.

Decorative topstitching with topstitching thread is usually placed $\frac{1}{8}$ to $\frac{1}{4}$ of an inch from finished seam edge with another parallel row $\frac{1}{4}$ inch from the first if desired.

When topstitching a notch collar, topstitch lapel edge, making a right angle to end topstitching at joint of collar and lapel. Hand walk stitches in seam to resume topstitching again on collar (Illustration 3).

Flashy Seam Finishes

Unlined jackets join the ranks of quality garments if the jackets are finished properly on the inside. Three choices are available for quality seam finishes: Flat fell seams, Hong Kong finished seams, and seam binding edge enclosures. Let's first examine ready-to-wear's current one-step favorite using seam binding.

While you may not have bought a package of (2.75m) seam binding recently; a very professional one-step seam wrap is possible with its use. Since only three yards come to a package and each side of the seam must be wrapped, double the length of seams is needed, plus extra length for facing and hem finishing. Press seam binding in half lengthwise with one half slightly wider. Use enough heat and steam to make a lengthwise crease.

After the garment has been fitted and seams are pressed open, trim off any notches which stick out or any place where seam allowances are wider than 5/8 inch. With fat half of seam binding against wrong side of seam allowance, position folded seam binding so that the raw edge of the seam allowance butts against the lengthwise fold of the seam tape. Pin in place. Enclose raw seam edge by sewing through both sides of the seam binding at once. Repeat process for other side of the seam as well as facing and hem edges. Black seam binding makes a wonderful contrast on a linen or flannel fabric in a different color.

The above seam binding finish is actually a substitute for the Hong Kong finish, which has been around for a long time. The difference in the technique is that bias strips of fabric are used for the Hong Kong finish instead of seam binding; and the Hong Kong finish is a two-step operation compared to a one-step operation for seam binding. If your garment has many curved seams, the Hong Kong finish will give more flexibility around the curves.

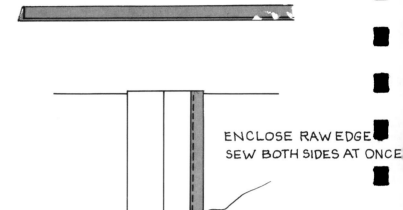

PRESS SEAM BINDING IN HALF

ENCLOSE RAW EDGE
SEW BOTH SIDES AT ONCE

SEAM BINDING FINISH

Flashy Seam Finishes

For the Hong Kong finish, cut bias or well off grain 1 inch wide strips in lightweight fabric—lining or cotton batiste make good choices. Each side of the seam allowance will be wrapped separately as in the seam binding wrap illustrated on page 64. Place the right side of the lining strip against the right side of one side of the seam allowance. Sew a $\frac{1}{4}$ inch seam. Trim seam to $\frac{1}{8}$ inch. Press lining and seam allowance flat. Wrap lining strip around raw edge of seam allowance. Pin into position in the well of the seam. Anchor lining wrap into position from the top side of the seam allowance by sewing in the well of the seam. For both techniques no stitching is visible from the right side of the garment. Both finishes are done to a single thickness seam allowance. While the flat fell seam is a seam finish alternative, it is limited to lightweight fabrics and not nearly as attractive.

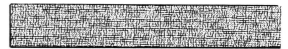

CUT 1" BIAS STRIPS

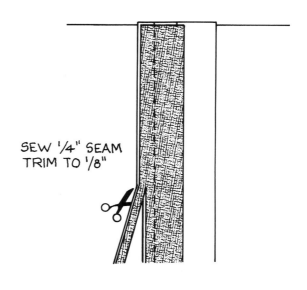

SEW $\frac{1}{4}$" SEAM TRIM TO $\frac{1}{8}$"

HONG KONG FINISH

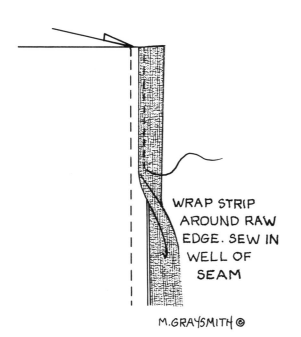

WRAP STRIP AROUND RAW EDGE. SEW IN WELL OF SEAM

M. GRAYSMITH ©

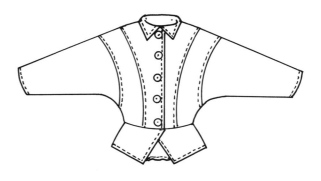

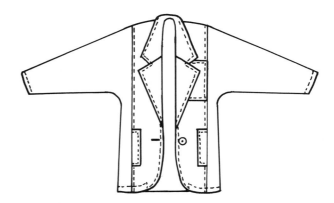

■ Check finished garment length on the back of the pattern. Don't save skirt and pant shortening for the last step. Cutting off more than 2 inches from the bottom distorts the silhouette. Determine length before you cut by comparing desired length to finished length indicated on the back of the pattern envelope. Shorten within the silhouette never more than 2 inches in one location.

TAKING IT ALL IN

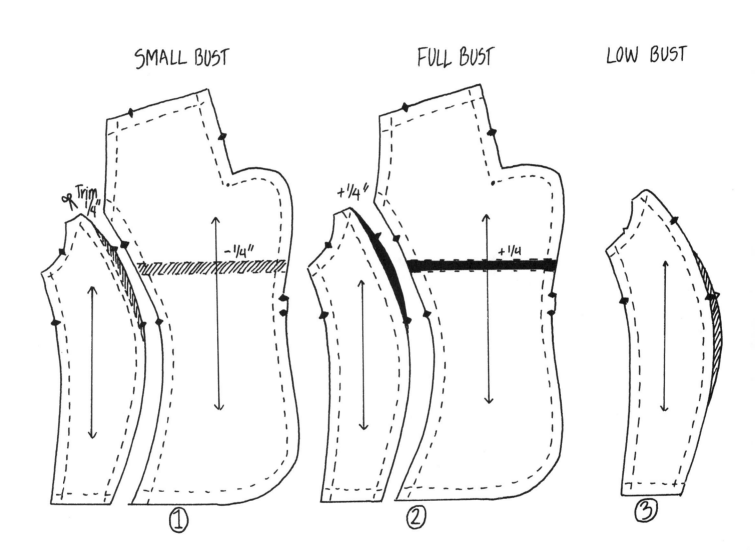

SMALL BUST   FULL BUST   LOW BUST

Trim 1/4"

−1/4"

+1/4"

+1/4

① ② ③

■ A smaller bust dictates less curve on side front princess seam. At the bust area on side front, trim off 1/4 inch from outcurve. On front and facing, fold out 1/4 inch horizontally in bust area. If both pattern pieces are not altered, the unaltered piece wrinkles from too much length.

Tucks Simplified

Is your fantasy of a beautiful pleated skirt or tucked blouse interrupted by a voice which says, "Forget it, pleats and tucks are too much work, remember making all of those tailor's tacks, trying to remove them after the pleat was sewn?"

How about a method for marking pleats which didn't involve tailor's tacks? For this technique, you will need a ruler and marking chalk or an erasable pen. For marking, place cut out garment with pattern attached on a padded surface such as a pressing board to which you can stick pins to anchor the pattern. Place pins at both ends of pleat, marking fold line and stitching line. Mark right side of fabric. Beginning at the first marking lines, pull pattern back away from fabric, leaving pins marking pleats in place. Using the end pins as a fence, push ruler against opposite end pins. Transfer pleat lines with chalk to the right side of the fabric. Differentiate fold lines from stitching lines by using different color marking chalk or using a solid marking line to indicate fold line and a spaced line to indicate stitching line. Unfortunately you can only mark one fabric layer at a time. Repeat marking process for second layer.

Perfect pleats are simplified with a little pressing before sewing. Fold pleat with wrong sides together. Press ¼ inch along the pleat fold line.

Form each tuck by matching stitching lines. Pin. Sew all tucks in the same direction. Lay tucks in the direction indicated on the pattern. Cover tucks with a press cloth. Press in the direction of the fold. Machine or hand baste tucks into position at top and bottom.

■ For tailor's tacks, use contrasting colors for squares, dots and triangles. Mates on different pattern pieces are easier to spot this way.

Perfect Pleats

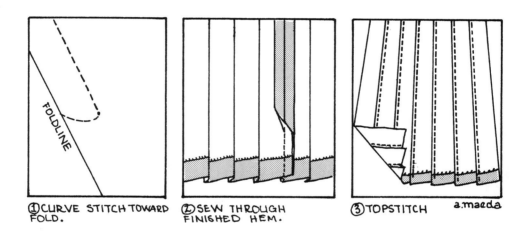

① CURVE STITCH TOWARD FOLD.

② SEW THROUGH FINISHED HEM.

③ TOPSTITCH

a.maeda

Pleats retain their memory best if the fabric contains at least 50 percent polyester. However, successful pleats can be made in many other fabrics including wool jersey and cotton knit if the procedure is done correctly.

Pleats which are released inches from the seamline should be sewn in a straight line with small stitches $\frac{1}{2}$ inch before the marking from the last stitch. Rather than ending the stitching at this point, curve the stitching up and away in a slight curve toward the fold (Illustration 1). This additional curve toward the fold helps lock the pleat into place, a tip shared by fabric sculptor Candice Kling.

Correct hem length must be determined initially if the pleated skirt is made in a heavy fabric. Hem each section of the skirt separately. Sew seams thorough all layers (Illustration 2). In lightweight fabrics, skirt sections do not need to be hemmed separately. Press seams in the hem open and trim to $\frac{1}{8}$ inch. Complete hem. Clip seams above the hemline so that the seams in the skirt can lie together. Pinch right side of garment together at hemline. Pin into place. Sew $\frac{1}{8}$ inch from pinched fold. To maintain a sharp pleat in any fabric, use the edge foot sewing machine attachment. Sew along the folded edges of the underside of the pleat always and topside if preferred. The edge foot allows you to sew within $\frac{1}{16}$ inch of the fold of the fabric. If your machine does not have an edge foot, sew a line of stitching $\frac{1}{8}$ inch from the fold. Edge stitching pleats on the underside forces the stitched edge to the underside, preventing the pleats from standing open. Edge stitching on the topside of the pleats gives a sharp crease and insures pleat memory (Illustration 3).

Use silk thread to baste pleats closed before pressing. Silk thread has elasticity and will not leave thread marks after pressing.

Make a solution of one tablespoon of white vinegar and one cup of water. Spray presscloth covering pleats with this mixture. Press and pound with a tailor's clapper. Allow pleats to dry thoroughly before moving off the ironing surface.

Ruffles and Gathers

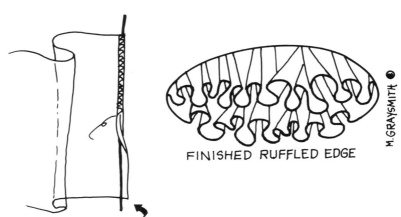

ROLL FABRIC EDGE OVER FISHING LINE.
NARROW ZIG ZAG STITCH

FINISHED RUFFLED EDGE

M. GRAYSMITH ●

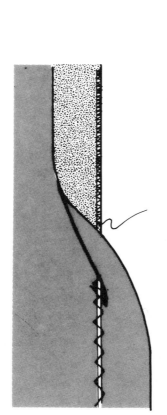

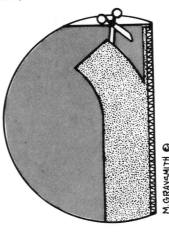

M. GRAYSMITH ●

BACK VIEW

Ruffles and Gathers

Interesting shaped ruffles can be created by zigzagging over monofilament fishing line along outside ruffle edge. The weight of the monofilament determines the sweep of the ruffle—40 lb. monofilament seems to work the best. A cording foot is helpful, not mandatory. On the wrong side of the fabric, using a long stitch and narrow width, zigzag monofilament line to fabric $\frac{1}{2}$ inch from the cut edge of the fabric. Trim excess fabric close to stitching. Now, using the edge foot, overcast fabric and monofilament by using a tight zigzag stitch. This step can be done on a serger with the rolled hem foot using wooly stretched nylon on the upper looper (if desired). Leave long tails on the overlock to hide end threads.

While gathers may seem haphazard on most ready-to-wear, any gathered portion whether large or small will be perfect and evenly spaced in a garment in the upper price brackets.

While this gathering process may take slightly longer, the results speak for themselves. If possible, allow a 1 inch seam allowance along the area to be gathered. Using a medium length stitch in a medium width zigzag, zigzag over fine cord within the seam allowance. Position the first row $\frac{1}{8}$ inch from the actual seamline. Moving over toward the cut edge of the seam allowance, complete another row parallel to the first. If you have allowed a 1 inch seam allowance, it will be possible to complete a third row parallel to the first. All rows are completed within the seam allowance. After all rows are complete, pull up gathering on each end by pulling all end strings at one time. Distribute gathers evenly. Wrap string ends around pin.

Move to the iron and flatten gathers slightly on both sides of the intended seam. Before moving gathered portion from the ironing surface, place Scotch tape $1\frac{1}{2}$ inches from cut edge. Tape will hold gathers into position while joining to second garment piece. Remove tape after completing seam.

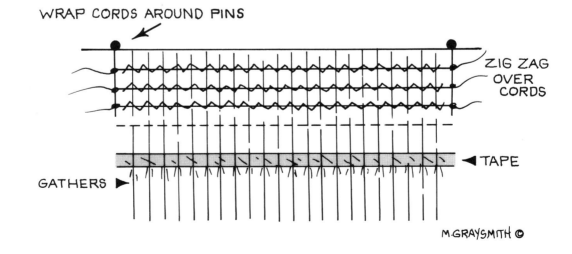

WRAP CORDS AROUND PINS

ZIG ZAG OVER CORDS

TAPE

GATHERS

M.GRAYSMITH ©

Framed Flap Pocket

While piping is capable of subtly outlining a pocket flap, greater attention can be drawn to this detail by framing the outside edge of the flap with a bias strip of fabric. Because wool jersey comes in a wide variety of colors, is lightweight and easily malleable around curves, it is often the choice for framing pocket flaps on jackets. Wool jersey can be repeated in a top, skirt or dress to complete the ensemble.

For this technique, $\frac{1}{4}$ inch seam allowances are used. If using a flap pattern, trim $\frac{5}{8}$ inch seam allowances to $\frac{1}{4}$ inch before cutting flap. Each pocket flap needs a top flap and an under flap, cut to the same size.

If you are using a sew-in interfacing, only the top flap needs to be interfaced. If you are using a fusible interfacing, it is advisable to interface both top and under flap with the fusible, since some shrinkage seems inevitable with fusibles. Trim is applied to the front pocket flap before pocket flap is constructed.

Cut a $1\frac{1}{4}$ inch wide bias strip of wool jersey. Some jerseys are pliable enough so that cross grain strips can be used. Press under $\frac{1}{4}$ inch along one long edge. Overlay wrong side of the strip against the right side of the pocket piece with raw edges in alignment. Start at top corner of the flap, go around the bottom edge of the flap ending atthe other corner of the flap. The top flap edge is left untrimmed.

Follow the outside edge of the pocket with raw edge of the contrasting strip. If the lower pocket edge is curved, clip the strip slightly within the allotted $\frac{1}{4}$ inch seam allowance to allow the outer raw edge of the strip to follow the shape of the pocket. With the iron, mold the folded inside edge of the pocket to lie flat and conform to the pocket shape. If the pocket flap is not curved and has corners, contrasting strip must be mitered at each corner. Naturally, a curved flap is easier to make and equally as effective. Pin in place. Machine stitch contrasting strip to pocket $\frac{1}{4}$ inch from outside edge. Invisibly hand stitch fold of contrasting strip to pocket.

Seam allowances are not visible around the outside edges of a well constructed pocket flap. To prevent their visibility, the underside of pocket flap must be made slightly smaller before flap construction. On underside of the flap, trim off $\frac{1}{16}$ inch from all sides except for the straight top edge.

After trimming under flap, place the right side of the decorated flap against the right side of the trimmed under flap. Place pins on flap side where machine stitching, which attached the contrasting strip, is visible. Using the machine stitching as a guide for $\frac{1}{4}$ inch seam, sew pocket flap around all decorated edges. Do not close top of flap. Press seams open. Grade fabric thicknesses. Turn pocket flap right side out. Press and pound flat with a tailor's clapper.

Flap can now be used to form the outside flap for an inside pocket (see page 76), or sewn onto garment as

---

■ Enjoy the clothes you wear. You only have yourself to please.

Framed Flap Pocket

a decorative touch only, eliminating pocket construction. This is accomplished by placing the right side of the pocket flap against the right side of the jacket with the finished edge of the flap facing up toward the shoulder. Parallel with the unfinished edge of the flap, sew a line of stitching ¼ inch from raw edge of the flap. Next to this line of straight stitching, sew a parallel line of medium width (3mm) zigzag stitching, which goes over the raw edge of the flap onto the garment.

Fold pocket flap down to its desired finished position. From the back side of the garment, hand tack the side ends of the flap to the garment for ½ inch. Press flap well in its finished position.

Special thanks to Barbara Kelly from the Sewing Workshop for perfecting this technique.

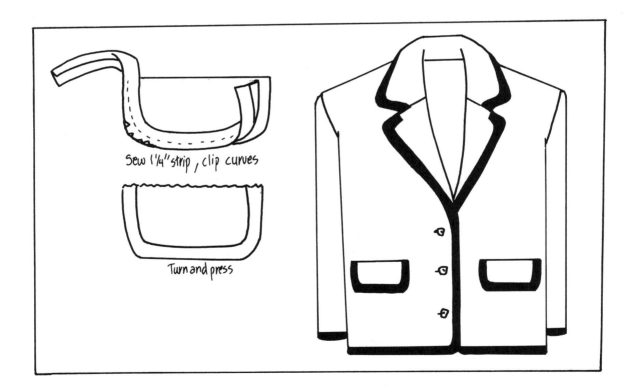

Sew 1¼" strip, clip curves

Turn and press

Skirt Opening
in Pocket

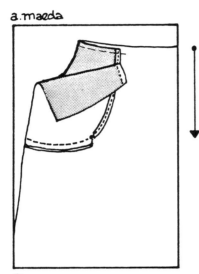

a.maeda

① FINISH RAW EDGES
SEPARATELY, LEAVE OPEN.
LEFT POCKET ONLY.

If you have ever owned a skirt with a hidden opening in the pocket, you may have searched pattern books to find that feature again. Any skirt pattern which features a set-in pocket can be adapted for this feature, which eliminates the zipper altogether.

Complete the skirt to the point where the inner pocket and outer pocket are joined. On the left pocket only, complete the seam joining the inner and outer pocket, leaving 6 inches free from the waistline (to about where the curve on the pocket begins). Sew small stitches for the last $\frac{1}{2}$ inch on the sewn seam to give reinforcement at the opening. Clip the seam once at the end of the stitching. Finish the raw edges in the opening by pressing in the raw edges at $\frac{1}{4}$ inch and again at $\frac{5}{8}$ inch. Enclose the raw edges with a machine or hand stitch.

The left side of the skirt now has a finished 6 inch opening inside the pocket (Illustration 1). Baste the inner pocket into place along the waistline. Do not include the back pocket in the basting. Complete the right pocket per usual pattern directions. Sew side seams and center back seam, eliminating the zipper. Press pockets and seams well.

You are now ready to apply the waistband. Cut the waistband length to your waist measurement plus 12 inches. Interface. Notch band $5\frac{1}{2}$ inches from end. Make sure that dot markings for left pocket placement are visible on the skirt. Run an easeline around the waist of the skirt.

Place the right side of the band against the wrong side of the skirt. Fit the skirt from the finished pocket edge of the left side to the pocket marking dot on the left skirt front, notch to notch on band. Use one $5\frac{1}{2}$ inch extension to extend from the marked dot to the newly finished pocket opening.

Extensions have been cut on both ends of the band so that you have the option of starting with the band

Skirt Opening in Pocket

and skirt—right sides together, finishing by hand, or starting with the right side of the band against the wrong side of the skirt, finishing by machine. The unused extension will be cut off with the waistband's completion. The band was notched to allow the skirt to fit to your waist measurement plus 1 inch ease.

The waistband extension is necessary to complete the left skirt front on the back side of the pocket. Finish the ends of the band in alignment with skirt. Pin finished band into place and try on. The end on the top side of the finished waistband should match up with the pocket placement dot at the waist, allowing an overlap of the waistband of perhaps 4 inches to 5 inches, depending upon the width of the pocket. Optional step: A zipper at the pocket seam is seldom necessary. Instead of finishing the raw edges at the inside pocket opening, simply insert a small zipper. Unzip the zipper and continue with the above instructions.

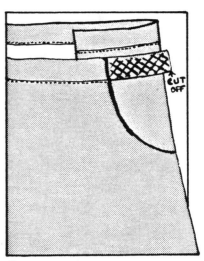

② WAISTBAND EXTENSION

■ Interface behind pockets on sheer or silky fabrics with narrow strips of fusible knitted tricot interfacing. Use straight grain strips for straight pocket areas and bias strips for lower pocket curves.

World-Class Welt Pocket

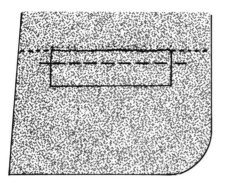

1

With a thorough understanding of the process, welt pockets can be repeatedly accomplished to perfection.

Stabilize the pocket area on the garment with a 2 inch wide strip of interfacing 2 inches longer than the intended pocket opening. Interfacing is needed to help support the weight of the pocket. Fold interfaced welt right sides together and stitch both ends of the welt. Trim seam to $\frac{1}{4}$ inch and corners diagonally to eliminate bulk. Turn welt right side out. Press and pound flat with a tailor's clapper. Topstitch if desired. Baste raw edges together.

Pocket placement should be well marked on the right side of the garment with contrasting thread. Begin pocket on the right side of the garment. Place raw edges of welt pocket along the bottom of the placement line. After the pocket is complete, the welt will turn up over the pocket opening. Hand baste welt into position $\frac{3}{4}$ inch away from raw edges (Illustration 1). Place pocket piece (cut from lining) on top of welt with straight raw edge of pocket piece in line with raw edge of welt. Baste into position $\frac{3}{4}$ inch away from straight raw edges, parallel with basted welt stitching. Place second pocket piece on the opposite side of the placement line so that straight edges of pocket and welt butt against each other along the placement line (Illustration 2).

2

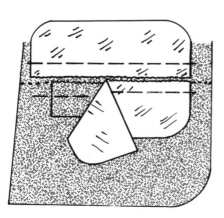

3

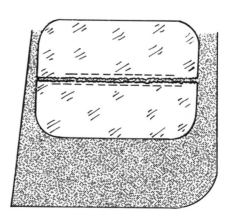

World-Class Welt Pocket

Machine stitch lower pocket and welt into position with small reinforcing stitches ¼ inch away from placement line and raw edges. Begin and end stitching one stitch beyond the ends of the welt. The ends of the welt are easy to identify under the pocket since the area before and after the welt has less bulk under the machine needle. Stitch upper pocket into position, with small reinforcing stitches, ¼ inch from placement line. This stitching line is parallel to the first which attached the lower pocket and welt. Start and end upper pocket stitching ¼ inch shorter on each end than lower pocket stitching (Illustration 3). A shorter line of stitching on the upper pocket piece is important to insure that the lining at pocket opening is not visible at ends when welt pocket is in its finished position.

Slash garment diagonally between stitching lines. Clip diagonally to form triangles in corners. Clip to within one thread of each end stitch. If clipping is not done close enough, pocket will not turn through smoothly. Carefully slash and clip garment only in this step. Do not cut welts or pocket pieces in this step or the buttonhole will be weakened (Illustration 4).

Pull pocket pieces through newly cut opening to the inside of the garment. Press welt up over opening. Hand baste welt in place. On the inside of the garment, attach triangles to pocket pieces on each end. Stitch triangles close to the end of pocket stitching. Lay pocket in finished position. Trim pocket pieces so that they are identical. Close pocket by stitching pocket pieces, sewing over clipped triangles once more. On the right side of the garment, handstitch ends of welt to garment with invisible stitching (Illustration 5). Press and pound into place.

4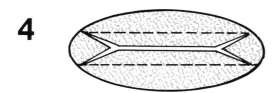

5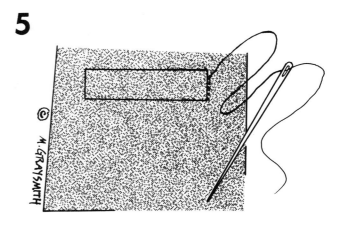

Tissue Fold Pocket

Perusing the racks of ready-to-wear, you will undoubtedly come across an ingenious pocket which is found in fine quality knit pants. Not only is this pocket an attractive design detail, but flat and unbulky as well.

Cut two pocket pieces 7 inches wide by 12 inches long. Interface with a lightweight press-on interfacing. Cut the bottom short edge into a V shape. The pocket piece now resembles a long pocket with a V at the bottom. Finish raw edges with an overlock or zigzag stitch.

Sew side seams from lower leg to 7⅝ inches from cutting line at waist. Sew last inch of seam with small reinforcing stitches. Do not backstitch. Cut four narrow strips ½ inch by 7⅝ inches in length of lightweight press-on interfacing. Press interfacing strips on wrong side of fabric, butting edge of strip against cut edge of unsewn side seam. Interfacing seam allowances will reinforce pocket openings and prevent stretching. Press back seam allowances on all unsewn side seams. Topstitch pressed back seam allowance into place on right side of fabric.

Center right side of 7 inch by 12 inch strip against wrong side of pants opening with pointed end toward hem. Topstitched seam allowances butt together and are vertically centered under 12 inch length pocket piece. Pin into position. Hand baste around outside edge. Topstitch pocket piece into position ⅝ inch from all raw edges of angled pocket shape. All pocket stitching is completed from the underside of the garment. Pocket is now complete.

Credit to: Marcy Tilton, founder of the Sewing Workshop in San Francisco.

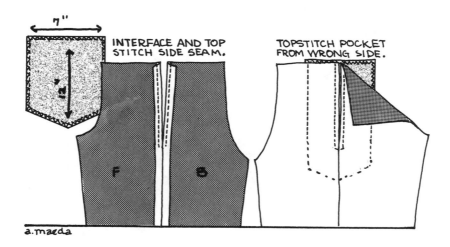

INTERFACE AND TOP STITCH SIDE SEAM.

TOPSTITCH POCKET FROM WRONG SIDE.

a.maeda

■ Reinforce pocket openings on well used pockets with bar tacks or small triangles.

CLOSURES

■ If you want an accurate, professional-looking fly front, don't leave topstitching to chance. Mark stitching line 1¼ to 1½ inch from center front. Don't forget to bar tack at the bottom.

In-Seam Buttonholes

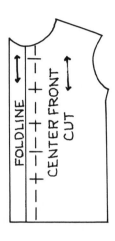

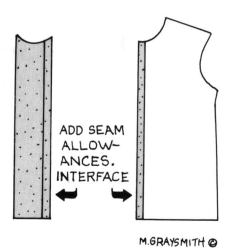

ADD SEAM ALLOW- ANCES. INTERFACE

M. GRAYSMITH ©

In-seam buttonholes can make a clean attractive opening for buttons which are quite large (in lieu of button loop or oversize buttonhole) or buttons which are quite small (in lieu of button loops on wedding gowns). In-seam buttonholes can also be used as a design feature. If you dread hand or machine buttonholes, in-seam buttonholes may be a solution. In-seam buttonholes can be used on any pattern where a newly created seam would be attractive.

If you were using a large button, the difference between the edge of the button and the edge of the garment must be half the diameter of the button itself. Therefore, the distance between the newly created seam and the garment edge would be larger than for a blouse. Since a newly formed seam will be created for the buttonhole, cut left and right sides of the bodice separately. For women's garments, cut the left side (where the buttons will be sewed) as per original pattern. The pattern will now be cut apart to form a seam line for button openings.

If the garment features a fold back facing, the next step is unnecessary. If the garment features a sew-on facing, to eliminate bulk, overlap seam lines joining the facing and the garment. Tape in place. The pattern now features a cut-on facing. Draw a new seam line on the pattern along the desired placement of the in-seam button opening. For most garments, button placement will be the most attractive along the center front line. On wrong side of garment, mark button placement along this line with perpendicular lines which intersect the placement line to indicate the beginning and end of the button opening. Make sure button opening markings are visible on both sides of the button placement line. Draw a parallel grain line marking on the garment section which will be cut off. Cut pattern apart along newly drawn button opening placement line (center front on bodice). Add desired seam allowance to each side of the newly cut line. This will form a seam allowance for the seam.

The narrower piece will now be referred to as the facing. Interface facing with fusible or nonfusible interfacing. Since some of the facing will be visible on the garment front, test fusible on a scrap before committing to the facing itself. Interface seam allowance on

In-Seam Buttonholes

bodice front with a $\frac{1}{2}$ inch strip of fusible interfacing to sharpen up seam edge.

Place facing and bodice right sides together. Sew seam with small stitches to reinforce beginning and end of buttonhole. Do not back stitch. Back stitching puts too much thread in the seam, causing seam not to press open uniformly. Reinforce with machine knot at beginning and end of button opening by holding fabric in place.

Fold facing into position. In-seam button openings will be approximately $\frac{5}{8}$ to 1 inch from the edge of the right bodice (further if a large button is used). Mark button openings from bodice front on to bodice facing by slipping pins through the ends of button openings. Mark button openings on facing. Sew button openings slightly larger on facing to make buttons slide in and out easily.

There are three options for finishing the button opening on the facing. One, repeat the process of the front adding a corresponding seam line to facing or lining. Two, create opening in facing by stitching an opening through a small bias rectangle of lining fabric. In either of the above methods, hand tack outer garment and facing button openings together at ends of button opening. Three, to eliminate bulk, slit fabric right behind buttonhole. Tuck under long sides of newly cut edge with part of the needle. Pin in place. Whip stitch with a single wax thread, using small stitches.

Credit to: Claire Shaeffer, author of *Fabric Sewing Guide* for her piece in *Sew News*, concerning topic. (See Sources).

M.GRAYSMITH ©

Hidden Buttonhole Placket

Many times a large button at the neck or an important accessory pin is the preferred closing on a pattern which features a row of visible buttons and buttonholes. A hidden buttonhole placket might also be the choice when buttonholes are less than perfect. Any pattern can be a candidate for a hidden placket with a few simple changes. Since women's garments traditionally button right or left, pattern changes will be made on the right side only.

If the fabric is not bulky and the outside edge of the facing is a straight piece, one simple operation makes it possible to add a facing and create a hidden buttonhole placket.

Placket addition is made on the right bodice side only. Feel free to cut the fabric double, adding placket addition to both sides—just remember to cut the left side per original pattern later. If the pattern has a fold back straight shaped facing, cut off facing along the

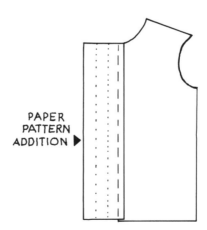

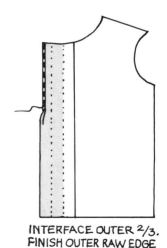

INTERFACE OUTER 2/3.
FINISH OUTER RAW EDGE

Hidden Buttonhole Placket

fold line. Tape on a wide piece of paper the length of the front. Extend paper into seam line 1 inch. Decide how wide you want the finished placket. A common placket width is 1½ inches. Multiply desired placket width times 3 (example 1½ inch times 3 equals 4 ½ inches). Make addition (in example: 4½ inches) to pattern along fold line.

Fold paper pattern addition into thirds and position at neck. Cut neck line shaping on pattern. Cut out garment. Mark front fold line on garment. Interface outer ⅔ of addition for buttonholes. Finish long outer raw edge.

If your pattern has a shaped facing that fits around the neck into the shoulder, cut pattern along fold line if it is the fold back type or make addition from the seam line if facing is cut separately. Decide on placket width. Add on only 2 times desired placket width. If facing is fold back type, tape facing into position after addition. Fold paper additions into position and cut neck line shaping. Interface facing on outer 1/3 of addition for buttonholes.

Press addition well along front fold line as per pattern. Press ⅓ of the placket addition into place. The second ⅔ of the placket is where the buttonholes will be made. Fold interfaced back half of placket into position, just a scant bit behind the first fold. Three fabric thicknesses will be formed behind the right garment front. Make buttonholes in back half of the placket through 2 fabric thicknesses. Secure hidden placket into place by sewing through all 4 thicknesses at neck and lower edge.

Hand tack facing layers together between buttonholes.

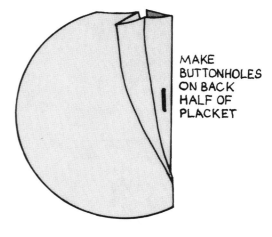

FOLD BACK HALF OF PLACKET INTO POSITION, A SCANT BEHIND FIRST FOLD.

BACK OF RIGHT FRONT

MAKE BUTTONHOLES ON BACK HALF OF PLACKET

M. GRAYSMITH ©

■ Betweens are hand sewing needles, sized 5-9 (the higher the number, the finer the needle), which are 3/8 inch shorter than sharps. Tailors love them because they go in and out of the fabric faster.

Flawless Machine Buttonholes

Even the best sewers are a bit timid when it comes to making buttonholes. Due to their function and placement, buttonholes are too visible not to be perfect. But how do we insure perfection? Many of us remember the buttonhole attachment that snapped on the Singer Featherweight being the closest to buttonhole perfection we have ever known. Two professional sewers I know refuse to give up their Featherweights and keep them set up for the sole purpose of making buttonholes. Most new sewing machines have built-in buttonholers that can be mastered with a sample or two. Here are some tips which can make your buttonholes worthy of praise and close inspection:

All buttonholes need the layer of interfacing for stability—no exceptions! Even a fine crepe de chine or silk chiffon blouse must be interfaced—silk or rayon organza are good choices for these fabrics. Interfacing does not have to be stiff to do the job! If the fabric is stretchy, such as a knit, a press-on interfacing is preferable, using the straight of grain parallel to the buttonhole to prevent stretching.

Extra-fine thread on top and bobbin produces less bulky, finer buttonholes. Madeira Cotona, 80 weight, is a very fine thread often used in heirloom sewing, which can also be used to make fine buttonholes in lightweight fabric. Gutterman and Sulky also produce fine threads (size 40) in a large color selection. Tighten bobbin screw slightly or thread through bobbin eye when using finer threads. For best buttonhole results use a 70/10 HJ or 70/10 N sewing machine needle.

If the fabric is washable, firm up the fabric for the buttonhole process with a fabric stiffener such as Perfect Sew or Sew Stable. If the fabric is dry cleanable, place a layer of Solvy between the buttonhole foot and the fabric. Between the feed dog and the fabric, slide in a piece of paper. These steps are necessary for accurate buttonhole size. Make buttonhole. Tear off paper and Solvy. Steam away excess Solvy or submerge garment in water to remove fabric stiffener.

Cut the buttonhole open with a pair of small sharp scissors or, better yet, with a buttonhole chisel. Fold the fabric back on itself so that the cut sides of the buttonhole are accessible to you. Trim fabric within the buttonhole as close as possible to the buttonhole stitching. After the buttonhole has been cut open, traces of interfacing are slightly visible. After trimming away as many threads as possible from within the buttonhole, color any visible interfacing with a felt tip pen. This step may come as a shock to many of you, but telephone calls to four professional dressmakers confirmed this as the method they all use.

Seal edges within the buttonhole with Fray Check or Fray Stoppa. This product seals the threads, providing a clear finish, seals in the color from the felt tip pen, and dries with a soft finish. Fabric glue makes the buttonhole too stiff.

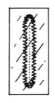  

M. GRAYSMITH ©

■ Whenever making a machine buttonhole on a jacket, don't trust the fully automatic buttonhole feature. Determine your own second bartack at the end of the buttonhole. This eliminates the machine's tendency to end one buttonhole prematurely when it senses extra fabric layers.

Buttonholes Near Bulky Seams

I do not know of any sewer, beginning or advanced, who does not dread putting in buttonholes. Since the buttonhole process is one of the finishing touches, this process can also ruin your whole project if not done properly. This problem often occurs on a coat or jacket where the fabric is slightly heavier, causing a bulky seam. Try these tips for success:

If you are having difficulty sliding the garment into position under the buttonhole foot, this buttonhole is on the fast track to disaster due to thickness of fabric. Home sewing machines are incapable of making a flawless buttonhole in two layers of melton or double-faced fabric plus interfacing. Pure and simple, these fabrics are too thick to permit the buttonhole function to operate properly. What are your choices in this instance? Consider making bound buttonholes, a loop closure or a hand buttonhole. You could also take your coat to a tailor and pay to have the task completed.

Success with other buttonholes can be obtained by following these tips. Insert a small strip of fusible web between garment and facing in the buttonhole area. Fusible web will prevent the layers from shifting during the buttonhole process and help seal threads after the buttonhole is cut open.

Varying top thread can change the look of the buttonhole. If you want a heavier looking buttonhole with a flat finish, use all-cotton Madeira's Cotona, 30 weight. For a glossy finish, try Sulky's rayon thread, 30 weight. Use these heavier threads on top only with a 80/12 N or HJ needle, to eliminate fraying. Use a lighter weight thread on the bobbin. If you want the buttonhole to be less visible, use a lighter weight thread, such as Madeira's Cotona, 80 weight, on top and bobbin with a 70/10 HJ needle. Higher numbers in thread denote lighter weight thread. Tighten bobbin screw slightly or thread through bobbin eye when using finer threads on bobbin.

If the fabric is spongy or the pile is deep, slide a piece of Solvy between the presserfoot and the fabric. This will keep the presserfoot moving and prevent it from sinking into the fabric. Bypass the automatic buttonhole feature, determining the bar tacks manually.

Better buttonholes near bulky seams, such as on jacket fronts and waistbands are made without the buttonhole boot, using the dual feed, says Jenny Haskins, training manager of Pfaff Australia. Slide a piece of paper between the feed dog and the garment fabric. Prop up the back of the presserfoot with cardboard or the "Hump Jumper," so that the foot is level to begin the buttonhole. Since you do not have the grooves on the buttonhole foot to help guide the buttonhole, guide the second row of stitching so that it is straight.

When making horizontal buttonholes by machine, do not start the buttonhole close to the seamed edge. Begin the buttonhole away from the seam, working toward the seamed edge. Premature buttonhole finishing does not happen when working in this direction.

Cut buttonhole open with a buttonhole chisel. Trim stray threads with small scissors. Color any interfacing which shows with color-matching felt tip pen. Use toothpick to seal buttonhole edges with Fray Stoppa or Fray Check.

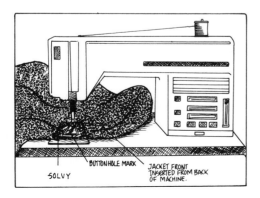

BUTTONHOLE MARK
JACKET FRONT INSERTED FROM BACK OF MACHINE.
SOLVY

■ If your fabric is very bulky, consider buttonhole alternatives before you begin the garment, avoiding disappointments later.

Determining Buttonhole Size

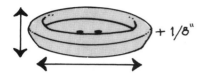

+ 1/8"

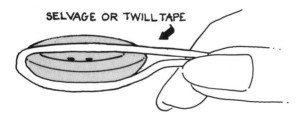

SELVAGE OR TWILL TAPE

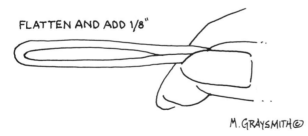

FLATTEN AND ADD 1/8"

M. GRAYSMITH©

The ideal way to determine buttonhole length is to make a series of buttonhole lengths by machine on a scrap, choosing the one with the best fit. Time being of the essence to most sewers, practice buttonholes are seldom made. A buttonhole is simply made in the garment in hopes that the fit will be adequate. If you know the length principle, all guesswork can be eliminated.

The formula for correct buttonhole length is: The width of the button plus the depth of the button plus 1/8 inch ease. Most sewers forget the depth of the button, making the buttonhole just slightly larger than the width of the button. This creates difficulty when using a large sculptural button because the buttonhole is too short to accommodate the depth of the button as well as the width.

Buttons are rather difficult to measure with accuracy using a ruler or measuring tape. Instead wrap the button snugly with a piece of twill tape or selvage. Slip out the button and flatten the tape in half. This represents the smallest opening the button is capable of entering. Make the buttonhole this length plus 1/8 inch ease. Making the buttonhole 1/8 inch longer allows the garment to button with ease and prevents the buttonhole from stretching out of shape during use.

Designer Celia Tejado creates a simple but interesting buttonhole in her sportswear line by creating buttonhole openings with contrasting fabric strips 2½ inches long and 2 inches wide. Press under ¼ inch seam allowances around entire facing strip. Facings are sewn, placing the right side of the facing against the wrong side of the garment, sewing a small rectangular opening for the buttonhole. After opening is clipped, turn facing to right side through the buttonhole. Press into position. Since raw edges on facings have been pressed under ¼ inch, topstitch facing into position near folds of rectangle.

■ Solution for imperfect completed buttonholes: Make a hand buttonhole with buttonhole twist over the imperfect buttonhole—all imperfections will be hidden behind hand stitches.

Button Choices

Which button is best—shiny or dull? A matte button is usually less obtrusive, and interferes least with the impact of bold accessories. Interesting shiny buttons can make a statement but they usually make the garment appear more dressy. Is that the effect you want?

What size button is best? This is purely up to you. If you want to use a lot of buttons, $1/2$ inch or smaller is best. Consider using one large button as a closure on a coat or jacket. The effect is more dramatic and can simply make the piece. My favorites come from Paco Despacio (see Sources), a buttonmaker from Oregon who sets semiprecious stones such as coral, jasper, and turquoise in silver bezels. Paco also makes buttons from horn, antler, antique coins, and fossils. Paco's buttons are recycled from year to year onto my current favorite garments.

Flea markets and antique shops are another source of interesting buttons. Occasionally some real treasures can be found. I found four matching antique amber buttons recently, perfect for a suede I'm working on.

Button choice may be the most important decision you make on a garment. Sometimes the size of the button can appear "out of scale." Small buttons from $1/4$ to $3/8$ inch are used on blouses, shirts and children's wear; $1/2$ inch button on dresses and blouses; $5/8$ inch buttons on skirts, dresses and vests. Generally, a $3/4$ to $7/8$ inch button is used on dresses, skirts and jackets, and a 1 inch button for jackets and coats. Buttons larger than $1\frac{1}{4}$ inch are usually limited in number or only one is used as a focal point on a garment. A long coat may feature one large (2 to 3 inch button) at the neck or a similar size button may be used as the one closing at the waist on a jacket.

Positioning the buttons correctly on a garment is important since the way a garment hangs on the body is affected. Lay the garment out on a flat surface. Pin the garment closed as you want it to look while you are wearing it. Pin garment together above and below the buttonhole. On a horizontal buttonhole, place a pin straight down through the end of the buttonhole, closest to the edge of the garment. On a vertical buttonhole, place the pin in the center of the buttonhole.

Often too little thought is given to the garment's final touch: the button. Many sewers buy the exact number of buttons the pattern calls for, make the exact length of button hole the pattern indicates and turn out boring garments. Where's your creativity? One spectacular button or a group of interesting buttons can turn an ordinary garment into an extraordinary one—a garment sure to elicit some comment.

Don't judge all buttons at their face value. Turn the button over and look at the back side. Very often an abalone button will be more interesting and of different coloration on the back side. If the garment fabric has a print motif, try to mirror the motif in the shape of the button.

Button Choices

Remove all pins except for pins which mark the actual button placement. If you are using more than one button, make sure that all buttons are placed the same distance away from the finished edge of the garment. Run doubled thread through beeswax to give it strength and to prevent knotting. Heavier thread such as buttonhole twist is preferable on coats and jackets. If you are using metal buttons, which tend to cut the thread, sew them on with dental floss.

Do not sew a button with holes tightly against the fabric. While sewing, create "extra play" which can be wrapped to form a shank, similar to that found on shank buttons. The shank behind a button is important as it allows the buttonhole to slide behind the button without puckering. Hold the button slightly loose agains the fabric. Make a pass through each hole in the button 4 to 6 times. Pull button away from the garment and wrap the thread against the previously sewn threads to form a shank. Pull needle to the wrong side of the fabric and knot.

■ If you machine wash purchased garments, check buttons periodically to make sure they are secure. A lost button is not easily replaced.

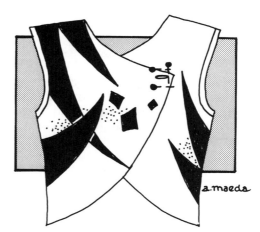

■ When sewing on a button, it is easy to create room for a shank by positioning a toothpick between the garment and the button as you sew.

Snaps as Button Replacements

After you do a beautiful job on a skirt or pair of pants, why not finish the waistband with a snap the way garments are finished in ready-to-wear? Hooks and eyes pull at the fabric and eventually fall off. Buttons are bulky under a belt. Buttonholes stretch and look messy after a few wearings if the waistband is snug. Snaps, if reinforced correctly, keep their shape indefinitely as well as providing a ready-to-wear touch.

After fighting with the Snap Fastener Pliers for years, I switched to a far simpler tool which sets snaps better, is less expensive and considerably easier to operate. This snap tool can be purchased from Bee Lee Company (see Sources), model #K810. Purchase a pair of junior punch pliers as well which will punch a clean hole through all fabric layers including interfacing, making th snap setting process far easier. Heavy-duty snaps are available from the same source in a wide

variety of colors. Use heavy-duty snaps regardless of fabric weight in order to accommodate the additional support needed.

Due to the way snaps are pulled open, additional reinforcement is necessary to keep the snap from pulling out of the fabric. In addition to the regular interfacing used in garment, cut a 1 inch square of Banroll (stiff, coarse waistband material) which will be placed between layers next to the interfacing before the snap is applied. Banroll was chosen because it has a dense texture, something the snap can sink its teeth into. Snaps in any fabric need this additional support. After the snap placement is determined, slide in the extra support before you put in the snap.

Using the hole punch, punch a hole for the decorative part of the snap in the outside of the garment. With scissors, clean out any threads which might pre-

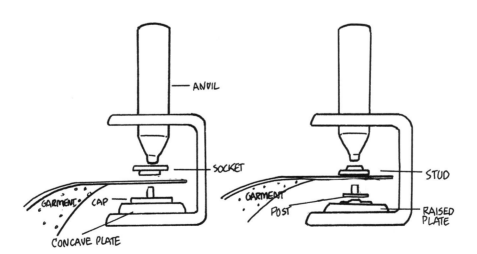

Snaps as Button Replacements

vent clean snap setting. Slip the cap (decorative part of the snap) into the hole punched into the fabric, so that the decorative side of the snap shows on the outside of the garment.

From the snap setting equipment, into the "U" shaped metal holder, slide in the metal disc which has a cup shape on one side and a slight protrusion on the other. Fit in with cup side up. Slight protrusion on the disc enables it to fit snugly.

Now slide the decorative snap, positioned in your garment, into the cup positioned in the snap setter. Fit the socket (a cup with round edges) onto the cap protrusion coming out of the fabric. To set the snap, lower the anvil into position. Pound hard on the end of the anvil with a hammer. The decorative half of the snap is set.

Rub chalk on the underside of the snap half you just set. Close the garment into the desired position. The chalk will mark the exact position for the other half of the snap. Using the hole punch again, punch a hole through all layers, for the bottom half of the snap. With scissors again, clean out any threads which might prevent clean snap setting.

Empty the cup shaped device from the "U" shaped metal holder. Position the other metal disc (which looks like a nipple on one side) into the holder. Slight protrusion on the disc enables it to fit snugly.

Fit the post (snap piece with the long shiny protrusion) through the hole punched in the garment, fitting the protrusion through the hole from the back side of the garment. Now slide the underside of the post onto the nipple position in the "U" shaped metal holder. Onto the end of the post, protruding out of the fabric, position the stud (flat bottom with wide ridge). Lower the anvil into position again, and pound hard with a hammer. The snap is now complete. Snaps should work smoothly. If your finished snap does not work smoothly, reposition in "U" shaped metal device and pound harder. Snaps will be difficult to snap if each side is not firmly in position.

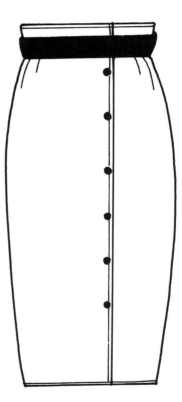

Demonstrated on *Power Sewing* Video #4; *Foolproof Pant Fitting.*

Placket from India

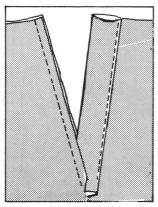 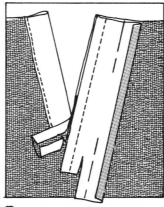 

a.maeda

①UNDER PLACKET FROM RIGHT SIDE.

②OUTER PLACKET FROM WRONG SIDE.

③FOLD EDGES UNDER AND TOPSTITCH.

Neckline and sleeve plackets have one thing in common: Everyone hates them, even the most experienced seamstresses. The unpopularity of the placket is well-founded in its persistence to pucker even under the most professional wielded needle. But the placket can be tamed with knowledge.

Custom dressmaker Tara Arnold from Berkeley generously shared a placket method used on Kuta, shirts worn by men in North India, which she learned during an 8 year stint there. This superior placket is easy, and both pucker and hassle free. Do placket construction on bodice before side seams are sewn or on sleeve before underarm seams are sewn—while garment is out flat.

On garment, cut slit for placket 1 inch longer than desired placket opening; the finished placket will be approximately $1\frac{1}{2}$ inches longer than the opening. Cut 2 placket strips per opening, double the width of the finished placket plus two seam allowances, and 2 inches longer than desired opening. For a typical sleeve placket with a $3\frac{1}{2}$ inch opening, cut strip $3\frac{1}{2}$ inches wide and $5\frac{1}{2}$ inches long. For a typical neckline placket, with a 10 inch long placket and a finished width of $1\frac{1}{4}$ inches,

cut two strips 12 by $3\frac{3}{4}$ inches. If your fabric is slippery or stretchy, interface with a lightweight interfacing.

Start under placket on the opposite side you want to overlap. For a woman's neckline placket, start on the garment left side; for a man's neckline placket, start on the garment right side. For sleeve plackets, start on side closest to the back of the sleeve.

Place the right side of the under placket against the wrong side of the garment, matching the lengthwise raw edge of the placket with the cut opening in the garment. Sew seam at 5/8 inch. Stop seam at end of the cut opening. Machine knot to reinforce stitching. Make a deep clip in seam allowances perpendicular to stitching line at the end of this stitching. Press under $\frac{5}{8}$ inch seam allowance on unsewn placket edge. Pull placket through to the right side. Pin pressed seam allowance into position on the right side so that it just covers previous line of stitching. Topstitch into place to the bottom of the sewn seam. Cut off $\frac{3}{4}$ inch at the unstitched end of the newly made placket (Illustration 1).

Place right side of the top placket against the wrong side of the garment, matching lengthwise raw edge of

Placket from India

the placket with unsewn cut edge of the garment opening. With sleeve side up, sew seam at $^5/_8$ inch. Stop seam $^3/_4$ of an inch past cut opening on top placket side. Make a deep clip in seam allowances diagonally to stitching line at end of the stitching. Press under a $^1/_2$ inch seam allowance on unsewn top placket edge. Make a 2 inch cut on the placket from the bottom of the placket to the bottom of the placket opening, parallel with the seam edge, 1 inch away from the raw edge of the sewn seam. Cut off excess fabric from bottom of top placket seam to original placket raw edge away from the newly folded edge (Illustration 2).

Pull top placket through to the right side of the garment. Pin pressed seam allowance in position on top placket side to cover previously sewn top placket seam. Fold bottom edge of placket under $^1/_2$ inch. Pin in position. Topstitch side of the placket to and from ends of opening. Fold under placket into position under top placket (Illustration 3). Sew end of placket. A decorative diagonal or stitch may be used in bottom placket box. Press and pound with a tailor clapper

■ Most garments made at home lack the sharp, crisp edges of their counterparts in the stores. The industry uses a 12 lb. steam iron to achieve this look. Combined with steam, use a tailor's clapper on plackets, collars, tabs, waistbands, lapels—virtually any area of detail. Do not use a clapper on seams because it will bring out an imprint in the seam allowance.

■ A jacquaid is any basket-, twill-, or satin-weave used to give the fabric a two-dimensional effect.

REALISTIC APPROACH TO PANT FITTING AND CONSTRUCTION

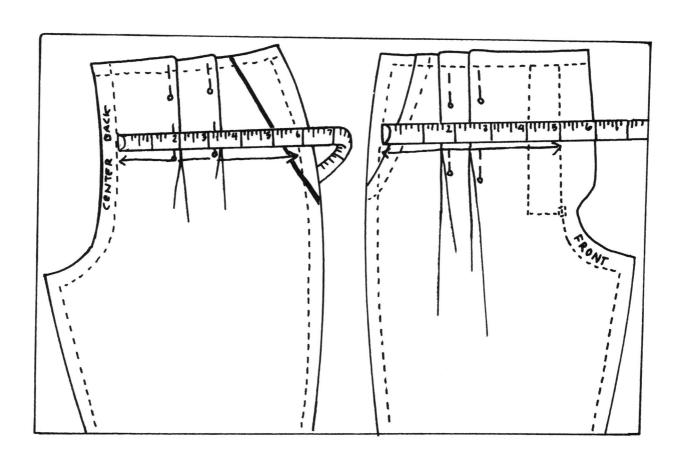

Choosing the Right Pant Style for You

If you are not happy with how you look in pants, even though they fit and are comfortable, perhaps the pants style is the problem. Since pants reveal many figure faults, everyone has something she wants to camouflage, so picking the right pant style is a critical decision.

Unless you are over 5 feet 10 inches, no legs can appear long enough in pants. Avoid cuffed and cropped pants which actually shorten the leg silhouette. Yoked pants shorten the leg and make hips appear larger as

well. The high-waisted pant lengthens the leg while shortening the waist and drawing attention to a smooth, sleek silhouette. Unless your figure is flawless and you are long-waisted, these are not the pants for you. Stirrup tights lengthen legs and can be worn by less than perfect figures if worn with a big loose top. Stirrup tights and narrow tapered legs are not flattering on an individual with full calves.

Unless you are tall, be careful of a pant leg that is too wide. Wide legs make you look shorter and wider.

Choosing the Right Pant Style for You

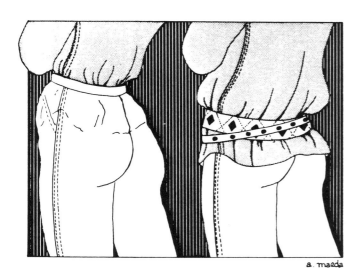

a. maeda

■ "Sure, deck your lower limbs in pants, yours are the limbs my sweeting, you look divine as you advance. Have you seen yourself retreating?" Ogden Nash.

Correct length is also an issue. Before hemming, try on pants with the shoes you intend to wear with them. Heel height affects pants length.

Pants should end at the break in front and be ½ to 1 inch longer in back, long enough to cover part of the shoe in back.

Although pants are not flattering to all women, you need a few pairs in your wardrobe regardless. Style choice is important in pants that are flattering. If you have fullness in the tummy or the hips, a style with deep front pleats will draw attention to the pleat and away from the problem. Pocket placement should be carefully considered if your hips are wide. Slant hip pockets that end at your wide hip act as an arrow pointing to the problem. Loose styles conceal figure faults, whereas snug styles draw attention to them.

If your hips are wide and your fanny protrudes, a straight leg pant with deep soft pleats will be the most flattering. Pleats combined with a fly front create vertical lines on the pant which lengthen the leg, making the figure appear less broad. Hips always appear narrower if balanced by a broader shoulder—available to everyone in the way of shoulderpads. Dolman sleeves, lapels, and pockets create volume on the upper half of the body while diminishing volume on the lower half. The flat seat should choose a fuller pant style draped or with soft gathers. Gathers fill in the space in the back while softly disguising a fully tummy in front. If your figure is smooth and well proportioned except for the flat seat, a jodhpur pant will be flattering as well.

If you have a flat seat and a tummy, close fitting pants can be flattering if they are worn with a high hip length or longer sweater or loose shirt worn out. The full top which covers the tummy eliminates side view comparisons of the protruding tummy and the flat seat.

If your tummy is full or your hips are large, avoid a tight-fitting waistband. A looser fitting waistband helps straighten out unwanted curves rather than emphasizing them. Tight-fitting pants are usually accompanied by wrinkles at the crotch in the front and back; these create horizontal lines which widen the figure. If you are considering shorts for summer, a deep-pleated tapered pair of Bermudas are kinder to most figures than a boxy pair or short-shorts. If your legs are good and your shoulders are broad, try a pair of full short-shorts for a long-legged silhouette. If you would rather cover the leg, try a wide-legged, fully-gathered pair in a soft drapey fabric such as Austrian cotton knit. The knit pants will be cool and hang in soft folds close to the leg.

Finally, how you wear pants is extremely important. Tops tucked into pants are only for the very slim. If you have any tummy fullness or love handles, do not tuck in your shirt.

Choosing Correct Pant Fabric

Fabric choice for pants is important. For tailored pants, choose a fabric with body so that the pants will hold their shape—light- to medium-weight wool flannel, lightweight wool tweed, wool crepe, wool double knit, rayon twill, cotton chino, cotton poplin, linen silk noil, silk pongee, tussa, dupionni or shantung. While wool gabardine makes an excellent tailored pant, knowledge of working with wool gabardine is essential for professional looking results. Be careful of corduroy—this is one fabric which adds weight.

Full pants and skinny pants come and go in fashion, but one pant style is always "in"—the classic four front-pleated trouser. If you really want to make a pair of pants you will get a lot of wear out of, make a classic trouser in black or cream wool gabardine or wool crepe. Both of these fabrics are wrinkle-resistant and trans-seasonal. Line the pants in Bemberg rayon, a lining which breathes. Send both wool gabardine and wool crepe to the cleaners for a good steaming before you begin. Preshrinking will eliminate puckered seams from forming as you sew, as well as giving a long-lasting perfect fit. If you neglect this process, be prepared to wear your wool crepe pants 2 inches shorter for the rest of the season. Wool crepe is one of the few fabrics which work in many pant styles.

Good fabric choices for full pants are drapey rayons, soft silks, silk velvets, wool crepe, lamb-suede, with enough weight to give good drape. Four-ply silk crepe de chine is another good choice, but often hard to find. Imported cotton knits with good drape will work for full pants if the knit does not stick to itself, preventing the drape necessary for these big pants to work.

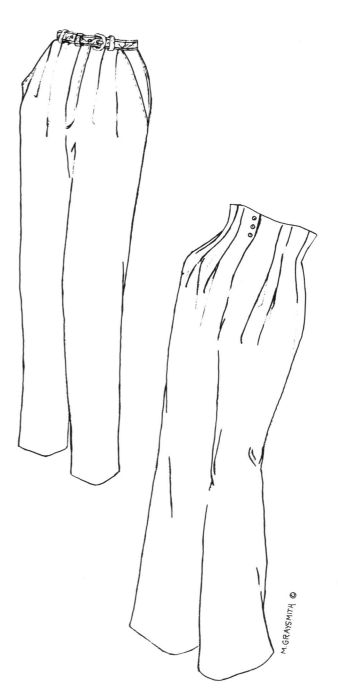

M. GRAYSMITH ©

96

Gold wool gabardine takes a different look when made into this Burda
pattern embellished with trim (see pages 208-209). Read about taming
gabardine (page 142) before you begin. **Pull on skirt** in pre-pleated
polyester (see page 151) makes a great travel piece. Pleats never come out
even after hand washing. Hat from Coup de Chapeaux in San Francisco.

Cranberry wool crepe (see page 144) jacket is underlined in pima cotton from a Style pattern. Pima cotton front and side fronts interfaced with fusible knit tricot and facing is fused with Whisper Weft (see pages 8-9). One half yard of Persian Lamb fake fur imported from Germany is cut on the crossgrain and used for collar and cuff contrast (see page 25 for fur technique). Color contrast hand worked buttonholes (see page 152 in **Power Sewing***) are made with black buttonhole twist.*

Silk chiffon blouse with dolman sleeve is tamed (see pages
152-154 for chiffon tips) in an Issey Miyake pattern by
Vogue. **Lambsuede pants**, made from five skins (technique
page 168 in **Powing Sewing**) have elastic waist (page 113-
114).

Leopard jacket is made from a Burda pattern in fake fur imported from Germany (see page 155 for fur tips). Entire front is interfaced with fusible knit tricot, facing fused with Whisper Weft (see page 8). Antique ivory pin made by Navarro Alternatives.

Well Fitting Pant Sloper

After teaching pant fitting classes for 15 years, I have come to the realization that the easiest way to get a close fitting pair of pants without horizontal wrinkles anywhere is to start with a European pant pattern.

The European pant pattern sloper is cut differently. Instead of the inner leg seam falling in the center of the leg, the inner leg seam falls toward the front of the pant. This is caused by a longer back crotch curve and a shorter front crotch curve. This seam configuration has several advantages: The longer back crotch prevents the pants from pulling down in the center back when you sit. The longer back crotch curve fits around the seat, curving under the seat. By curving well under the seat to the front, the leg can be well-tapered right under the crotch in back, eliminating the extra fabric sewers refer to as "baggy seat." The short front crotch eliminates excess fabric above the crotch in front when you sit or walk.

These so-called "fitting problems" are not actually fitting problems but problems caused by the sloper itself. If you are planning to go to all the trouble to make a master pant pattern, why not start with a sloper which helps rather than hinders the process? Unless you particularly like a very basic style with no design details, I would recommend making a basic pattern which fits you perfectly from a classic four-pleat, slant pocket trouser pattern. This pant is always in fashion in one form or another. Slight style changes to conform to fashion can be made by tapering the inner and outer leg seams in or out. A good classic pants pattern is Burda No. 6866.

Rather than making the pants from checked gingham or muslin—both uninspiring—why not make them from preshrunk wool crepe or lightweight wool flannel? Use 1 inch seams on inner and outer leg and considerable excess (2$\frac{1}{2}$ inches) above the waist to allow for varying crotch length.

Taking the Stride

Stride measurement plays a key role in comfortable, well-fitting pants. Stride measurement is the measurement taken through the legs from the front waist to the back waist. Place a piece of 1 inch elastic or Banroll around the waist and slide it into a comfortable position exactly at the waist. (String or ¼ inch elastic is a little too flexible for reliable waist determination.)

Be aware that your waist may drop in back and rise in front; this is quite normal. Tie a small weight (fishing weights are great) or an old key ring to the center

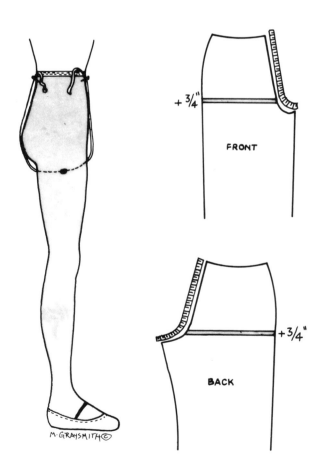

M. GRAYSMITH©

FRONT

+ ¾"

BACK

+ ¾"

of a 36 inch piece of string. Position the weight at the crotch on the body. If you are using a European pattern, the crotch point falls about ½ inch closer to the front than the actual crotch point on the body. With the weight in position, drop the weight away from the body ½ to ¾ inch, the distance from the body for a comfortable crotch seam on a finished pair of pants. Mark the weighted string with a pin where the string meets with the bottom of the waistline elastic or Banroll on front and back.

Remove the weighted string from the body. Measure the distance from the weight to the front waistline pin and the distance from the weight to the back waistline pin. You will arrive at two separate measurements, indicating front and back stride measurements.

If you are using a Burda pants pattern, the crotch length will be approximately ¾ inch shorter than the crotch length in the same size American pants pattern. If you have not had crotch length problems in the past, lengthen the front and back pant pieces on a Burda pattern ¾ inch to give yourself the same fit you are accustomed to.

If you know from past experience that you are short in the crotch, leave the Burda pattern as is and the crotch length will be shorter without adjustment. If you are long in the crotch, add ¾ inch plus whatever you normally add to an American pants pattern. For example, if you normally lengthen the crotch ½ inch on an American pattern, lengthen the Burda pants pattern 1¼ inches. Make crotch length adjustments horizontally at the hip, just under the pocket, to avoid changing the length and shape of the pocket

Flat pattern measure front and back stride on the pattern by placing the tape measure on end for accuracy around curves.

Compare stride measurement from your body (string and weight measurements) to the pattern. Compare front and back separately.

If the difference between the pattern and you is more than 1½ inches, add or subtract a bit more to the crotch length.

Adjusting the Crotch Length

Where to adjust crotch length on a pants pattern depends whether or not you want to adjust the length of the fly as well. If you are tall or have a small waist in comparison to the hip, you may want to use a longer zipper to make the pants easier to slip in and out of. If this is the case, the crotch should be lengthened before the end of the fly extension. Unfortunately a vertical cut across the pattern front in this area results in lengthening the pocket as well. Length must then be added to the pocket facing and side front as well. Unless you are tall and like deep pockets, lengthening the pocket is usually undesirable. The pant can be lengthened within the fly area without lengthening the pockets, by lengthening the front pant piece on two different areas.

Draw a line vertically across the pant front $1/2$ inch under the fly extension. Intersect this horizontal line with a vertical line $1/2$ inch toward the center front after the pleat markings. Draw a vertical line 2 inches above the end of the fly front extension. Cut pattern apart at vertical and horizontal lines. Move pattern up the same length in fly extension area and below fly extension for the rest of the pant. Crotch length additions will have a step pattern.

To lengthen crotch without lengthening fly facing or shortening crotch, simply draw a horizontal line across the pant front piece a half inch under the fly extension. Shorten or lengthen crotch in this area. Don't forget to lengthen back pattern pieces as well. Avoid hip distortion by drawing a vertical line to lengthen or shorten back at the same place with regard to the notches on the side seam.

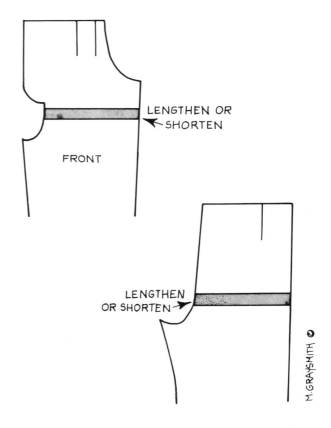

LENGTHEN OR SHORTEN

FRONT

LENGTHEN OR SHORTEN

ADD

1/2"

1/2"

ADD

FRONT

■ For a perfect centered zipper, center a piece of cellophane tape over the right side of the basted seam. Stitch along each taped edge.

Customizing the Crotch Curve

Stride is a measurement which not only involves crotch length but crotch depth as well.

If your front thigh is full, resulting in "smiles" under the front crotch on your pants, make an addition of ½ to ¾ inch on the front inner leg only, tapering to zero about 7 inches down to the inner leg from the crotch point. If your inner leg is full all the way to the knee, taper off the addition by midcalf. If your calves are well developed as well, make the full thigh addition from crotch point on front inner leg all the way to the bottom of the pant. If the leg is full and not enough addition is made, the front leg will twist.

If the reverse problem is true—thighs are thin—it will result in a vertical wrinkle which goes from about mid-thigh to around the bottom of a front fly opening. Cut off ¼ to ½ inch from the front inner leg seam, tapering back to the original by the knee. In addition, it helps to lift the center back of the pant slightly to pull the inner leg seam slightly more to the back, removing vertical wrinkles at front thigh.

If the seat protrudes, resulting in "frowns" under the seat on your pants, lengthen the back crotch slightly by adding ½ inch or so to the back inner leg seam at crotch point, tapering back to the original 7 inches down from the crotch on inner leg. If your seat is more rounded than the back crotch shape appears to be, scoop out the back crotch curve ⅛ to ¼ inch to tailor the shape more to the seat. Return to the original shape 2 inches from crotch point and 7 inches from waistline on back crotch curve.

More common is the fitting problem of a flat seat. To begin with, the Burda pant sloper will give a closer fit under the seat than an American pant pattern. Additional shaping may be desired if the seat is quite flat. Trim off ¼ inch from the back inner leg seam at crotch point, tapering to original 7 inches down the inner leg from crotch point. A flat seat is often low as well, requiring a shaping of the back crotch curve. Lower crotch curve ⅛ to ¼ inch about 1 inch away from crotch point into the back curve. Lower the curve in this area only. Gradually reshape back curve to the original crotch curve.

The individual with a flat seat often complains of much fabric under the seat. One additional adjustment can be made to sculpt the area under the seat. On the back pant piece, draw a horizontal line across the back leg, 2 inches down from the crotch point. Draw a parallel line ½ inch above this line. Fold out the pattern between these two lines. Re-draw the inner leg so that the cutting line is smooth. During pant assembly, stretch the back leg to the front leg for a 5 inch area below the crotch on inner and outer leg seams. This technique works well on most fabrics, but will look puckered on any fabric which doesn't ease well, such as gabardine or Ultrasuede®.

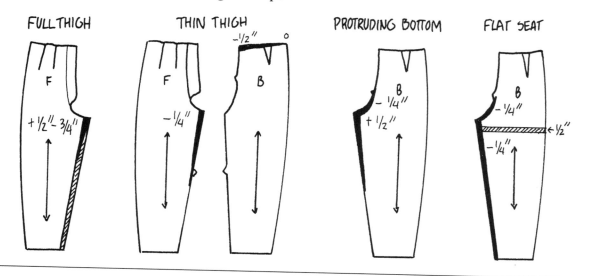

FULL THIGH   THIN THIGH   PROTRUDING BOTTOM   FLAT SEAT

Demonstrated on *Power Sewing* Video #4: *Foolproof Pant Fitting.*

Halving the Body for Pant Fit

If you take a careful look in the mirror from the side view, you may find that your body is not divided at the side seam into equal halves. If you have a large tummy and flat seat, the front of your body is much larger than the back. If the bulk of your weight is carried in the seat, your body will be larger in the back than the front. In addition to taking waist, high hip and full hip measurements in the round, Jane Whitely, an extremely knowledgeable fitting teacher, suggests measuring the body in halves for critical areas such as high hip and full hip.

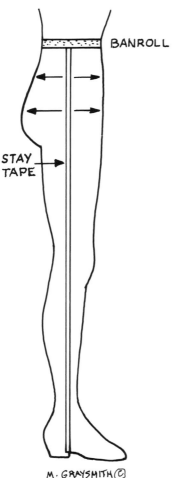

BANROLL

STAY TAPE

M. GRAYSMITH ©

Standing before a mirror, observing the side view, determine the ideal side seam placement on the body if the side seam extended from the middle of the leg to the waist. With a length of twill tape, pin the tape at the side of the leg, starting at the knee. Extend the tape from the knee to the waist in a straight line. It is difficult to ignore the actual side seam if you are wearing a garment during the measuring process, so take measurements in hose or a leotard. With the twill tape pinned in place on both side seams, measure the high hip area (which includes the tummy) across the front from tape to tape. Repeat this process for the back.

Record front and back measurements separately for high hip and full hip. For high hip ease, add $\frac{1}{2}$ to 1 inch to the front high hip measurement and $\frac{1}{2}$ to 1 inch to the back high hip measurement. The amount of ease across the tummy and back love handle area is a personal preference. A looser fit tends to give an illusion of slimness to the figure, especially for pot-bellied figures. For full hip ease, add 1 inch to the front full hip measurement and 1 inch to the back full hip measurement. If the hip is large, add an additional $\frac{1}{2}$ to 1 inch ease on front and back full hip. A looser pant is more flattering on an individual with full hips.

Using the pattern size guide sheet, determine the size which corresponds to your full hip measurement. Trace along this size with a felt-tip marker. If your waist or legs are small in comparison to hips, cross over size line and trace on smaller size in these areas. Make size transition smoothly. Assuming you are using this procedure for pants, pin out front pleats on pants from waist to the crotch. Even though the pleats will be sewn only a short distance from the waist, measuring the pattern with the pleats closed prevents you from counting on pleat spring for fitting. If the pants fit correctly, the front pleats stay in place and do not spread open.

Halving the Body for Pant Fit

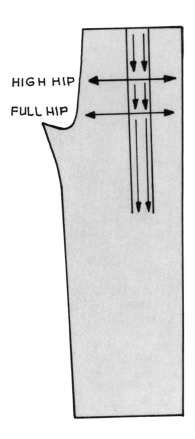

HIGH HIP

FULL HIP

in back. For the full-seated figure some addition may be needed in back and perhaps some subtraction in front. Make all additions and subtractions at the side seams and taper back to the original by mid-thigh. If the high hip is full and the full hip and seat are small in comparison, consider eliminating the back dart—pinning out the width of the back dart from the waist to the hemline, on the pattern. Naturally this scales down the whole back, just what many of the flat-seated figures need.

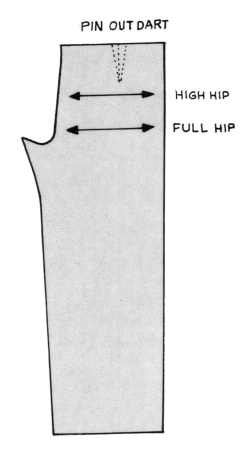

PIN OUT DART

HIGH HIP

FULL HIP

On back pant piece, pin out dart. Flat pattern measure front and back pattern pieces separately for high hip and full hip.

Remember to multiply each measurement by two, since the front and back pattern pieces represent only one leg. Compare your flat pattern measurments to your measurements for corresponding areas plus ease. Make a decision now about adding or reducing at side seam. If the pant pattern you are using is very full, 2 to 4 inch style ease may have been added to the full hip measurement plus 2 inch fitting ease. Take this into account before altering. For a full pant to fall properly, additional ease—over the 2 inches already needed for fitting ease—is required.

For the full-tummied figure, some addition will probably be needed in front and maybe some subtraction

Pant Fitting for the Large Woman

Perhaps the most important change a large woman needs to make in regard to pants is a change in attitude. Not wanting to appear "big," the large woman often makes or chooses body-hugging pants to wear under a big top. For such a woman, pants fitting closely over the tummy will actually accentuate the area she is trying to hide. The most flattering pant is one which hangs straight off the tummy to the top of the shoe. This type of fit may take some getting used to—at first it will feel baggy. In time, the large woman will come to regard this as her most flattering look in pants.

Gale Hazen, a large and extremely attractive California woman and owner of The Sewing Place in San Jose, teaches pant fitting for large women. Try this well-tested method when making pants for the large figure. The large figure is best suited to an American-made pant pattern. Buy the pant pattern two sizes smaller than you actually wear. The smaller pattern will give a better fit in the leg and under the seat. Most women with large tummies have small legs and seat in comparison.

Four back crotch angles will give the best fit to the full tummied figure. Begin the pant fitting process by making a second back pattern piece. Cut away the bottom of the front pattern piece, below any design details you wish to retain. Tape this design detail section over the second back piece, matching at the top of the pant.

Before cutting, flat pattern measure the pattern at tummy and hip. Because you purchased a smaller size

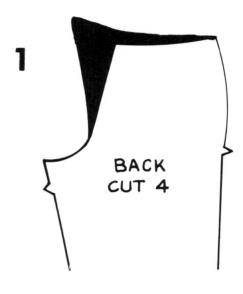

than you measure, additions will have to be made at the center front and the side seams. Any addition made at side seam should be tapered by mid-thigh.

Never cut the center front or center back on the straight of grain for the large figure. A slight bias cut gives more comfort and less pull during sitting. Take

■ The best fitting pant for the larger woman is obtained by drafting a pattern to the individual's body measurements. An easy to use drafting system is offered by Sure Fit Designs (see Sources).

Pant Fitting for the Large Woman

stride measurement through the legs, from center front waistline to center back waistline 1 inch below the crotch. Compare this measurement to the stride measurement of two backs. Add the difference above the waist on front and back. If your waist slopes upward in front, make most of the addition on center front, tapering the addition at the side seam to the same amount you are adding at the back. If you like a slightly tapered leg, add a 1 inch dart at center front and center back at hem (Illustration 2). Sew dart ½ inch in

width at hem tapering to zero 5 inches up the leg (Illustration 3). To make legs appear longer, cut pants 1 to 2 inches longer than needed and let pants bunch gently at ankle.

Fabric choice is very important for the large size woman. Soft, drapey fabric is a must. Invest in a good quality wool jersey or imported rayon twill and you will have a well fitting, comfortable pant which will last for years.

2

3

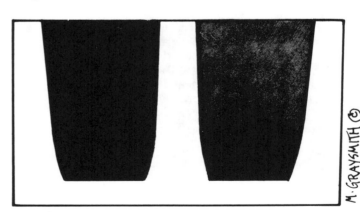

M. GRAYSMITH ©

Pant Altering and Construction Sequence

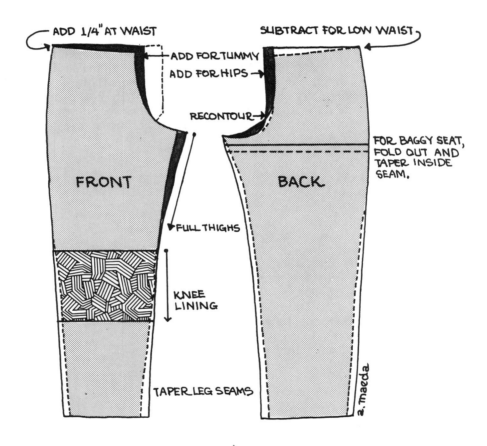

ADD 1/4" AT WAIST

SUBTRACT FOR LOW WAIST

ADD FOR TUMMY

ADD FOR HIPS

RECONTOUR

FRONT

BACK

FOR BAGGY SEAT, FOLD OUT AND TAPER INSIDE SEAM.

FULL THIGHS

KNEE LINING

TAPER LEG SEAMS

a. maeda

The sequence for altering and construction of pants remains a mystery to many sewers. Keep this for reference when you try your next pants pattern.

Unless you are using a Burda pattern, buy one size smaller than your hip measurement if you like a close-fitting leg and narrow seat.

If you are using a Burda pattern, use the pattern guide sheet to determine the the size which corresponds to your full hip measurement. Trace along this

size with a felt-tip marker. If your waist or legs are small in comparison to hips, cross over size line and trace on smaller size in these areas. Make size transition smoothly. Alter the crotch length first. Measure a distance fron waist to knee. To retain drape of pant leg, alter pants for finished length both above and below the knee.

On the pants front, alter full tummy as well as for full or narrow thighs. On pants back, change crotch

Pant Altering and Construction Sequence

curve in harmony with the shape of your bottom by filling in, scooping out, or lowering crotch curve.

If you are trying to eliminate a baggy seat, fold out $1/2$ inch horizontally, 2 inches under back crotch, as well as scooping out $1/2$ inch along waistline at center back tapering to zero by side seams. This lifts back crotch slightly, permitting the back leg to hang more on grain.

Flat pattern measure the pattern at key points, hip and high hip, to determine how much alteration is needed at side seams. Don't forget to alter pocket and pocket facings if additions were made at the side seams.

Compare your waist measurement to that corresponding to the size pattern you are using. Determine waistline alterations, altering at side seams. Dart and pleats can be narrowed or deepened slightly if waistline alteration is a big one. Alter waistband at double dot markings indicating side seams.

Measure a favorite pair of pants for finished pant width at bottom. Compare your findings to pattern. Taper pant legs at all four seams ending taper by mid thigh.

If you are uncertain about fit, use 1 inch seam allowances except crotch until after the first fitting.

Now you are ready for pants construction. Sew front crotch, from $5/8$ inch from inner leg to waistline at center front. Use a basting stitch at zipper opening if fly front will be used. Insert fly front and fly facing. Construct all pockets. Sew side seams, basting for initial fitting. Sew inner leg seams. If you are using 1 inch seams, sew crotch seam as a four point closure. Turn one leg right side out and slip into other leg. Sew remainder of crotch seam using twill tape or selvage as seam reinforcement. Baste on waistband. Try on for fitting. Make final alterations. Trim and overlock lower half of crotch seam at $1/4$ inch to eliminate bulk.

If you plan to line the pants, cut out pattern pieces, eliminating pockets. Cut lining to the finished length of the pants to enable the lining to fit inside each pant leg. For a smoothness inside, sew lining with $3/4$ inch side seams rather than $5/8$ inch—this makes the lining slightly smaller. Trim down crotch seam and press all lining seams open.

Slip lining inside of pants, wrong sides together, anchoring at zipper and waistband only. Hem pants and lining separately.

To eliminate fitting on the next pair of pants from this pattern, write down all pattern alterations including any findings in the final fitting.

■ Avoid the stuffed sausage look in pants. Use clingy knits for full styles only.

Seat Stretch Prevention

Although a pant may hang and fit beautifully when new, the seat of the pant always seems to stretch out slightly after the first wearing. Lining the pant may prevent wrinkling, extend pant life and prevent stretching in all other areas, but is unable to prevent the inevitable stretch which comes after the first wearing. Try this ingenious solution from a San Francisco designer.

After pants are cut but not yet assembled, remove back pattern piece from cut back pant pieces. Using plenty of steam on the wrong side of each back pant piece, start a press and stretch motion from the area halfway across the pant back right under the crotch. The point of the iron reflects the direction of the back crotch point. Working from the center of each back pant piece, press and stretch fabric toward the point of the crotch with each motion. Some fabrics stretch more than others. Do not press and stretch so much that the area has a slight transparency. Allow pant piece to dry thoroughly before moving off the pressing surface.

Reposition back pattern piece on to each newly pressed back pant piece, matching side seam waist, hem and inner leg seam to within 5 inches of the crotch point. You will notice that the pant is slightly larger along the inner leg near the crotch and along the lower back crotch curve as well. The mount may vary from $1/8$ inch to $1/2$ inch depending upon the amount of stretch in the fabric. Wool gabardine stretches very little ($1/8$ inch), while wool flannel may stretch up to $1/2$ inch. Cut off all excess fabric which extends beyond the cutting line of the pattern. If you are using a European pattern, remember that your cut pattern edge will not reflect seam allowances. Cut off any excess which has been pressed and stretched in the crotch point area.

Assemble the pants. Don't forget to stay tape the crotch under the zipper. Merely apply a strip of stay tape to the crotch seam as you sew.

Since your pants were prestretched with heat at the ironing board to assimilate the heat of the body and the stretch on the back crotch during seating, the stretching that usually occurs after the first wearing has been cut off. Therefore the shape of the pant will remain perfect from the first to the last wearing.

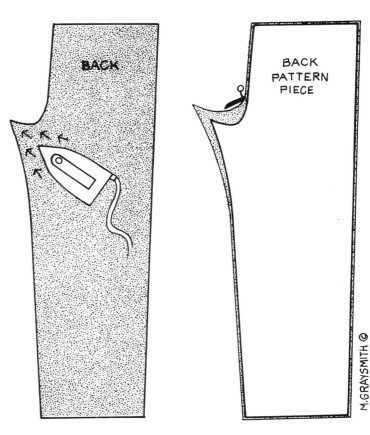

■ For pants which hold a crease and resist wrinkles, underline pants with Armo Press soft. Mark or press front crease. Machine sew underlining to outer pant along front creaseline with medium-small stitches. Machine stitch disappears in fabric and allows you to get a sharp front crease.

Crotch Reinforcements

If you have ever closely examined a pair of expensive men's trousers, you will notice that both the front and back pant pieces are reinforced with triangular wedges of lightweight cotton pocketing fabric or silk broadcloth. The purpose of the triangular wedge is to preserve the shape of the crotch in a stressed position such as sitting. Anyone who wears trousers and sits most of the day at a desk would be wise to add this reinforcement to preserve the shape of the pant.

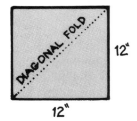

Cut four 12 inch squares of fabric. Fold square in half on the bias. Slide the bias fold under the back pant pattern pieces so that the fold begins approximately 4 inches from the back crotch point along the crotch curve and 6 inches from the crotch point along the back inner leg seam. Pin in place. Cut bias square of fabric folded on the diagonal to fit crotch curve and inner leg.

Repeat for other back leg. Machine baste into place along crotch curve and inner leg.

For front crotch reinforcement, slide 12 inch piece of fabric folded in half on the bias under front pant pattern piece so that the fold begins approximately 2 inches from the front crotch point along the crotch curve and 6 inches from the crotch point along the front inner leg seam. Pin in place. Cut bias square of fabric folded along the diagonal to fit crotch curve and inner leg. Repeat for other front leg. Machine baste into place along crotch curve and inner leg.

With folded crotch reinforcements basted to the wrong side of the fabric on each leg piece, continue pant construction.

This tip will preserve the shape and life of the finished pant.

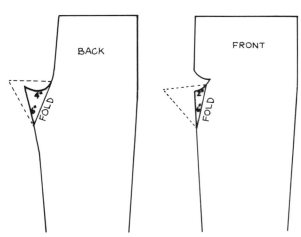

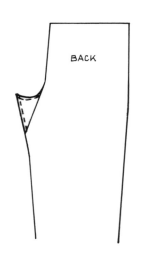

Pant Front Stay

Better pant manufacturers increase the desirability of their product with the use of a front stay. A front stay is merely an extension of the pocket across the tummy to the fly front cutting edge. A front stay enables a pair of pants to look new indefinitely by preventing the fabric from stretching in the tummy area as the pant is worn. Wearers of pants which include front stays claim they look slimmer as well.

Over the years a limited number of patterns have included a pattern piece for the front stay. Any pants pattern can be made to include a front stay by merely substituting the pattern you're about to make for the side front piece. Pin out any darts or pleats on the front pant piece. Superimpose the side front piece onto its designated placement position on the pant front.

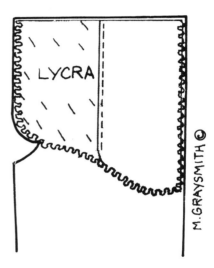

WRONG SIDE OF PANTS

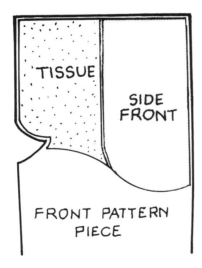

FRONT PATTERN PIECE

After this piece has been superimposed trace the bottom curve shape of the pocket. Continue across the front of the pants arching slightly as you cross the pant front to $\frac{1}{4}$ inch below the zipper opening. If you are using a 7 inch zipper, the front stay will have a depth of $7\frac{1}{4}$ inches. If you prefer a longer zipper, adjust the depth of the front stay to extend $\frac{1}{4}$ inch past the bottom of the zipper.

The pant front stay is the same shape as the pant front along side seam, waistline and fly front exten-

sion. The lower edge of the pocket stay extends from approximately $7\frac{1}{4}$ inch at the fly front extension across front, curving down to mimic the lower edge of the pocket. For added tummy control, interface the entire side front piece. For maximum tummy control, use an extension of lycra from the end of the side front to the edge of the fly front extension.

Continue pocket construction by sewing the pocket facing to the pant front along slanted pocket edge. Don't forget to stay tape this seam. Press, trim, and edge stitch seam. Finish edges of pant side front with an overlock or alternative seam finish.

Place pant side front into position by matching dots. Close pocket by sewing pant side front to pocket facing along curved edge. Pin out pleats on pant fronts to crotch line. Allow pocket stay to relax across pant front. Baste into position along the cut edge of fly.

■ Wool crepe is not strong enough to support a pant stay without extra support. Underline stay with pocketing fabric or finely woven cotton. Failure to do this results in seams which pull away from the fabric.

Pant Pattern Overlay

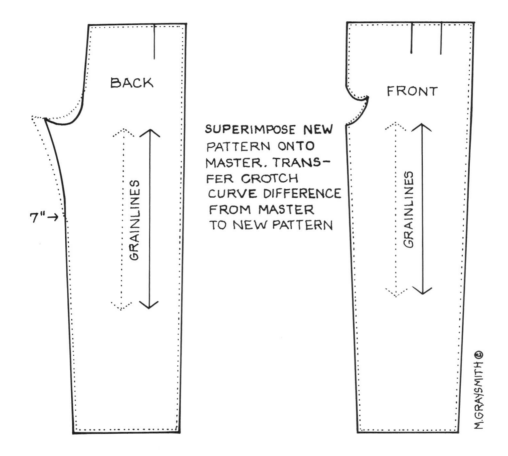

BACK

7" →

GRAINLINES

SUPERIMPOSE NEW
PATTERN ONTO
MASTER. TRANS-
FER CROTCH
CURVE DIFFERENCE
FROM MASTER
TO NEW PATTERN

FRONT

GRAINLINES

M.GRAYSMITH ©

After you have made a master pattern for the classic trouser or basic pant, how can you translate this information to another pattern? Can you use the well fitting pattern as an overlay?

Different pant styles require different amounts of ease for the pant style to be successful. While one style pant fits well with 2 inches of ease, another pant style may need 6 inches of ease to hang well. Therefore, using the master pant pattern as an overlay will not be successful. What is the solution?

Slopers vary between pattern companies. If you stay within the same pattern company, all pant patterns are drafted off of the same pattern sloper within that pattern company only.

Therefore, if you make the identical changes on a new pattern from the same pattern company as well as using the same size, the pants will fit. Make every addition or subtraction that was made on your master to the new pattern. Since fabrics vary and personal tastes vary in style, cut 1 inch seam allowances on the

Pant Pattern Overlay

side seams. If the pant style is quite fitted, cut 1 inch seam allowances on side seams, inner leg seams and waistline seam. If your master pant pattern is a classic trouser, a very fitted pant may require slight additional fitting in the crotch or inner leg to get each curve perfect.

Suppose you fall in love with a pant pattern from a different pattern company from your master pattern. Perhaps your master pattern is from a European pattern and the pant style you now want is from an American pattern. If you follow the process just described, the pant will not fit since the new pant was drafted off of a different sloper.

Crucial to well fitting pants is the shape of the crotch curve. Since quite a bit of time was spent on the master pattern perfecting the crotch curve, this well fitting curve should be transferred on to the new pattern from the different pattern company. If the pattern you now want to use is from a different pattern company than your master follow this plan: Overlay of the master pattern is useful for crotch curve to the waist and 7 inches of inner leg seam only. Lay the master pant pat-

tern on the table. Matching pattern at seam lines, superimpose the new pant pattern on to the master pant matching crotch curves and "direction of" grain line. Grain lines do not have to match up exactly but must be parallel. Transfer any crotch curve differences from the master pattern to the new pattern. Most likely the back crotch curve of the new pattern will need to be extended 1 to 1½ inches, if your master pattern is a European pattern. The front crotch curve may differ slightly as well in the shape of the curve itself. Transfer these changes on to the new pattern. Trace 7 inches of the inner leg seam near the crotch from the master on to the new pattern on front and back. Put away the master pattern.

Now compare your measurements to those measurements indicated on the size of the new pattern you have purchased. Make necessary alterations at the side seams. Cut out the new pant with 1 inch seam allowances on the inner leg and side seams, 2 inches on the waistband. Wider seam allowances give greater flexibility for final fitting. Construct new pant. You will be pleasantly surprised by the results.

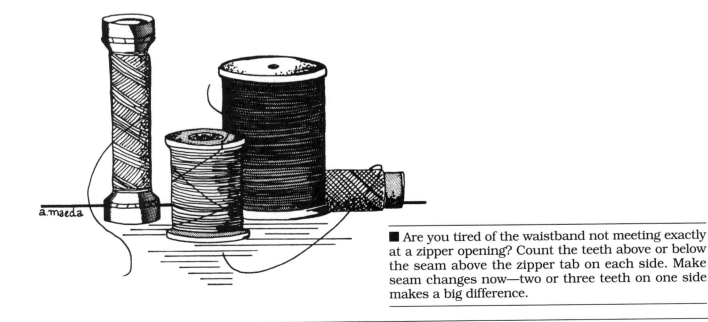

■ Are you tired of the waistband not meeting exactly at a zipper opening? Count the teeth above or below the seam above the zipper tab on each side. Make seam changes now—two or three teeth on one side makes a big difference.

Stirrup Pants

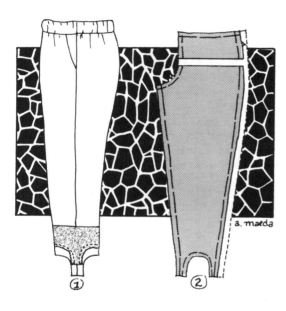

① ②

The popularity of stirrup pants is based on the fact that so many women look good in them. Stirrup pants work best with oversized tops unbelted such as a big shirt, longish sweater or elongated jacket, crotch length or longer. A big shirt or oversized sweater can hide a multitude of sins, so if you haven't tried the look perhaps you should try a pair on.

"But I have big thighs," you say. If your thighs are not your best feature, choose your oversized top a little longer. The sweater can be tunic length and the oversized shirt can fall a few inches above the knee. Most figures can wear stirrup pants if paired with an oversized top. What makes stirrup pants work is the contrast between the oversized top and the skinny bottom.

For flexibility in getting the fit you want, use a one inch seam allowance at side seams. Machine stitch side seams in contrasting thread to determine final fit. Since fabric stretch varies, this policy is good insurance.

Alter the pattern pant legs the same amount you would for an ordinary pant pattern for yourself. If the alterations for lengthening or shortening are more than one inch, divide the alteration into smaller increments distributed evenly in the leg. This technique is the most effective for maintaining the original shape of the pant leg.

To eliminate popped stitching lines, use a narrow stretch stitch for seams after fitting; then overlock seams together close to original stretch stitch, letting the overlock cut off excess seam allowance. For a slimming effect, top stitch creaseline on front of pants. Use narrow stretch stitch for creaseline as well or topstitching will break the first time you sit down.

"But my legs are short and stirrup pants can't be shortened," you say. Yes, they can. Merely fold out a tuck in the pants on one thigh until you can feel the stirrup against the arch of your foot. The amount of the tuck is the amount the stirrup needs to be shortened.

Remove the stitching at the base of the stirrup, making it possible for the stirrup shaped part of the pants to lie flat. Recut the shape of the pants along the lower edges shortening the pants the amount determined by the tuck. Finish the raw edges of the stirrup curve. Resew the seam at the bottom of stirrup.

Most of the stirrup pants patterns are designed for stretch fabric, offering little or no ease. With a slight adjustment, your stretch stirrup pant pattern can be used for woven fabric as well. This does not apply to patterns designed for four-way stretch with minus ease built in for a very close fit. In addition to your normal pattern adjustments, customizing the pattern to your figure, add ½ inch at each side seam, returning 2 inches of ease back to the pattern. In addition, add ¾ inch of crotch length to the front and back (Illustration 2).

This is needed for sitting ease since you cannot rely on fabric stretch in woven fabric. If the stretch pant pattern does not include a zipper, insert a zipper and waistband for a smooth fit in a woven fabric.

■ Four-way stretch fabrics make the most comfortable close-fitting pants. If your fabric has two-way stretch only, use the greatest stretch up and down on the leg.

$100 Pair of Pull-on Pants

Since a good pair of pull-on pants now costs about $100, why not spend an hour and a half sewing and save $70? The most flattering pull-on pants feature full gathers around the waist and nicely tapered legs. Good fabric choices for this style are: wool jersey, cotton knit, wool double knit, wool crepe and rayon or wool challis. Purchase 1 or 2 inch wide webbed elastic the length of your waist measurement.

After cutting out the pants, finish all raw edges with an overlock stitch. Using the overlock stitch as a seam finish rather than the seam itself allows you to press seams open, giving a flatter, ready-to-wear quality seam treatment. Cut back pocket pieces out of the fashion fabric and front pocket pieces in a slippery lining fabric. If both pocket pieces are cut from the fashion fabric, the pocket fabrics tend to stick together and bulge in the pocket area.

Attach pocket pieces to side seams, using stay tape to stabilize seam joining front pocket and front pants pieces.

If you are not planning to line the pants, cut two 10 inch pieces of lining fabric the shape of the pant front in the knee area. Finish knee lining pieces with overlock stitch. Baste knee lining to pant front at inner and outer leg seam allowances.

Do not attach knee lining except at side seams. Knee lining eliminates baggy knees.

Join front leg to back leg at inner and outer leg seams. Press seams open. Turn one leg right side out. Slip this leg into the other one so that right sides are against each other. Pin crotch seam. Stabilize crotch seam by sewing on a piece of stay tape as you sew the crotch seam. A good stabilizer substitute for stay tape is a $\frac{1}{4}$ inch width of selvage cut from lining fabric. Cut off lining selvages and keep in a plastic bag for color coordinated seam stabilizers. Clip seam in the area of the crotch curve, front and back; press crotch seam open above the crotch curve. Cut $\frac{5}{8}$ inch seam down to $\frac{1}{4}$ inch in the lower curved crotch area. Zigzag or overlock lower curved seam.

If the outer pant fabric is a knit, use a stretch stitch or a narrow zigzag when seaming knit.

If you plan to line the pants—suggested for wrinkle and sag resistance—cut lining from the same pattern as the outer pant, minus the pockets. Instead of $\frac{5}{8}$ inch seams, construct pants lining with $\frac{3}{4}$ inch side seams. The larger seam makes the pants slightly smaller, enabling them to slip into the outer pant effortlessly. Join lining and outer pant at waistline before inserting waistband. For a smooth fitting pant, hem outer pant and lining separately.

For the waistband in a knit, the crossgrain of the knit has the greatest amount of stretch. If wool ribbing or cotton ribbing, with 10 percent more lycra, is available which coordinates with your fabric, ribbing could be an excellent choice. If ribbing is unavailable, cross grain knit is your best bet. If you are using 2 inch elastic, cut waistband 5$\frac{3}{4}$ inches wide. If you are using 1 inch elastic, cut waistband 3$\frac{3}{4}$ inches wide. Measure your hips. Cut waistband length your hip measurement plus 2 inches if fabric is non-stretchy. For stretch fabric, cut waistband your hip minus 2 inches. Pin into a circle. Try on waistband. Re-pin to the smallest circle which you can comfortably slip over your hips. The smallest circle will be the least bulky.

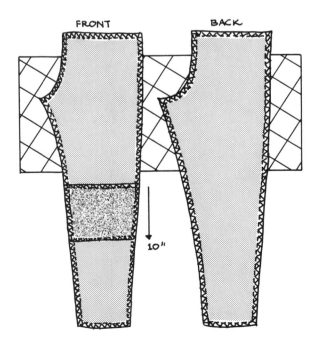

FRONT   BACK

10"

$100 Pair of Pull-on Pants

If the pants are very full at waist, gather pants before putting on the waistband to your hip measurement plus 2 inches. With right sides together stretch waistband to match pants.

Cut elastic to your waist measurement minus 2 inches. Sew in a circle. Use Nancy Zieman's (see Sources) trick of butting edges over a piece of non-fusible interfacing for less bulk or overlapping ends. Insert elastic between waistband and seam allowance. Wrap waistband around the elastic toward the inside of the pants.

Create a tight fit of waistband over elastic. Anchor waistband into place by sewing in the well of the waistband seam from the right side of the pants. If you are using webbed elastic, two or three parallel lines of stitching can be made around the waistband through the elastic, giving the feeling of "ruching." If you are using regular elastic, sew vertically through the elastic and the waistband at the side seams, to prevent the elastic from rolling.

Hem pants with a 1½ inch hem, ½ inch longer in the center back than at front to cover the heel of your shoe.

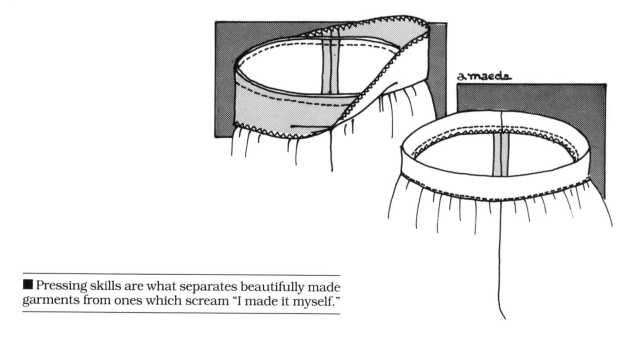

a.maeda

■ Pressing skills are what separates beautifully made garments from ones which scream "I made it myself."

Saddle Bags

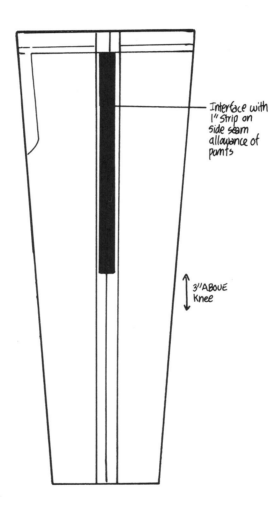

Interface with 1" strip on side seam allowance of pants

3" ABOVE knee

■ If the side of your body curves in and out between tummy, hip and thigh—camouflage this figure problem by fusing a 1-inch strip of medium weight interfacing to pressed-open seam allowance from waist to knee.

Slit Skirt with Mitered Corners

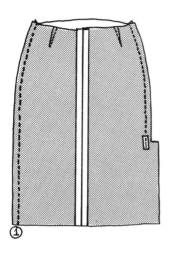

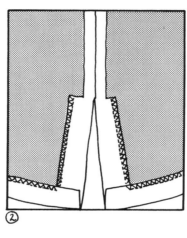

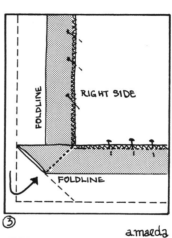

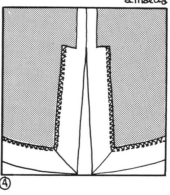

a.maeda

A straight skirt with a slit can be made sleek and smooth by mitering the hem. To prevent the slit seam tearing higher from walking or sitting, reinforcement is necessary. Sew the seam with a regular length stitch except for 1 inch before the slit opening begins. Place a small strip 1 inch long of stay tape or closely woven cotton selvage over the last 1 inch of the seam to be sewn. Switch the stitch length to small reinforcing stitches, sewing over the extra fabric strip for the last inch. Machine knot at the end of the seam (Illustration 1). Small stitches combined with the reinforcement fabric strip enable seam stress to be confined to the stabilized seam and prevent tearing of the fashion fabric itself.

Bulk is eliminated at the slit seam with a mitered corner. Fold back the cut on facing and press into place. Fold up the skirt hem and press into place. For the miter technique to work, the facing and the hem must be the same width. Overlock or finish the facing and hem raw edges before sewing the miter (Illustration 2).

Unfold hem and facing pressed edges. Fold up the corner diagonally so that the facing foldline and hem fold creases meet. Press. Unfold corner. This diagonal pressed line now becomes your guide. Placing right sides together, pin the hem and facing together matching your newly creased diagonal line (Illustration 3). Sew along diagonal crease-line with reinforcing stitches. Trim to $1/8$ inch. Turn right side out and press (Illustration 4). If this is your first miter, machine baste and turn right side out before trimming. Check your end result before doing permanent sewing.

Streamline Straight Skirt

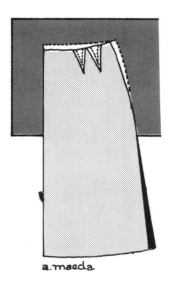

a. maeda

With the return of more fitted garments, the straight skirt becomes a pivotal wardrobe piece. Proper fitting is mandatory for both comfort and style. Unless you are adept at fitting, buy a straight skirt pattern by the hip size and alter the waist by deepening pleats or narrowing darts.

If you have a defined tummy, add $1/4$ inch at the center front tapering to zero by the side seam, along the waistline of the skirt. This will prevent the skirt from hiking up in the center front to accommodate the fullness there.

For a skirt to hang properly on a body whose fullness starts right under the waist, ample fabric must be added at the side seam. Measure your body $1\frac{1}{2}$ inch under the waistline. Measure the pattern in the same area, $1\frac{1}{2}$ inch down from the waistline seam. Eliminate seam allowances and darts from measurement. Compare your measurement to this flat pattern measurement. For the skirt to hang properly, the skirt must be $1\frac{1}{2}$ inches to 2 inches larger than your measurement over the tummy.

If the pattern is not large enough, sew darts narrower and/or add fullness at the side seam.

Before cutting, be sure to flat pattern measure the straight skirt in the full hip area between the seamlines. An average figure requires 2 inches ease; a large figure requires 3 to 4 inches ease at the full hip. Compare your measurement plus needed ease to the flat pattern measurement. The difference between the two is the total alteration. Divide the total alteration by 4 to calculate the amount to add to each side seam. After the skirt is assembled, run an easeline $1/2$ inch from the cut edge around the waist of the skirt to ease in the fullness. Compare to waistband. If more ease is needed, run a second easeline around the waist in the vicinity of the first. Using a press and lift motion, flatten the eased fabric before applying the band. Easing the skirt to the band eliminates tiny folds in the skirt under the waistband.

Determine finished skirt length before cutting out the skirt, allowing for a 2 inch hem. A straight skirt will need either a slit or a pleat for ease in walking. Reinforce the final $1/2$ inch of the seam before the slit opening with tiny stitches and a small piece of twill tape. A pleat can be held into position with edge stitching $1/8$ inch from pleat fold along creaselines. Give pleats a memory by pressing with a damp presscloth moistened with a solution of two tablespoons of white vinegar to one cup of water.

In ready-to-wear skirts, side seams are tapered to give a slimmer look near the knees. If you like this silhouette, taper side seams from $5/8$ inch at hipline to $1\frac{1}{8}$ inch near the hem. Eliminate baggy seats by lining skirts. Use rayon or silk lining; polyester linings trap warmth. To enable the lining to fit inside the skirt smoothly, sew side seams at $3/4$ inches rather than $5/8$ inches. A lining cut on the crossgrain will prevent rump spring more than one cut on the lengthwise.

■ Paring down accessories rather than adding usually leads to elegance.

Wrap Skirt

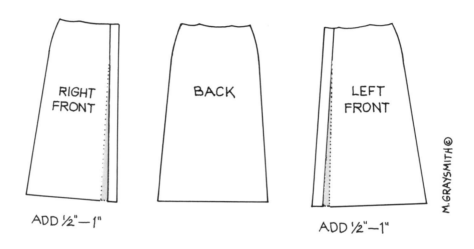

RIGHT FRONT

BACK

LEFT FRONT

ADD ½"—1"

ADD ½"—1"

M. GRAYSMITH©

Difficulty in making a wrap skirt which stays wrapped while wearing has led many people to give up on wrap skirts all together. With a few precautions, a wrap skirt can be entirely successful.

To begin with, compare your full hip measurement to the measurement given for the pattern size you purchased. Compute the difference. Divide the total amount by 4 to arrive at the amount which will be added to each side seam. Pattern alterations for hips larger than the pattern "as is" are a must for the wrap skirt. A wrap skirt which is not full enough at the hip will start unwrapping before you even take a step.

To prevent the skirt from pulling apart as you walk, walking ease must be added. Walking ease allows extra fabric at the hemline for movement. On both front skirt pieces—outer and underwrap—2 inches away from outside seam edge, slash the pattern from hem to waist. Spread the pattern ½ inch for above knee length skirt,

3/4 inch for below knee length skirt and 1 inch for mid-calf length skirt. If you are lining the skirt, identical additions must be made to the lining.

When cutting out the skirt, use the original skirt grain line for pattern placement. Walking ease does not change the grain of the skirt, merely the grain of the vertical front edges. Therefore, this technique is not suitable for lengthwise stripes or prominent lengthwise plaids.

Once you make a wrap skirt with walking ease included, you will never make one without it. English designer Sara Sturgeon solves the problem of the short wrapped skirt by making a pair of matching footless tights which are sewn in with the skirt at the waist. This not only solves the problem of the short skirt unwrapping but the question of what to wear under as well.

Circle Skirt

a. maeda

Just because you're hippy doesn't mean that you can't wear a circle skirt. Make your first circle skirt in a soft drapey cotton knit or wool jersey. Make it in black or charcoal. Any figure type can wear this skirt, providing the fabric is suitably drapey and the skirt is long enough. Because of the circle skirt's volume, careful fabric choice is mandatory. Not only must the fabric have drape but some weight is preferable so that the fabric will drape closely around the legs, hanging in soft folds.

Good fabric choices are: Austrian knit, wool and rayon crepe, wool jersey, and rayon challis. Rayon fabric blends can also be successful. I recently used a rayon, linen, and silk blend which combined the texture of linen and the lustre of silk with the drape of rayon. Most circle skirts need 4 yards, but you might want to buy 4½ yards if you plan to cut the skirt longer.

For the circle skirt to hang properly, measure the circumference of the circle at the waist along the seamline. Accomplish this by holding the tape measure on its side. Do not include seam allowances in the measurement. For a smooth fit, the skirt must be 2 inches larger than your waist along the seamline before the skirt is put on the band. If the pattern is smaller, cut down ¼ to ¾ inch from the waist to increase the circumference. Run an easeline along the waistline before adding to a waistband which is notched your honest waist measurement plus 1 inch.

If you are hippy or have a large tummy, a circle skirt will be more flattering if it features some gathers under the waistband. Choose a circle skirt with gathers or increase the circumference at the waist to accommodate the gathers.

The best circle skirts in ready-to-wear feature details such as welt pockets or side buttons. To create side

Circle Skirt

button detailing, simply cut an additional 2 inches past the front and back seam allowances on the left side. Finish raw edges. Press added 2 inches facing into place. After the initial pressing, deliberately stretch both faced sides slightly in the pressing process. This will prevent stretching between the buttons later. Interface behind facing. Sew all vertical seams with a tiny (.05) zigzag stitch of medium length to allow the seams to relax with the cut of the skirt. Stretch seams slightly as you press.

For an even hemline, a hem marker must be used. Due to the cut of the skirt, you will notice considerable difference in the excess amounts cut off from the bottom. A narrow non-bulky machine hem is the best choice for the circle skirt. Finish the skirt bottom with an overlock stitch. Press up a hem of $3/4$ inch. If you have difficulty pressing the $3/4$ inch, run an easeline $5/8$ inch from skirt bottom. The easeline prevents stretching and allows you to press up the $3/4$ inch easily. From the right side, run two lines of stitching $3/8$ inch from the folded edge. A double needle works perfectly here, eliminating the effort of trying to get two rows of stitching equally spaced.

■ Never use selvages as a seam finish on a circle skirt. Selvages prevent the fabric in a circle skirt from relaxing uniformly, resulting in seams which draw up and are shorter than the rest of the skirt. To prevent this, cut off lengthwise selvages and $1/2$ inch beyond before pattern layout.

■ Hem width continues to be a mystery for many sewers. The following are standards used in the industry: Straight skirt—$2^1/2$ inches; A-Line skirt—$1^1/2$ inches; Very full skirt—$1/2$ inch; Pants—$1^1/2$ inches; Shirt—$1/2$ inch; Blouse—1 inch; Sleeves—$1^1/4$ inches; Jacket—2 inches; Coat—3 inches.

Easy Tube Skirt

For a garment you will live in happily, try a narrow tube skirt with elasticized waist in a soft cotton knit or wool jersey. The narrow silhouette is a perfect balance for oversized tops. The combination of soft fabric and elasticized waist makes the skirt more comfortable than a pair of pants.

If your hips measure 39 inches or less, and the fabric is 45 inches or wider, a tube skirt can be made from one yard of fabric. If your hips are wider than 39 inches, buy one yard of 54 to 60 inch fabric or two yards of narrower width fabric. Buy one yard of webbed elastic for a special elastic treatment which will be described later.

For a narrow tube skirt with comfortable walking room, cut skirt your hip measurement plus 6 inches. Seam skirt in center back, leaving the last 5 inches of the seam free for a slit if the skirt fabric is a woven. If you are adept at mitering (see Slit Skirt with Miter) allow a wider seam allowance (the same width as hem). For knits, a slit seam is necessary.

If you are using 2 inch webbed elastic (my favorite), finish raw edge at top of skirt with overlock or alternative seam finish. Fold down $2\frac{3}{4}$ inches for casing on wrong side of skirt. Sew casing $\frac{3}{8}$ inch from finished edge leaving a 2 inch opening at center back for inserting elastic. Cut webbed elastic your waist minus 2 inches. Insert elastic through casing. Overlap ends of elastic and anchor with two rows of zigzag stitching. Close opening in casing. Sew elastic through casing vertically at center back to keep from twisting. Distribute fullness evenly around elastic.

For an attractive finishing touch, sew elastic horizontally at $\frac{1}{2}$ inch intervals through casing and elastic, stretching elastic as you sew. Stretch elastic as you sew for each row. Absolute even spacing is not necessary but the perfectionist might want to draw on stitching lines with chalk before the elastic is inserted.

Hem skirt to desired length. For an interesting sportswear touch at center back, zigzag over a 6 inch piece of $\frac{1}{4}$ inch width elastic gathering up 12 inches of length in the center back seam, slightly draw up the center back and hem (see Illustration).

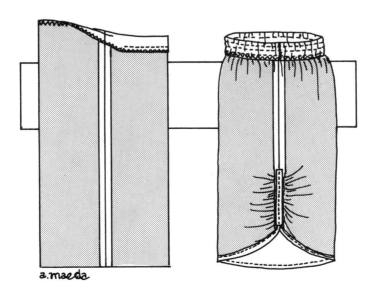

a. maeda

When to Line

Nothing is more disappointing than discovering at the completion of a garment that it should have been lined. Few seamsters go back and insert the lining, so the garment hangs in the closet, worn once, waiting for lining fabric to be purchased or uninterrupted sewing time to be available, neither of which is likely. Linings are little more work than seam finishes, provided you have purchased the lining fabric and altered and cut it out while cutting out the garment itself.

If you do a lot of sitting in your job or in airplanes, lining a skirt or pants will cut down on wrinkles. If the garment is narrow, the lining can be cut identically to the outer fabric and machine hemmed separately, hanging $7/8$ inch shorter than the outer garment. If the skirt has a slit, vent shaping is cut off the lining, allowing a $5/8$ inch seam on lining for turn back. The lining is then attached to the sides of the slit. Pants lining is left loose at lower edge, anchored at seams only with $1/2$ inch thread tacks.

A jacket will always slide on and off more easily if the sleeves are lined in a slippery fabric. If the fabric is likely to ravel, lining will enclose raw edges and reduce raveling. If the fabric is likely to wrinkle, jacket lining will cut down on wrinkles. If you have spent more than $20 per yard on fabric, why not line the jacket and move its value up a notch? You may decide not to line a jacket if the effect you want is that of a loose sweater.

Another decision not to line may be based on heat. If you plan to wear a linen jacket in a hot climate, lining will cut down on the wrinkles but will keep in body heat. One possible alternative would be to leave the back unlined but double the jacket front during cutting. Front facing is eliminated and a second front is substituted, attached by hand at the side seam. Double jacket fronts get around the problem of facings that won't keep to the inside of the jacket, and they eliminate the need for construction detailing on the under side of the pocket.

If you are sick of sleeve linings that pull out after a few wearings, try this. Instead of cutting a $5/8$ inch seam allowance along the sleeve lining cap, cut a 1 inch seam allowance. When attaching sleeve lining to jacket at cap, fold under $5/8$ inch, giving an extra $3/8$ inch play within the sleeve. Sleeve lining length is cut to the finished length of the sleeve. Fold under the sleeve hem when cutting sleeve lining. To attach sleeve lining to sleeve at lower edge, fold under $5/8$ inch from sleeve lining. Hand-tack lining fold to the upper edge of sleeve hem allowance. The sleeve lining fold covers the raw edge of hem fold by $1/4$ inch.

Demonstrated on *Power Sewing* Video #6: *Easy Linings.*

Silver Lining

Although lining a jacket can give a beautiful finish to the inside of the garment, if the lining is not cut correctly it can detract from the outside of the garment by pulling up the hem.

A jacket lining can be attached at the hem or hang free. In either case the lining is cut to the length of the jacket minus the jacket hem allowance. If a lining pattern is provided, fold up the hem allowance (with any alteration for length) on the jacket pattern pieces. Compare lining and jacket pattern pieces. The length of the lining should be the length of the jacket pattern minus the hem allowance.

If the lining pattern piece does not feature a 1 inch pleat in center back, allow for one when cutting out. Sew up the pleat from hemline to waist and for 2 inches in center back from the neckline. The pleat is left free in the broad back area to allow for movement.

To prevent pulling at armhole, extend the shoulder seam (front and back) by $\frac{1}{4}$ inch, tapering extension to zero. Add height to shoulder seam by adding $\frac{1}{2}$ inch to shoulder seam at armhole, tapering to zero at neck.

If the jacket is made from somewhat unstable fabric such as a handwoven or loose weave, allow 1 inch extra length when cutting the lining. Attach the lining at the neck and front facing. Before attaching the lining at the hem, let the hemmed jacket hang and relax for 48 hours. From the outside of the coat, trace the bottom of the hemmed coat to the lining. Use this line as a guide for cutting off excess lining. Fold under $\frac{1}{4}$ inch on bottom edge of lining. Attach the lining to the jacket hem. Attach $\frac{1}{2}$ inch fold line on the bottom of the lining to $\frac{3}{4}$ inch from the top of the jacket hem. When the jacket lining is allowed to relax inside the jacket, a slight fold in the lining will form between the bottom of the jacket and the place where the lining is attached. This fold is necessary to allow the lining to move within the jacket.

Sleeve lining is cut to the finished length of the sleeve and attached to the top of the sleeve hem allowance in the same manner as the rest of the jacket. Hem sleeve first. Attach $\frac{1}{2}$ inch fold at bottom of lining to $\frac{1}{2}$ inch from the top of hem on the garment sleeve.

Lining Decisions

Although not mandatory, lining a skirt or pants is preferable since a lining prevents stretching in seat and knee areas, prevents static cling to hose, makes the garment more comfortable to wear, cuts down on wrinkles if you sit a lot and gives a quality, finished appearance to the inside and outside of the garment.

Buy two yards of lining for pants and one yard of lining for back zippered skirts. A simple tube lining in a skirt will cut down on bulk and provide all of the above lining characteristics. A side pocket opening skirt requires approximately the same amount of lining as the outer skirt, since a tube lining cannot be used. A slippery lining is a must—Bemberg rayon by Skinner is a favorite. Natural fibers breathe and will produce less heat than their polyester counterparts—especially important in pants linings.

Cut lining exactly the same as the outer garment with darts and pleats, eliminating style details such as pockets. Pocket pouch hangs between outer garment and lining. Fold up the hem allowance on the pattern so that the lining will be cut to the finished garment length. Sew side seams in lining at ¾ inch rather than ⅝ inch, making the lining slightly smaller to fit inside the garment. To allow the lining to sit above crotch seam in pants, sew lining seam at ⅜ inch from notch to notch along crotch bottom (Illustration 1).

If the skirt or pants closes with a zipper, leave an opening 1 inch longer than the zipper in the lining (Illustration 2). If the skirt or pants opening is inside of the left pocket, leave the lining open 1 inch below the bottom of the pocket. Attach a back pocket piece cut in lining to the back seam allowance.

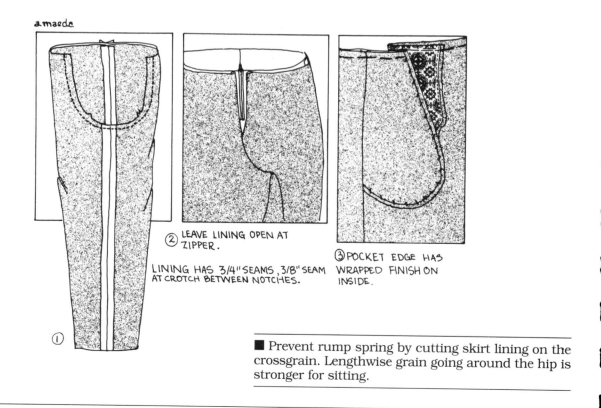

amaede

② LEAVE LINING OPEN AT ZIPPER.

LINING HAS 3/4" SEAMS, 3/8" SEAM AT CROTCH BETWEEN NOTCHES.

③ POCKET EDGE HAS WRAPPED FINISH ON INSIDE.

①

■ Prevent rump spring by cutting skirt lining on the crossgrain. Lengthwise grain going around the hip is stronger for sitting.

Demonstrated on *Power Sewing* Video #6: *Easy Linings.*

Lining Decisions

Both the lining and the outer skirt or pants should be eased and pressed separately at the waist before attaching the waistband. Place the wrong sides of lining and garment together. Sew lining to the zipper placket by hand. Pin the right side of the lining seam to the right side of the garment at the waist.

If the skirt or pants closes through the left pocket, attach the back pocket lining to the back pocket along the outside edge. Finish the raw seam with a wrapped seam finish (Illustration 3). Attach front lining at side seam pocket opening by hand. Wrap front pocket around lining. Baste in place at waistline.

Baste lining and outer garment together at waist. Sew on waistband. Hem separately. Attach lining at side seams on skirt and inner leg seams on pants at lining bottom with a French tack.

Cut skirt lining tube your hip measurement plus 4 inches in width. For example, a 38 inch hip would need a piece of fabric 42 inches wide by 31 inches long (for desired 31 inch length skirt). Sew ¾ inch center back seam starting 8 inches from each end of center back, leaving an 8 inch opening for zipper and an 8 inch

opening for ease in walking. Press back ¾ inch seam allowance for zipper opening.

Nancy Zeimen in *The Busy Woman's Sewing Book* (see Sources) gives this tip to round corners for slit in center back. Measure up 7 inches from lining bottom at center back, measure across 7 inches from center back, cut edge along hemline. Measure 3 inches from point in corner which intersects center back and hemline. Mark dots on fabric, connect the dots to form curved hemline at center back (Illustration 1). If the outer skirt has a back slit, no handtacking is necessary at the slit since the lining is curved and prevents peeking out from behind the slit. Additionally, a curved hem in a lining is easier to sew than one with mitered corners.

Take out some of the fullness at waist in lining tube with a series of darts at side seams, front and back. Slip lining inside constructed skirt, wrong sides together. Handtack lining to zipper. Baste waistline of lining and skirt together (Illustration 2). Attach waistband. Hem lining and skirt separately. Let lining hang free.

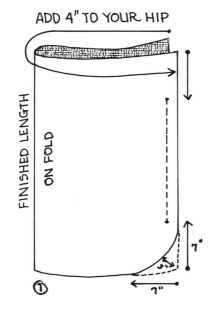

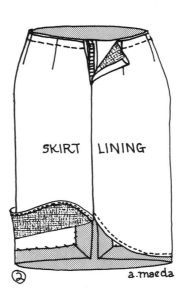

a.maeda

Lining Around the Kick Pleat

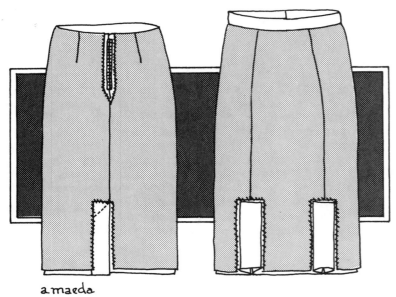

a.maeda

Lining in a simple straight skirt is easy enough, but how about lining a pleated skirt, a skirt with open flaps or a kick pleat? For openers, choose a soft lining fabric which will hide construction details and keep the skirt from stretching out of shape without causing problems such as wrinkling. Lightweight Bemberg rayon lining shrinks considerably and softens after washing so be sure to preshrink if you plan to wash the garment.

For a pleated skirt, simply use a straight tube lining which you can cut from a straight skirt pattern or make a simple tube 3 inches larger than hips with a deep slit for walking in center back. Fit at waist with darts for smoothness.

For a straight skirt with pleat or open flap detailing, cut the lining from the same pattern as the outer skirt. Sew side seams with a ¾ inch seam allowance to make lining a tiny bit smaller than outer skirt, allowing a smooth fit when slipped inside. Hand tack lining at zipper and include lining in waistline seam with the waistband.

Skirt linings are most successful when they hang free at the hem. If a slit or pleat is involved, the lining must be hand tacked vertically along the sides of the opening but still be allowed freedom along the bottom edge. Do not put a pleat in the lining. Simply fold under the ½ inch raw edges of the lining and hand tack lightly along inner edges of the pleat. Allow the pleat in the fashion fabric to work independently without the bulkiness of extra fabric.

Lining a skirt with flaps which open near the knee requires the same vertical tacking at the side of the flaps, allowing the bottom edge freedom. If the flap is a narrow flap in center front or center back, the lining could be tacked vertically at sides of flap and horizontally for the distance of the narrow lap, making a "U" shaped hand tack.

■ Never pull thread too tightly when hemming. The result is slight puckering which cannot be pressed out and is very visible.

Slick Quick Jacket Lining

To attach a jacket lining need not be time-consuming. Several methods are acceptable. Try this method for speed plus excellent results. Before a lining is inserted, the jacket should have all design details completed: Be hemmed; shoulder pads inserted; and be well pressed. A good pressing is difficult once the lining has been slipped into place.

Lining front and back should be joined at shoulders and side seams. Sleeve linings should not be inserted. Place right side of facing against the right side of lining matching shoulder seams. Cut a long strip of ¼ inch Pellon Save A Stitch Fusible Web. Place the strip right over the intended seamline on the facing side of the seam. While sewing the facing and lining together, sew through the strip of fusible web simultaneously. The web will help anchor the facing to the jacket in the final pressing.

Sew one long continuous seam up one side of the jacket front, across the back neck and down the other side of the jacket. Start at the top of the jacket hem and end at the same place on the other side. It usually appears that the jacket lining is too long. The correct length for the jacket lining unhemmed is the finished length of the jacket. The seemingly excess length is used in a small take-up tuck at the bottom of the lining. This allows movement in the lining without stress at the seams.

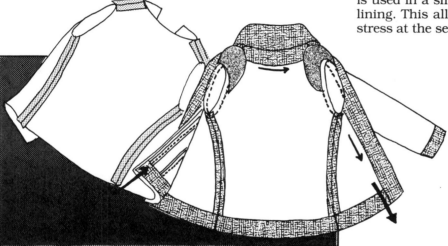

① SEW CONTINUOUS SEAM FROM HEM TO HEM USING SMALL FUSIBLE STRIP.

② HAND SEW SLEEVE AT CUFF AND ARMHOLE.

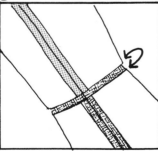

a. maeda

Turn under the raw edge of the lining and hand stitch to ½ inch from the raw edge of the jacket hem. A take-up tuck will form naturally.

Hand stitch the lining at the armholes to the armhole seam of the jacket. The sleeve lining is attached separately. The sleeve independence helps prevent the lining from tearing away at the armhole. Fold under ½ inch at the bottom of the sleeve lining. Hand stitch to the top of the jacket sleeve hem. Attach sleeve cap to armhole with a hand stitch using waxed thread for strength.

Final press. The ¼ inch of fusible web will melt in this process and invisibly anchor the facing to the jacket.

Long in the Crotch

If you are long in the crotch, you probably have a closet full of pants which not only wrinkle in the front but are uncomfortable as well. You may hate the thought of making pants or a jumpsuit because you can never decide how much to add, and too much is visually worse than not enough. Not only is there a solution for this dilemma but you can pull every ill-fitting jumpsuit and pair of pants out of your closet and fix them all at once, spending about 10 minutes a pair. Sound unbelievable? Try this:

The reason the pants ride too high in the crotch and are uncomfortable is that the crotch needs to be lowered. This can be accomplished by merely sewing a lower crotch in the pants.

Slip one leg inside the other so that the crotch curve is visible. The point at which the curves join and the inner leg meets the outer leg is called the crotch point. At this point, from the seamline, place a mark ¾ inches lower on the inner leg seam with chalk. Connect this mark to the crotch curve gradually on both sides so that the curve appears similar to the original curve but is actually ¾ inches lower. Sew the new lowered crotch curve connecting with the original crotch curve 3 to 4 inches from the crotch point on either side. Sew a smooth seam. Trim away the old crotch seam. You have now created more length for your body.

When I first heard about this technique, I, too, was skeptical; it seemed too easy. I lowered the crotch in a pair of pants by sewing a lower crotch seam. I tried the pants on. They looked the same. Until you trim away the old seam allowance, more room cannot be made in length. I trimmed away the seam allowance. I tried them on again. They were much better but still a little short as I am very long in the crotch.

I repeated the process again, lowering the seam an additional ½ inch for a total of 1¼ inches. This time I trimmed away the seam before I tried them on. They were perfect! The moral of the story: You won't see a difference until you trim away the old seam.

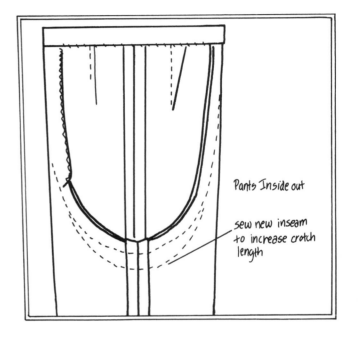

Pants Inside out

sew new inseam to increase crotch length

■ "Your personal style is who you are. Your lifestyle is what you do. Both are part of your total image. Over 65 percent of all American women work outside the home and more are entering the labor force daily. This lifestyle transition has created major wardrobe requirements for many women," says Clare Revelli, author of *Style & You.*

Short in the Crotch

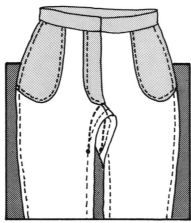

TO SHORTEN CROTCH, DEEPEN INNER LEG SEAM.

Knowing how difficult it is to buy or sew well-fitting pants, here's a tip for an easy way to shorten or lengthen the crotch on a bought or finished pair. To fit well, pants should have a crotch which lies $\frac{1}{2}$ to 1 inch lower than the body.

If the pants are long in the crotch, you may have felt the only way to shorten the crotch was to remove the waistband and shorten from the top. Not only is this time-consuming, but shortening from the top shortens the zipper and pockets as well, usually an undesirable side effect.

Leave the waistband intact and shorten the crotch by sewing the inner leg seams deeper into the crotch area. Turn pant wrong side out. Start new stitching 7 inches down from the crotch seam on the inner leg. Gradually taper the seam up the leg and into the crotch seam. Be conservative at first. Sew seam deeper into the crotch repeating identical stitching on second inner leg as you did on first. Unless you have thin legs, try to take out as little as possible in the inner leg seam. Remember your goal is to shorten the crotch and leave the leg size intact.

Try on the pants before you trim out the excess. A trial fit gives you an opportunity to correct a too short crotch or sew deeper for a crotch which is still too long.

■ Transparent Scotch tape can be used as a guide for topstitching on fly front zippers. Do not sew through the tape.

Final Word on Waistbands

One waistband is too tight, the next waistband is too loose. What a hassle! When it comes to measuring the waist, many of us refuse to believe the tape measure. Instead, we make the waistband the size we wish our waist was, cinching in an additional 1 inch to 2 inches from the actual measurement. After the garment is finished, you look in the mirror and exclaim, "This makes me look fat!" The real reason the skirt or pants in question makes you look fat is that the waistband is too tight. A tight waistband pushes bulk below the waist, causing a pot belly to protrude and "love handles" to be more pronounced. One of the secrets to looking slim is making a waistband which fits comfortably—even if it's a bit loose.

Try this method for slimming results: If you prefer a finished waistband width of 1 inch, cut a lengthwise strip 3$\frac{1}{4}$ inches wide, using a selvage edge if possible. If no selvage is available, overlock one long edge or finish by wrapping long edge with lining, producing what's known as a Hong Kong finish. If you are forced to use a crosswise strip of fabric for the waistband, make sure you interface it so that it will have no stretch.

Cut waistband length your comfortable honest measurement plus $\frac{1}{2}$ inch ease, plus 4 inches to finish ends. For example, a 29 inch waist measurement results in a waistband 33$\frac{1}{2}$ inches long and 3$\frac{1}{4}$ inches wide. Notch the cut band 2 inches from each end. Divide the band in half and mark front and back halves of the waistband. By studying body proportion, we know that the front waistline is at least $\frac{1}{2}$ inch larger than the back. Therefore, move waistband markings indicating the front $\frac{1}{2}$ inch toward the back ($\frac{1}{4}$ inch on each side), making the front slightly larger than the back. Indicate center front, center back and side seams on the waistband.

One of the real secrets to a smooth, well-fitting skirt or pants is having enough fabric at the waistline of the garment to ease to the waistband. The garment must be 1$\frac{1}{2}$ inches to 2 inches larger than the waistband between markings to allow enough fabric for easing. If the garment and the waistband are exactly the same size, the garment will not be able to fall smoothly over the tummy and high hip. The result is a slight fold all around, right under the waistband.

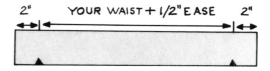

YOUR WAIST + 1/2" EASE

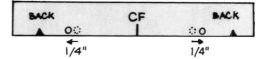

WAISTBAND WITH CENTER BACK OPENING

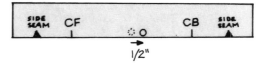

WAISTBAND WITH SIDE OPENING

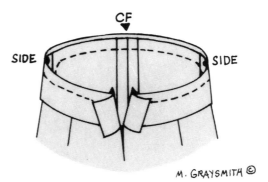

M. GRAYSMITH ©

Final word on Waistbands

Before applying the waistband to the garment, measure the garment around the waist, from zipper teeth to zipper teeth or garment opening to garment opening If there is no zipper. For a smooth fit, the garment should measure $1\frac{1}{2}$ to 2 inches larger than the waistband between end notches. If you find that you are shy this amount, reduce the side seams slightly or sew the back darts slightly smaller. If you find that your garment measures larger than the recommended amount, slightly deepen the side seams and back darts.

When your garment measures $1\frac{1}{2}$ to 2 inches larger than the waistband between end notches, it's ready for the ease process. Run an easeline around the garment waistline approximately $\frac{3}{8}$ inch from the cut waistline edge, within the seam allowance. After eas-

ing, compare the garment to the waistband, between end notches. If the garment still seems a bit large, run another easeline over or near the first. If the garment seems a bit small, pop a thread or two to release some of the ease.

Before joining eased garment to the waistband, use a press-and-lift motion with an iron to flatten eased portion. Join waistband to the garment by matching center front, center back, side seam and end markings on waistband to corresponding area of the garment. Machine baste waistband in place. Try on garment. Let the mirror tell you how slim you look. Now is the time to make any final adjustments on fit as well as to determine hem length. Finish the waistband.

■ Solution for small selection of men's patterns: Choose loose styles, use size 16 pattern, cut 1 inch seams, reverse buttons, lengthen pattern between shoulder and armhole, lengthen cap to accommodate lengthening between shoulder and armhole in bodice, and lengthen sleeves. If you take accurate body measurements and compare them to the pattern—you won't have a problem.

■ When sewing skirt or pant dart, start stitching darts from fat to skinny end at the waistline seam placement ($\frac{5}{8}$ inch from cut edge). Darts closed up to the waistline cut edge result in a smaller circle and inaccurate waist measurement.

Designer Waistband Which Grows

Many women experience a change in waist size at different times of the month or during different times of the day. Appropriate for this figure is a smooth fitting waistband slightly elasticized, allowing for weight fluctuation, comfort while traveling or simply an end to binding waistbands forever. Marcy Tilton, founder of The Sewing Workshop, swears by this waistband.

A waistband which feels comfortable in the morning is often tight and binding in the evening. If you travel, or sit in an office, a comfortable waistband is a must. Knit skirts and pants with elasticized waists are popular for this reason. Woven fabrics present a slightly different problem which can be solved by the technique below. Construction of a slightly elasticized, smooth-fitting waistband combines the comfort of a pull-on elasticized waist with the styling of a tailored waistband. This waistband is designed not for pull-on garments, but fitted garments with darts, tucks, pleats or gathers with zipper or side pocket opening. Any weight fabric, including denim or pigskin, can be used successfully.

Compare your honest waist measurement to the measurement of the garment at the waist before the waistband is applied. The garment should measure 1 to 2 inches larger than the waist measurement. If the garment does not measure 1 to 2 inches larger than

waist measurement, decrease side seams and darts slightly. If your garment is slightly larger, run an easeline around the waist to remove some of the fullness. Cut elastic Dritz flat rib or Banroll honeycomb to your waist measurement minus 3 inches, plus underlap, plus 2 seam allowances. Mark seam allowances and underlap on elastic, with blue water soluble pen. Divide remaining elastic in quarters to establish center front, center back, and side seams. Since the body is $\frac{1}{2}$ inch smaller in back than front, move side seam marking $\frac{1}{4}$ inch toward back of garment. This prevents side seams from pulling toward the front of the garment. Mark designations on elastic. Cut waistband the garment waist measurement (1 to 2 inches larger than actual waist measurement) plus underlap plus 2 seam allowances. If possible, use selvage for one long side of the waistband. If no selvage is available, finish one long side of waistband with overlock or Hong Kong finish. If you are using 1 inch elastic, cut waistband $3\frac{3}{8}$ inches wide; $1\frac{1}{2}$ inch elastic, cut waistband $4\frac{3}{8}$ wide; 2 inch elastic, cut waistband 5 3/8 wide.

Complete garment including zipper and pockets up to the waistband application stage. Apply right side of unfinished long edge of the waistband to the right side of the garment with a $\frac{5}{8}$ inch seam. Press.

Sandwich elastic between the wrong side of the waistband and the seam allowance joining the waistband to the garment. Match elastic markings with corresponding garment locations. Pin elastic to seam allowance at center front, center back and side seams. Elastic will extend into the ends of the band in underlap and into seam allowances on ends, but will not be stretched in these areas. Anchor elastic to seam allowance by sewing the long edge of the elastic to the seam allowance with a long zigzag stitch, stretching elastic to fit between pins designating center front, cen-

WAIST MEASUREMENT + 1-2"

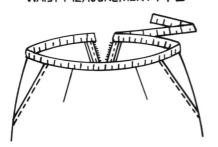

■ If your pant or skirt features a fly front, be sure to determine "center front" and "center back" before you begin. Zipper teeth are not the indicator here.

Designer Waistband Which Grows

ter back and side seams. Edge of elastic is placed along stitching line.

With right sides together, fold waistband in half lengthwise. On the back half of the waistband not joined to garment, trim away $1/8$ inch from the ends of the band. This trimming will create favoring, which when the waistband is completed will pull the ends of the band slightly toward the inside of the garment, keeping the edges smooth, preventing roll to the outside. Pin ends of the band together, forcing ends meet, despite the fact that one half was trimmed by $1/8$ inch. Complete

each end separately by sewing ends right sides together, including end of elastic in seam. Trim seam, turn and press.

Fold waistband into place, wrapping elastic and folding to the inside of the garment. Pin waistband in place in the well of the seam. With a straight stitch, sew in the well of the seam from the right side of the garment, stretching the waistband as you sew.

Although your waistband will have a slight puckered effect on the hanger, it will be smooth and comfortable on the body.

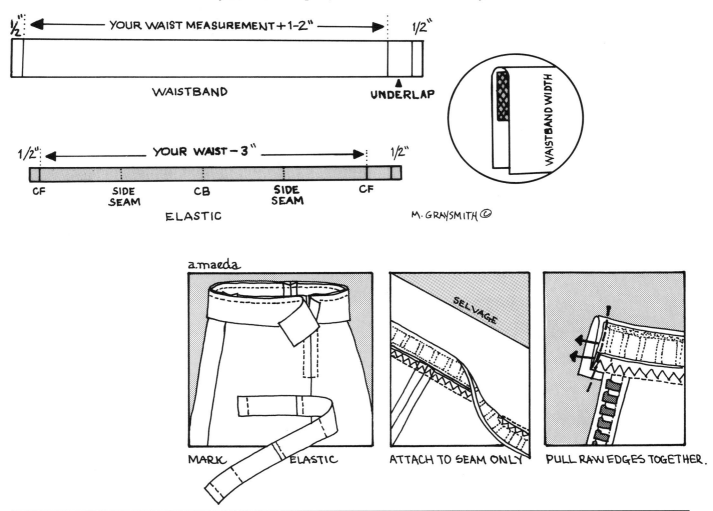

½" ← YOUR WAIST MEASUREMENT + 1–2" → 1/2"

WAISTBAND   UNDERLAP

WAISTBAND WIDTH

1/2" ← YOUR WAIST – 3" → 1/2"

CF   SIDE SEAM   CB   SIDE SEAM   CF

ELASTIC

M. GRAYSMITH ©

a.maeda

MARK   ELASTIC   ATTACH TO SEAM ONLY   PULL RAW EDGES TOGETHER.

SELVAGE

Waistband for Pull-ons

Pull-on pants and skirts look attractive only if the waistband is not bulky. The following waistband technique, developed at The Sewing Workshop in San Francisco (see Sources), is designed to fit over hips and add minimum bulk at the waist. This technique is ideal for knits, but may also be used for soft woven fabric as well. Cut waistband $4\frac{1}{2}$ inches wide if you are using 1 inch elastic. Waistband may be trimmed down later, but some fabric narrows as it stretches.

Cut waistband length your hip measurement plus $3\frac{1}{4}$ inches (2 inch ease plus 2 seam allowances). The least bulky waistband is one which has the greatest stretch; therefore, a waistband cut from ribbing or crossgrain knit is preferable, but lengthwise grain can be used if ribbing or crossgrain knit is not available or compatible with your fabric.

Join waistband at ends, forming a circle. Try on waistband. Make the circle smaller until it slides over hips snugly, and smoothly. Press seam open, trim to $\frac{1}{4}$ inch and topstitch with a wide zigzag stitch.

Divide and mark waistband in quarters. Pin waistband to garment right sides together, matching quarter points with seams, placing waistband seam at center back. Sew waistband to garment right sides together with waistband on top, stretching as you sew to match garment. Use a narrow zigzag (.5) stitch of medium length. Press seam up into waistband. Turn waistband to the inside, forming a casing for the elastic. Make casing slightly larger ($\frac{1}{4}$ inch) than elastic. Pin in place. Trim and overlock unfinished side of waistband. From the outside of the garment, sew in the well of the seam around the waist, at the bottom of the casing. Leave 2 to 3 inches open at center back to insert elastic.

Depending upon how snugly you like your waistbands to fit, cut elastic to your waist measurement minus 2 to 3 inches. To prevent twisting elastic when joining ends, mark ends of elastic on the same side before inserting. Insert elastic into casing with bodkin or closed safety pin. Join ends of elastic by overlapping. Sew back and forth on elastic with zigzag or serpentine stitch. Close opening in casing with a hand or machine stitch.

To prevent elastic from twisting in the garment, sew vertically through elastic and casing at waistband on side seams.

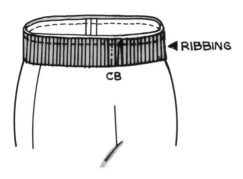

RIBBING

CB

PANTS SIDE VIEW

M. GRAYSMITH ©

■ If you like the look of several rows of topstitching on your waistband, both Sport and Ban Rol elastic retain their original elasticity.

Elastic Mystery

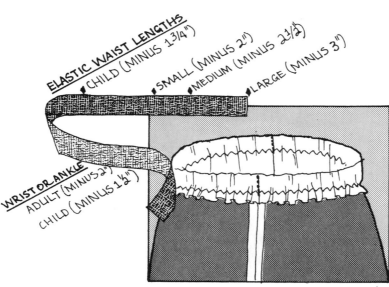

ELASTIC WAIST LENGTHS
CHILD (MINUS 1¾")
SMALL (MINUS 2")
MEDIUM (MINUS 2½")
LARGE (MINUS 3")

WRIST OR ANKLE
ADULT (MINUS 2")
CHILD (MINUS 1½")

a. maeda

Elastic continues to pose a mystery for many people. Purchase a good quality elastic. Webbed and woven elastics have a higher recovery and will maintain their shape for the life of the garment. If you want to eliminate the risk of elastic which becomes too tight after the garment is laundered, simply preshrink the elastic by hand in a basin of hot water. If the garment will be machine dried, run the wet elastic through the dryer cycle in a mesh bag.

The cut length of waistline elastic is determined by the size of the individual. A large figure should cut elastic 3 inches smaller than waist measurement, a medium figure 2 inches less, and a child 1¾ inches less than waist measurement. Wrist or ankle elastic should be cut 2 inches less for adults and 1½ inches less for children than the wrist or ankle measurement. Narrower elastic—¼ to ⅜ inch—is more comfortable at the wrist or ankle.

Wrist and forearm elastic is a sore subject for some children. Consider using elasticized thread on the bob-bin only. Wind the elastic thread onto the bobbin by hand, stretching slightly as you wind. Sewing from the right side of the garment, use a wide zigzag in the area to be elasticized. The drawback to elastic thread is that it rarely lasts the life of the garment. Since application is simple, it is often worth re-application to avoid battling the getting dressed factor with a child.

Before you begin elastic application, determine whether the elastic can stretch enough to pull in the entire length of fabric. If not, gather the fabric to be elasticized slightly before you apply elastic. To insure uniform fullness, divide the elastic—minus ½ inch on each end—into quarters. The ½ inch at each end will be used as overlap to attach the ends of the elastic into a circle. Overlap ends ½ inch and sew back and forth several times.

To prevent cased elastic from rolling during wear, anchor elastic at the side seams by sewing through all thicknesses at the well of the seam.

Shirred Waistbands

Skirts and pants with elastic waistbands were often bulky and unflattering. Not so with the shirred elastic bands on much of today's sportswear. The secret to success with shirred elastic is the combination of lightweight fabric and webbed elastic. Although the shirred band appears to have 4 to 8 separate channels filled with separate individual lengths of elastic, the shirred effect is actually accomplished with one wide strip of special honeycombed elastic. Made by Banroll, it's offered in a variety of widths from ¾ inch to 3 inch. While most elastic loses recovery when stitched lengthwise, honeycomb elastic retains 90 percent recovery with four or more rows of topstitching.

If the fabric is quite lightweight, it is feasible to add 4½ inches above the waistline if you plan to use 2 inch wide elastic. For the least bulk and the most flattering results, a separate cutout waistband is recommended. Cut waistband length to hip measurement plus 6 inches, and waistband width to twice the width of the elastic plus 1 inch. Finish one long side of the waistband by using a selvage or overlock. Sew waistband in a circle. Press open seam. Gather garment to fit waistband. Apply unfinished edge of waistband to garment, right sides together.

Cut honeycombed elastic to waist measurement minus 4 inches. Topstitching reduces elasticity 10 percent. Sew elastic in a circle by overlapping ends ½ inch. Divide elastic into quarters and mark. Insert circle of elastic between wrong side of waistband and seam allowance, joining waistband to garment. Use the seam allowance as a shelf for the elastic. Match quarter markings on elastic with center front, center back and side seams. Wrap elastic snugly by bringing the waistband around the elastic toward the inside of the garment. Place pins vertically at center front, center back and side seams through both sides of waistband and elastic. Do not move these pins. If you find it easier, hand baste vertically through all layers with double thread at center front, center back and side seams.

Stretch waistband one section at a time, placing pins horizontally in the well of the seam, joining the waistband with the garment. Make sure that waistband seam goes up into the band. Finished side of waistband is pinned down, extending about 3/8 inches

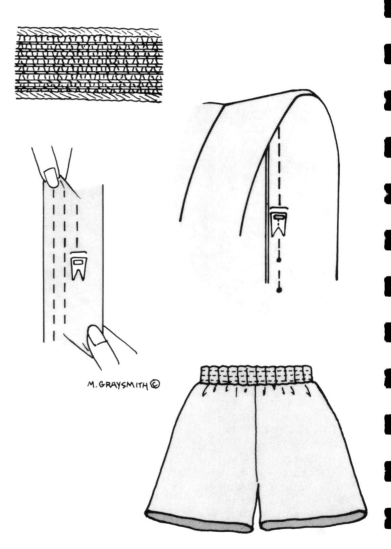

M. GRAYSMITH ©

below the waist seam. Form casing by sewing in the well of the seam around the waist. Do not remove vertical pins or basting holding elastic in place.

To give the waistband a shirred effect, the waistband is topstitched at approximately half-inch intervals, forming 4 to 8 parallel rows of even topstitching. Continue to stretch elastic to match waistband for all rows of parallel topstitching.

No Waistband at All

If you hate waistbands and would like an attractive, comfortable option, try a deep-faced yoke which rides on, or $\frac{1}{2}$ inch under, the waistline itself. This style skirt looks best with a bodysuit, a well fitting sweater or with an overblouse. Tuck-in blouse styles will not stay tucked into this style skirt.

Since the waistband is eliminated, the yoke must be faced to finish off the upper waistline edge. Consider a lightweight fabric for the facing such as pocketing or lining fabric to eliminate bulk. To give the firm sculpted shape of the yoke, interface the outer yoke itself. If you would like to use a press-on product, try the product on a sample scrap before committing yourself to a press-on for the yoke. Check to make sure the press-on results are truly invisible. To eliminate innate press-on bubbles, use a dry iron for first contact with the fashion fabric and the press-on product. The dry iron will not promote shrinkage during adhesion. After the press-on is firmly applied on the wrong side, turn the yoke to the right side; cover with a presscloth; press well with steam. This final pressing assures long-lasting adhesion.

Using the yoke pattern pieces as guides, cut stay tape the exact size of the pattern at the waist. Apply premeasured stay tape to each outer yoke piece. Stay tape will prevent the waistline from "growing" during wear (Illustration 1).

Trim $\frac{1}{8}$ inch from all three sides of yoke facing pieces, except waistline seam side. This trimming will make the yoke facing a tiny bit smaller than the outer yoke, consistent with the "turn of cloth" principle. Trimming for the turn of cloth eliminates wrinkles in the yoke facing. Apply the yoke and yoke facing. Grade seams to eliminate bulk, Press with steam and pound with a tailor's clapper.

With or without a yoke, it is possible to face a waistline with $\frac{1}{2}$ inch grosgrain ribbon. Stay tape waistline to insure a stable fit. Sew grosgrain and skirt right sides together with a $\frac{5}{8}$ inch seam. Clip and trim seam. Understitch waistline seam to ribbon. Finish ends. Shape and press over tailor's clapper (Illustration 2).

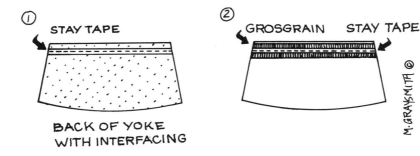

① STAY TAPE

BACK OF YOKE WITH INTERFACING

② GROSGRAIN   STAY TAPE

M. GRAYSMITH ©

■ Waistline shaping becomes a design focal point with English designer Sara Sturgeon's $\frac{1}{4}$ inch pin tucks sewn to the outside. The pin tucks form a ridge and do not lie flat.

Fabric Friends

Let's face it—some fabrics are a pleasure to sew on. They are not only pleasant to touch (known as "nice hand"), they don't stretch while sewing or wearing, are not prone to ravel, resist wrinkles, hang and drape well on the body to create a flattering silhouette. What are these fabrics?

For the best in drapeability, choose wool jersey, Austrian cotton knits, wool crepe, imported rayon challis, cashmere knits or wool challis. Any garment with fullness will be flattering in these fabrics.

For blouses, try fine Swiss, French and German cottons which have silk-like qualities—without the dry cleaning bills. For a slightly more structured look, use linen blends.

For jackets, soft wool flannels, Harris tweed and raw silk make good choices. Without expertise, avoid "hard-finished" wools, worsteds, and gabardines. If your sewing skills are not the best, fabrics with texture tend to hide mistakes.

In many climates, fabrics such as Viyella (wool and cotton blend), wool jersey, wool crepe, wool and rayon challis, and cotton knits are multiseasonal, which makes the time and money investment worthwhile. To avoid disappointment, preshrink washable fabric by washing, and dry cleanable fabric by preshrinking at the dry cleaners. Once you sew with these fabrics, you will find favorites to which you will gravitate season after season. Say "good-bye" to trial and error.

■ If you are having difficulty fitting yourself, set up a private appointment with either a dressmaker or a sewing teacher from a local community college.

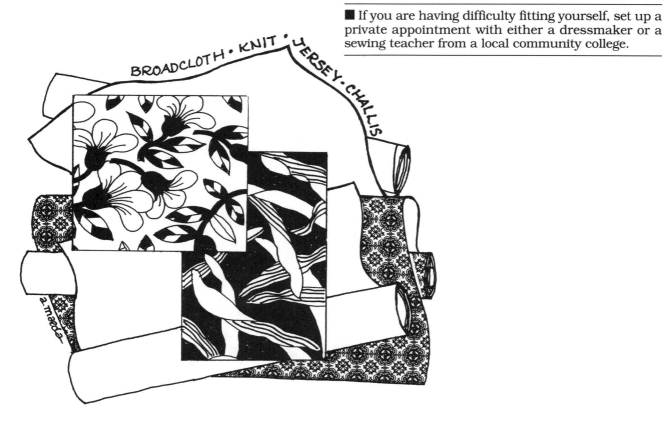

Coming to Terms

To be a knowledgeable sewer is to be knowledgeable about fibers and fabrics as well. Here are a few terms that you may be unfamiliar with:

DENIER is the yarn count of the fabric. High denier refers to a fine fabric. Denier usually refers to silk or silk-like fabrics.

THREAD COUNT refers to the number of crosswise and lengthwise threads per square inch. A fine weave will have a high thread count. Oriental rugs and sheeting often show notation of thread count.

MERCERIZATION is a process used to strengthen and give luster to cotton threads.

LOFT refers to the recovery or resilience of a fabric.

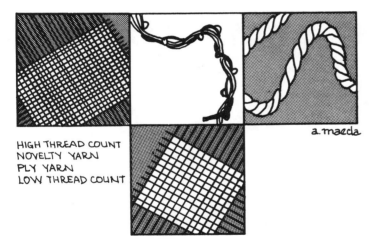

HIGH THREAD COUNT
NOVELTY YARN
PLY YARN
LOW THREAD COUNT

a. maeda

HAND refers to the feel of the fabric.

DRAPE refers to the hang of the fabric.

PLY YARNS are two or more strands of yarn twisted together to give durability and interest.

SLUB YARNS are unevenly spun yarns which have irregular knobs on the yarn surface.

NOVELTY YARNS are a combination of tightly twisted yarns which have been spun together to give a knotted or looped effect.

SPUN YARNS are short staples of yarn in varying lengths spun into a continuous strand.

COMBED YARNS are regular even yarns of rayon, cotton, or wool which have been carded and combed.

FILAMENT YARNS are long continuous fibers.

STRETCH YARNS are chemically processed yarns produced to give from 4 to 10 times stretch-and-return from their original size.

TENACITY is a term used to measure yarn strength.

FABRIC TEST

Very often one can find bargains in fabrics in "off the bolt" sales, but fabric knowledge is mandatory. Sometime or other, we have all heard someone refer to the "burn test" to determine fiber content. This test is not 100 percent reliable but in more cases than not, it can solve fiber mystery.

Those of you who stockpile fabric might wish to perform this test on a few of your mystery fabrics bought years ago. Cut off a small piece, put a match to it and observe the behavior of the flame and smell created. (I recommend performing this test carefully, over an empty metal trash basket.) The following observations can be made.

ACRYLIC: Melts in flame and leaves a hard black bead.

NYLON: Pulls away from flame, burns slowly and melts (will not continue to burn when flame is removed), smells like celery, leaves a hard gray bead.

SILK AND WOOL: Sizzle and burn slowly, curl away from flame, smell like burning hair, leaves gray ash.

COTTON, LINEN AND RAYON: Burn quickly with a bright flame, glow after flame is removed, smell like burning hair, leave gray ash.

POLYESTER: Shrinks away from flame, burns slowly, smells slightly sweet, leaves hard black bead.

ACETATE: The best test for acetate is not the burn test. Instead, test it in a bit of nail polish remover, in a dish. If the fiber is acetate, it will disintegrate.

Beaded Fabrics

If you find yourself fondling beaded fabrics, but are afraid to commit to buying a piece, Bobbie Carr, national lecturer, offers the following techniques for buying, cutting and sewing beaded fabric.

For openers, your pattern must be pre-tested. Forget about letting out beaded seams—the let-out portion will be devoid of beads and the alteration obvious. Choose a pattern with as few seams and as little darting as possible.

Underline beaded fabrics with silk or cotton tulle, found in bridal departments. Silk tulle is much softer than synthetic tulle, adapting better to beaded fabrics. If silk tulle is not availble in a compatible color, it can be dyed at home with Rit dye. Line with silk chiffon, organza or charmeuse. These fabrics are capable of stabilizing without imposing, allowing the character of the beaded fabric to be maintained. Experiment with different colors for lining, choosing the one which enhances the beaded fabric.

Cut out the lining fabric from the pattern. Pin lining fabric to tulle. Baste lining to tulle within seam allowances using one long and one short stitch for basting. Do not go around corners with hand basting. Clip thread at corner and continue basting. After lin-

ing is basted to tulle, cut out tulle using lining as a pattern.

Place beaded fabric on table with the wrong side up, beaded side against the table. Place tulle side, which is basted to lining, against the wrong side of the beaded fabric. Consider placement of major beaded designs so that they are not cut off in neckline or at armhole if possible. Pin tulle and lining to beaded fabric so that tulle is sandwiched between beaded fabric and lining. Hand baste tulle band lining to beaded fabrics. Cut out beaded fabric using lining and tulle pieces as the pattern (Illustration 1). You may hear the beads cut in the scissors; it's okay, you can't avoid it. Use old scissors.

Machine staystitch 15 stitches per inch layers together ½ inch from cut edges with color contrasting bobbin thread on all seams, not hems (Illustration 2). Have plenty of size 80/12 H and 90/14 H needles on hand since beaded and sequined fabrics are famous for needle breakage. Ravel beads out from seam allowances beyond staystitching line. Staystitching prevents beads from ravelling into the body of the garment.

Get seams ready to sew. Pin with right sides together.

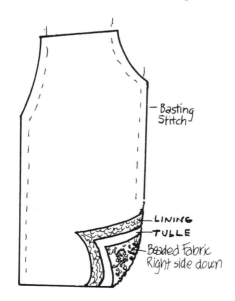

Basting Stitch

LINING
TULLE
Beaded Fabric
Right side down

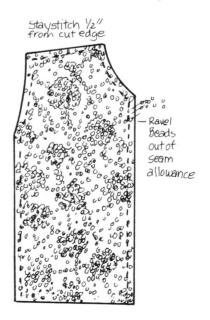

Staystitch ½"
from cut edge

Ravel Beads out of seam allowance

Beaded Fabrics

Hand baste seams within seam allowances. Sew seams; breaking one needle per seam is par for the course. Remove staystitching from seam allowances to prevent seams from looking overworked and puckered. Finger press seams open. Beaded fabrics do NOT like irons.

Stabilize and cushion shoulder seams with 2 inch wide strips of tulle, one on each side of the seam (Illustration 3). Cotton tulle is stronger than silk tulle, giving support to an area which is responsible for the weight of the beaded garment, which is substantial. Apply tulle strips as you sew shoulder seam.

Finish beaded seam allowances by overlocking each side of the seam allowance separately. Finish seams with wide strips of bias silk lining (raw edges pressed under) which are placed over the open seams. Whip-stitch bias strip to lining (Illustration 4). Finish neckline with a narrow strip of bias binding from lining material. Position binding on the inside so that only beaded fabric shows at the neck from the outside.

Give a better drape to beaded fabric by using a strip of drapery weights along the fold in the hem (Illustration 5). Hand stitch the strip to the fold of the lining. Finish raw edge of hem with a Hong Kong finish. Hem stitch is attached to the tip of the hem and the lining, not the beaded fabric itself.

See these techniques demonstrated in Bobbie Carr's video, *Couture Techniques for Special Occasions*—see Sources.

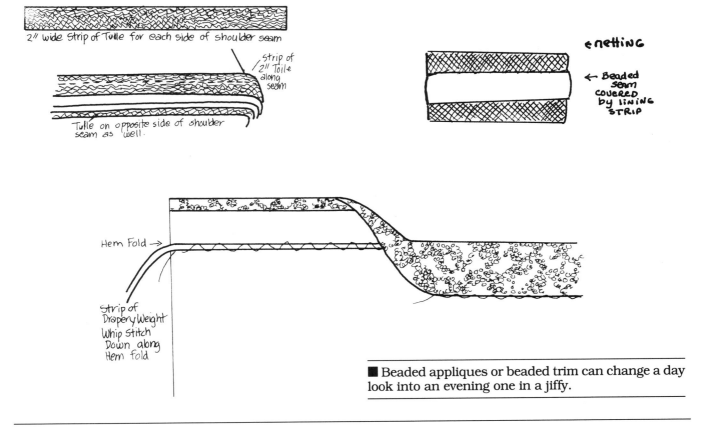

2" wide Strip of Tulle for each side of shoulder seam

Strip of 2" Toile along seam

Tulle on opposite side of shoulder seam as well.

€ netting

← Beaded seam covered by lining strip

Hem Fold →

Strip of Drapery Weight Whip Stitch Down along Hem Fold

■ Beaded appliques or beaded trim can change a day look into an evening one in a jiffy.

Gabardine Can Be Tamed

Resistance to wrinkling and stretching makes gabardine a favorite for pants and skirts created by better ready-to-wear designers here and abroad. Although a gabardine garment may "seat out" slightly, its strong twill weave gives the fabric recovery when allowed to relax on a hanger overnight.

However, despite its attributes, gabardine has a reputation for being difficult to sew. The following tips will help you conquer the demons and tame gabardine into professional-looking garments. Although gabardine may be handwashed in cold water and allowed to drip dry, you may prefer to have the fabric preshrunk at the dry cleaners. Some shrinkage should be anticipated, so do not eliminate the preshrinking process.

Since gabardine will not ease without leaving a slightly puckered appearance, choose patters carefully. A jacket with a raglan or dropped shoulder will yield far more professional-looking results than a set-in sleeve.

Since gabardine is not a porous fabric, making long-term interfacing fusion a problem, a sew-in medium-weight interfacing such as Stay Shape is preferable. Include interfacing into the seam allowance about $1/8$ inch to give strength to the seam.

Cut interfacing from the garment pattern piece and trim off $3/8$ inch to $1/2$ inch from the interfacing before sewing to the fashion fabric. For machine sewing, use a size 80/12 H needle with a medium length stitch. If your seam puckers slightly as you sew, loosen the top tension slightly or use an even feed foot. Thread choices include both cotton and polyester. You may prefer poly-

■ Trenchcoat pictured is Shermaine Fouché's trenchcoat pattern (see Sources).

Gabardine Can Be Tamed

ester if you need black thread, since black polyester is more colorfast long-term than black cotton. Be sure to wind a polyester bobbin slower to avoid stretching of the thread, often responsible for puckered seams.

Grade seams in areas of bulk, trimming the center seam of three the shortest to cushion edges when pressing. Get in the habit of using a presscloth with steam throughout the pressing process. No presscloth results in flattening the twill weave, creating a shine on the fabric. Use a press and lift motion as you press at all times to prevent stretching. A hard edge from seam imprint on the right side can be avoided by using a point presser. Since the width of the pressing surface is only half an inch, a ridge at the edge of the seam allowance will not be visible. Pressing with the point of the iron will eliminate seam allowance ridges on most fabrics, but will not give the heat necessary to open seam allowance on wool gabardine.

Due to the weight and strength of wool gabardine, you may prefer not to line the garment. Tip for those with sergers: Experiment with wooly nylon on the underloopers for serged edges with a lush finish. If you do decide to line the garment, medium weight Bemberg rayon lining is a good choice.

Credit to: Shermaine Fouché, couture designer based in San Francisco, who is responsible for some of the outstanding ball gowns on the opening night at the opera.

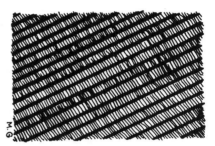

WOOL GABARDINE – CLOSE UP

■ To imitate better ready-to-wear and save time sewing hems, use a Schmetz "ZWI" needle. It ensures even rows of topstitching while creating attractive detailing. If you like topstitching with heavy thread but hate frayed threads, use a Schmetz "N" needle, which has a long eye to accommodate the thicker thread without piercing large holes in the garment.

Mastery of Wool Crepe

If you have never worked with wool crepe, you are in for a real treat. Not only is this fabric a pleasure to wear, but a pleasure to sew with as well.

Always buy an extra ⅛ yard for every 2 yards needed to allow for shrinkage. Although you might get away without preshrinking some wools, wool crepe is definitely not one of them. Wool crepe shrinks in both length and width and should be preshrunk by a dry cleaner. Wool crepe is not washable and must be preshrunk properly for a long term reliable fit.

Among the more popular style choices for wool crepe are tailored pants, culottes, straight skirts, fitted jackets and full skirts—cut on the bias. Wrinkle resistance, trans-seasonal properties and ability to hold a crease account for much of wool crepe's popularity. Ability to mold and tailor, nice hand and interesting weave make additional points for wool crepe during the construction process. The price per yard ranges from $25 per yard for domestic to $70 per yard for the imported Italian. The imported wool crepe may seem expensive, but once you own a garment in it, whatever you paid per yard seems worth it. Price similar garments in ready-to-wear and you will see that your time and money is well spent.

Guard against ravelling by cutting and sealing the raw edge with fray check, or overlocking cut pieces before sewing. Stay tape all areas of stress: pocket openings, crotch, shoulders and angular neckline cuts. Due to its porous nature, wool crepe makes a good candidate for fusible interfacings. Before committing a garment to a fusible, always try a sample to determine whether the fused fabric has the property you want.

Although lining is not mandatory, lining is advisable to give depth to the fabric as well as preserve the life of the garment. Bemberg rayon by Skinner® makes a good lining choice for its wrinkle resistance and breathability. Exceptions to lining might be a wool crepe blouse or tailored pants made in lycra and wool crepe blend with multi-stretch. A lined wool crepe blouse would be too warm and lined pants in a multi-stretch fabric would defeat the purpose of using a stretch fabric for an action garment.

Pressing must be done with steam and a presscloth to prevent shine on dark crepes or stains from potential steam iron leaks on light crepes.

Suggestions for 3 garment pieces you will wear to death are: tailored pants, straight skirt and a straight or fitted jacket. Make all 3 pieces in black wool crepe. After you see how much you wear these pieces, because they always seem appropriate and can be dressed up or down, make yourself another 3 in cream wool crepe which can be mixed with pastel silks and linens for spring or cream cashmere for an elegant cool weather look.

Cashmere Opulence

Cashmere knits and wovens may be fashion news, but high prices associated with cashmere are not. Perhaps by becoming more knowledgeable about the origin and scarcity of cashmere, you might be tempted by a piece of cashmere yardage for one of your next projects. In addition to its supple nature, allowing for a sensuous drape over the figure, cashmere is three times warmer per ounce than the finest wool.

The best quality cashmere today comes from China, Afghanistan and Iran. Cashmere is actually the downy undercoat of the Cashmere goat whose average yield is between three and four ounces per year. Every spring, the fleece is combed by hand. The fine fleece fiber is measured by the thousandth of an inch. Cashmere

goats grow the soft fleece as a protection against extremes of temperature. Although several attempts have been made to raise this goat in other parts of the world, these attempts have been unsuccessful.

When a cashmere shipment arrives in the United State or Europe, the fleece is washed and combed to remove the coarse guard hairs and excess oils. The finest cashmere is then dyed, teased so that all the hairs lie in one direction and oiled to protect the fiber during spinning. The fiber is then combed, stretched and spun into yarn. During the spinning process, millions of tiny air pockets are formed, giving the cashmere fiber its greater insulation. The yarn is then knitted or woven into yard goods.

If you are fortunate enough to afford a piece of cashmere woven or knit, treat the fabric gently during construction, folding the cut pieces flat on the table. Due to their fragile nature, cashmere knits should never be hung on a hanger.

Always make a pretest of a pattern intended for cashmere. If you can't bring yourself to do a pretest, hand stitch side seams to try on. The fragile fiber does not take kindly to ripped stitches and may hold a memory of the old stitches, especially if the seam has been pressed. Use an 80/12 H needle and medium stitch length for wovens and 70/10 H/S needle and slightly smaller stitch for fine knits. For pressing, use a press-and-lift motion with little steam on a medium setting. No fusible interfacing for cashmere, it flattens the hairs. Always use a presscloth, and be careful not to use too much iron pressure, or you will flatten the delicate hairs.

If you want to make an epic piece in cashmere, make yourself a cashmere topcoat or blazer. Underline with 100 percent cotton batiste, china silk, or Armo Press soft. Underlining creates dimension for cashmere and gives an anchor for hand stitches, making them invisible. A lightweight hair canvas makes a good interfacing for a coat or jacket. After pressing or wearing, if the fabric seems flat anywhere, brush with a baby's hairbrush in the direction of the nap.

Sand-Washed Silk

If you have been craving the look of sand-washed silk used in better sportswear, a similar look can be achieved at home with a little premature aging of the fabric. For best results, use Fuji silk, commonly known as silk broadcloth. Crepe de chine is a bit too thin and silk Dupionni remains a bit too stiff for most garments. China silk, commonly used as lining material, remains pretty much the same before and after washing, but is too thin for use in outer garments.

In addition to being washable and soft to the touch, sand-washed silk looks slightly faded as well. At-home washing will achieve a similar effect; be certain you can accept a slightly muted color before you try this process.

Using warm water and detergent, wash silk fabric with some towels which are color compatible, as the silk will lose some of its color. Put fabric and towels in dryer and run through normal heat drying cycle. After this process is finished, you are ready to view the results. If you would like a more aged, softer silk, repeat the process using a cup of fabric softener in the rinse cycle. Put towels and fabric in the dryer with a pair of tennis shoes or two tennis balls.

If you have never seen sand-washed silk or prefer to see the results before committing yourself to an entire piece of fabric, buy ¼ yard of Fuji silk and experiment. I loved the results of the above process when used on black Fuji silk. It removed the harshness of the pure black, leaving a soft grey/black color.

Silk pretreated in this manner makes an excellent pair of soft pleated summer pants lined in China silk, a soft multi-pocketed blouse, or a loose blouson jacket.

Sew garments with a fine needle—60/9 or 70/10—with cotton or long staple polyester thread. Preshrink interfacing as well so that garments can be machine washable and dryable. Pressing may or may not be required depending upon personal taste.

a. maeda

■ Considerable pressing as well as wear and tear on garments can be eliminated by hand washing and air drying on a hanger. Never machine wash or dry black fabric unless you don't mind the grayed-out look.

Linen Luxury

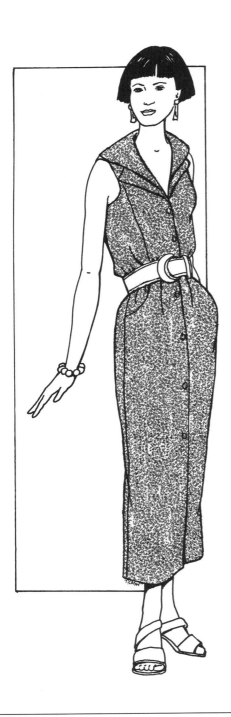

Most sewers have a love/hate relationship with linen. No one ever claimed that linen didn't wrinkle. Linen purists like the wrinkles. Wrinkles let the world know your garment is 100% linen. Linen is an ideal fabric for hot weather climates because it breathes, absorbs body moisture and is quick drying. Perhaps the most difficult thing about linen for the home sewer is choosing the correct weight for the garment piece. While handkerchief linen makes a beautiful full cut skirt or blouse, this same weight is unsuccessful for pants due to its slight transparency and lightweight nature. For pants to hang properly, choose a mid-weight linen such as moygashel or white Irish linen. Mid-weight linens can be used for jackets, straight skirts and pants. Heavy-weight linen is best for home furnishings.

The finest linen comes from Ireland with a higher price reflecting its source. Irish linens are soft to the touch, a pleasure to wear and extremely strong. Belgian linen is slightly less expensive; Polish linen the least expensive. If you have ever owned a garment of Irish linen, you will agree that the price differential is worth it. The best styles for linen are simple ones.

Linen can be dry cleaned, hand or gentle cycle washed in warm water. Do not put garment linen in the dryer since it weakens the fibers. Hang to dry. To get the best press—dampen linen slightly; put in a plastic bag; refrigerate for an hour or more; iron with a hot iron. Hand wash or dry clean linen to preshrink.

Linen is a pleasure to sew on. Simply use a sharp (H) needle suited to the weight of the linen: 70/10 for handkerchief; 80/11 for mid-weight.

Many linen blends are available combining the look of linen without so many wrinkles. Although these fabrics make up well—to the purists, they are not linen.

Linen Know-How

Purchasing linen from a fabric store to create the same effect as linen garments in ready-to-wear can be difficult, without some knowledge about the types of linen which are on the market. Sometimes it is difficult to find the exact product that you see in the ready-to-wear. Look at the label carefully on the garment you are admiring. Since Irish linen is the best, the label will usually will reflect this. Irish linen is the softest and most pliable of the 100% linen products. Irish linen is available is various weights from handkerchief to suit weight. If Irish linen is what you want, check the bolt to make certain this is what you are getting. Moygashel is the trade name for the best quality Irish linen used in ready-to-wear.

Since handkerchief linen is slightly transparent, I often eliminate the facing on a blouse and cut the front double. The fabric remains soft, but the end result has less transparency, often desirable on the front of a blouse. If interfacing is visible between the two fabric layers, consider interfacing with another layer of the linen itself, under the buttons and buttonholes as well as the collar.

Ready-to-wear jackets in Irish linen often have a softer hand than the linen found in fabric shops. If you machine wash and dry the linen, while it does weaken the fibers slightly, it often gives the look you want. Since an investment in Irish linen is not a small one, I suggest purchasing a quarter of a yard. Throw it in the washer and dryer with some other clothes to see il this treatment gives you the effect you want. Off-season is a good time to purchase linen in fabric stores, since prices are usually well reduced.

If you feel you are unwilling to buy the best in a pure linen, Oatmeal linen, usually imported from Poland rather than Ireland is slightly less expensive. This linen is the color of oatmeal and is coarser and less expensive than Irish linen. Between these two grades of linen comes a third called Belgian linen, not as fine as Irish, but not as coarse as Polish either. Because of its desirability, Irish linen is the most available. If you fall in love with a piece of fabric which is not marked Irish linen, let your hand decide.

Because so many people love linen but would like a product which is less prone to wrinkles, linen blends are available. If a linen blend is 75% rayon and 25%

linen, the fabric will have a linen-like appearance, but drape better and wrinkle less. Because of the addition of rayon, the fabric is not as strong as pure linen and machine washing is definitely not recommended. Hand washing and air drying is suitable.

A combination of polyester and rayon can be created to give the appearance of linen. While this fabric looks good on the bolt, it breaks down with wear and may not be worth your time to construct. If you see a fabric described as silk linen, this is not a silk and linen blend, this is silk made to look like linen. Perhaps the best of the linen blends is a cotton and linen blend, usually 60 to 80% cotton blended with linen as the remainder. The higher the linen content, the more expensive the product. Because both linen and cotton are natural as opposed to man made products, this combination is comfortable to wear. The addition of cotton helps considerably in reducing the wrinkles.

In my opinion, for longevity, you are better off with a genuine linen product. Pure linen will always be in demand.

Don't try to force a fabric to behave against its nature. Soft fabrics rarely tailor and crisp fabrics rarely drape. If you love linen but hate wrinkles, underline the entire garment with fusible knitted tricot interfacing. Underlining white linen pants accomplished two things: It cuts down on wrinkles and prevents "see-through," in white fabric.

■ Have you ever noticed how joining the facing to the jacket shortens the jacket in this area? This is caused by not lengthening your machine stitch when joining the facing to the jacket. If the same stitch length was used to join the facing as was used in other seams, the stitch length is shortened in this seam because the stitch itself has to go through more layers. In addition to the jacket and facing fabric, usually both the front and the facing have been interfaced which adds two more layers. If you are adding piping to the seam, even more depth has been added. Experiment by adding .5mm stitch length to an unpiped seam in this area and 1 mm stitch length il the seam is piped. You will see that the problem disappears.

Active Sports Fabrics

If you have always wanted to make clothes for biking, camping, skiing, swimming, or river running, try these excellent tips from Arlene Haislip from The Green Pepper, Inc.

There's no need to preshrink nylon. Nylon is a fiber with much give, but it will not shrink when washed.

Always use a sharp needle for woven nylon fabrics. Small sizes are better than large because they go through the fabric easier.

If your stitches start to skip during your project, your needle may need changing. Nylon dulls needles quickly.

Use a small size ballpoint needle for Savina DP. It is so tightly woven, a sharp needle might break the fibers. Hold your fabric taut, not tight, while sewing.

Use all polyester thread. Polyester fibers are longer and usually smaller in diameter than cotton fibers. When twisted, the larger fibers won't break as easily as shorter fibers.

Polyester thread will go through layers of tightly woven nylon and insulated garments easily.

When sewing with uncoated nylons (nylon taffeta) sear or zigzag your seam allowances. They will fray if you don't! To sear, hold fabric edge taut and quickly pass close to base of candle flame.

If you are using coated nylon, the coating side should be inside, or wrong side, of your garment. The double polyurethane coating must be protected from abrasion. If scratched it may leak! These fabrics do not ravel, so seam finishing is unnecessary.

The polyurethane coating on fabrics somewhat alleviates the importance of grain. For loose fitting garments, you can lay pattern pieces crosswise to grain if this saves you fabric.

When sewing with coated fabrics, pin pattern within seam allowance to prevent punching holes in garment.

Apply seam sealer on wrong side of coated fabrics, on each side of, and down the center of seams. Two thin coats of seam sealer are more flexible than one thick coat.

Mountain cloth has a water repellent finish on it. After a few washings you can put more finish on with Wash Cycle, a Keynon product.

Additional tips for active sports fabrics:

Do not use fusible interfacing on coated fabrics.

Seal seams in waterproof garments with a bead of Seam Sealer on the wrong side of the garment.

If skipped stitches occur, try a layer of Tear Away between the fabric and the feed dog. Gortex® is less of a problem than some other laminated varieties.

For patterns, notions and fabric, see Sources.

M. GRAYSMITH©

■ Eliminate saggy crotch on aerobic and cycling pants. Take a crotch measurement on body from front waistline to back waistline. Measure front and back crotch measurement on pattern by placing tape measure on edge for accurate crotch measurement around curves. Take crotch measurement on seamline. For proper fit, adjust crotch length on pattern so that it measures 1 inch less than crotch length measurement on body.

Custom Pleating

For sculptural and supple pleated clothing, Japanese designer Issey Miyake is the master.

If you like permanent-pleated skirts and are unable to find them in your best length (always either too long or too short), have hips disproportionate to waist, or simply find the fabric selection too limited, custom pleating is the solution for you.

Check your phone book for a local fabric pleating source. If you fail to find one, and that may be the case since very few cities offer custom pleating, you might try the San Francisco Pleating Company (see Sources). This company offers printed instructions and has been very helpful to home sewers.

Although most fabrics will take a pleat, some fabrics maintain the pleat better than others. Synthetic or natural fiber and synthetic blends pleat best. A blend of cotton and synthetic pleats well, but 100 percent cotton is quite unsatisfactory.

Fine-weight wools and wool blends also pleat well. Rayon is capable of maintaining a pleat but has a tendency to shrink in the process. Allow for this when cutting out.

Although paper pleat molds are used, a variety of fabrics in lightweights may be pleated, such as fine suedes and leathers. Fine knits are also successful as long as the fiber is synthetic or a natural and synthetic blend. Because of the variance in fabrics and dyes, you are taking a small risk in fabric pleating. This can be minimized by a well informed staff at the pleating company. If you are uncertain, send a fabric sample. Contrary to popular opinion, custom pleating is quite reasonable. The price ranges from $1.50 to $2 per yard, with a $6 to $8 minimum.

The amount of fabric before pleating must measure three times the desired finished amount. For example, a 36 inch hip would require 108 inches of flat yardage plus 2 inch ease and seam allowance. If the fabric is stable, crossgrain and lengthwise grain fabrics are suitable.

Garment pieces should be joined at the side seams and hemmed before pleating, leaving one last seam open so that fabric pieces will lie flat for the pleating process. Pleating is most successful on a length of fabric. Hems and seams should be pressed flat before being sent to the pleaters. Knife pleats can be made in any size from $1/8$ inch to 2 inches. On pleats smaller than $1/2$ inch, lightweight fabric must be used. Waist taper can be done with knife pleats $5/8$ inch or larger. Box pleats can be made in size 1 inch to 4 inches with or without a tapered waist. Allow three times the finished length. Very fine crystal pleating is available in one size and must be done only in lightweight fabrics.

One of the most flattering pleated garments is the circle skirt.

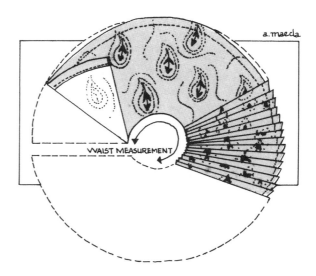

The waist before pleating should measure your waist size. After the circle is pleated, merely flatten out the pleats at the waist before you put on the waistband. If you have a tummy, cut waist circle 2 inches bigger than your waist. This will allow slightly pleated ease over the tummy area. After cutting, press well and hang overnight. From the hem, trim off bias hem drop, then hem skirt. Do not join the last seam, add zipper, or apply waistband until after the pleating process.

San Francisco Pleating Company needs ten working days for a job and will be happy to answer your questions.

Pre-Pleated Fabrics

Intimidating but tempting are the new permanent pleated polyesters in metallic and satin finishes. The most successful creations in the mini-pleated fabrics have simple styles, showing the pleats off to their best advantage.

Avoid interfacings since they will not respond to pleat movement.

Eliminate facings wherever possible, use bias trim or overlock raw edge and turn under.

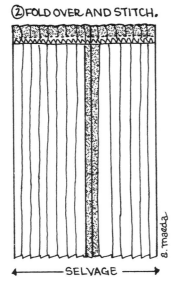

① SKIRT LENGTH PLUS 1 1/2" FOR CASING.

② FOLD OVER AND STITCH.

SELVAGE

If you care to tackle a shaped garment in prepleated fabric, hold pleats into position by sewing a narrow strip of Seams Great® within the seam allowance on each piece. This is especially important for a seam which will go across the pleat. Stabilizing each garment piece with Seams Great® prevents pleats from spreading open as seam is sewn.

Finish hems with the double needle. Push pleats into the presser foot as you sew.

Press very carefully, using low heat on the wrong side of the fabric. Too high a heat will flatten pleats.

A tube skirt, cut on the crosswise grain to take advantage of the flattering vertical lines of the pleat, is a perfect choice for these pre-pleated fabrics. If you don't want a clingy fit, buy enough fabric to go around your hips plus 3 inches. If you are more daring and want the result to be body conforming, buy your hip measurement minus 2 inches. The amount of fabric required is the fabric pleated, not stretched out. Most tube skirts will take about a yard of pleated fabric or 2¼ yards stretched out for measuring.

If you want a straight skirt that hangs close to the legs, use the selvage as a finished edge for the hem. Any hem treatment causes the pleated edge to flare out and should be eliminated unless you want the ruffled appearance seen on designer Mary McFadden's evening clothes.

Determine your finished skirt length and add 3 inches for elastic casing. For a 30½ inch finished length, cut skirt 33½ inches long. Form a tube by sewing one long seam at center back, parallel to pleating. Overlock raw edges of center back seam as well as newly cut edge, which will form the bottom of the fold-down casing. Pleating will flare out a little as you overlock. Fold down 1½ inches from overlocked edge. Let pleats release a bit as you sew. Leave a 2 inch opening. This forms the channel for 1 inch elastic.

Insert elastic and the skirt is finished.

For this tube skirt, little or no pressing is needed. If pressing is necessary for other designs, use light pressure without steam.

Credit to: San Francisco rainwear designer Babette.

Silk Chiffon Control

Why not grab the tiger by the tail and conquer your fears of sewing with sheers? Chiffons are offered in three different fibers: polyester, rayon, and silk.

Due to the fragile nature of silk chiffon, choose a pattern with simple styling; let the fabric make the statement over design detailing. To cut fabric double, hand-baste lengthwise selvage edges together 1 inch away from the selvage. Eliminate drawn-up lengthwise seams by cutting off $\frac{1}{2}$ inch from lengthwise edges, including the selvages. Save silk chiffon selvages to use as stay tape in area prone to stretch.

Polyester chiffon is the most practical since it is hand washable, drapey, and relatively inexpensive. Crinkled polyester chiffon is also available. Rayon has slightly better drapability but wrinkles. Fortunately, the wrinkles hang out in a damp bath room. Silk chiffon is the most expensive, must be dry cleaned, wrinkles, and is slightly harder to work with but yields beautiful results.

If you want a sheer fabric with slightly less transparency, consider georgette, a fabric with slightly more body, less transparency, and good drapability.

Before you leave the fabric store, purchase a packet of new schmetz needles. Number one choice would be 70/10 J needle for its extremely sharp point. Number two choice is 60/8 H or 70/10 H. If you don't own a satin edge foot or a triple lingerie needle (Schmetz 130/705 H DRI 2.5/80), you need one or the other for hemming.

If you are planning on making a skirt, the best chiffon skirts are two layers, so remember to double yardage requirements. The second layer need not be the same color. Try the effect of layering before you purchase. A georgette skirt can be successful using a single layer of fabric.

Hassle-free cutting is possible with a rotary cutter or Gingher micro-serrated knife edge bent trimmers. If you work with fine fabrics, these extremely sharp shears are a good investment ($30). Pick up a new box of 1BC glass head silk pins. Regular pins will snag the fabric. Sixty weight embroidery thread is preferable or use another fine thread alternative. If you plan to serge

seams, American and Elfird Inc. puts out a very fine weight serging thread called "Serge Well." Regular thread and wooly nylon are too heavy for professional results. On your way home pick up a package of tissue paper—an essential for accurate cutting.

After you have made the decision to tackle a chiffon skirt, here are some pointers. Cover your cutting surface with tissue paper and tape into place. Tissue paper helps control static electricity and eliminates snagging on the cutting surface.

Pin fabric to tissue before applying pattern. Now pin pattern to fabric with fine pins or use flat pattern weights. If you are using a rotary cutter, it is possible to get more accurate results by laying a grid ruler on the excess tissue along the inside seam of the pattern.

On the machine, cover the large hole in the throatplate with a thin $\frac{1}{4}$ inch strip of tape, being careful not to let the tape cover the feed dog. This procedure will prevent the chiffon from being pulled down into the throatplate as you sew. Your first stitch will make a small hole in the tape to bring up the bobbin thread. This method eliminates the technique of sewing chiffon seams through a layer of tissue paper. Switch needle position to the left for more control over stitches when using the all-purpose presserfoot.

Two methods for seams give professional results. French seams work well on blouses, but appear bulky on skirts unless you are very adept on fine French seams, pressing between the second stitch stage. Less bulky and easier: Sew a $\frac{5}{8}$ inch seam with fine thread and a very tiny zigzag in a medium stitch length. Using a slight zigzag enables the seam to drape with the fabric as it is pressed. Right next to the seam, sew another slightly wider zigzag. Trim off close to zigzag. Press well. If small hairs poke out between the zigzag, you might prefer to serge right next to the seam with three threads using only fine thread. Do one of these methods, not both. Always press well. Experiment first on scrap fabric after cutting. Cut waistbands double and baste together to prevent elastic see-through. Apply waistband.

Press skirt well and let hang overnight. For best

Silk Chiffon Control

results try a damp bathroom for polyester and rayon, not silk. Dampness fluffs up silk fiber. Using a hem marker, place fine pins where you want the fold of the hem. Go to the iron and press excess fabric under from the hem fold. Remove pins as you press.

This wealth of information was provided by fabric expert Barbara Kelly from the sewing workshop in San Francisco.

■ Allow twice as much time for a garment in chiffon than you would for anything else.

■ When working with chiffon, if you can't spare a sheet to pin the chiffon to, tape chiffon periodically to the cutting table—keeps slipping and sliding to a minimum.

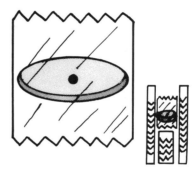

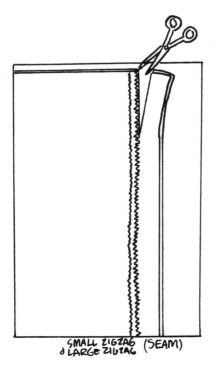

SMALL ZIGZAG (SEAM)
ð LARGE ZIGZAG

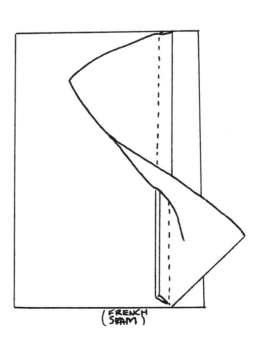

(FRENCH SEAM)

Hemming Chiffon

The most professional and least bulky hem results are obtained by using a satin edge foot with the needle one step from the center to the left position. Use a zigzag wide enough to go over the fold of the fabric when the fabric is guided along the satin edge knife. You are sewing a very narrow zigzag. Do not pull the fabric as you sew, unless you want "lettuce leaf" edging. Guide fabric into the needle with your right hand. If the fabric seems to be stretching as you sew, place your left index finger on the back of the presserfoot, acting as a fence, preventing the fabric from coming out as fast as it wants to. This easing technique is terrific for controlling stretch.

Another hem technique which also provides professional results is topstitching with a lingerie triple needle Schmetz 130/705 H DRI (2.5/80). Since you will be using an extra spool of thread you may need to buy a thread extender (about $6.00). After pressing up the hem fold, using the needle mentioned above, do three rows of top stitching near the hem fold.

For both hem techniques, carefully cut off excess fabric beyond hem fold. Press flat.

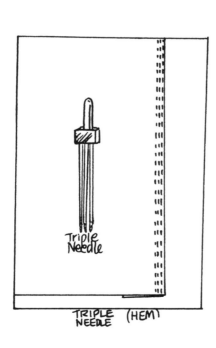

TRIPLE NEEDLE (HEM)

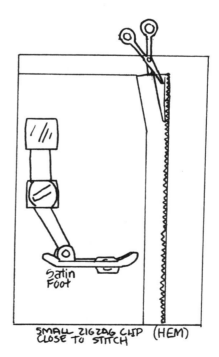

SMALL ZIGZAG CUP CLOSE TO STITCH (HEM)

Fake Fur Classics

Since most women either can't afford a real fur coat, or object to real furs on moral grounds, the excitement about fake fur is a welcome one. Fake fur no longer tries to imitate real fur, but makes a fashion statement on its own. To the industry's credit, fake furs are better than ever.

Choose your fake fur fabric carefully. If you are concerned about appearing heavy, a shorter fur will be more flattering.

Pattern choice should be limited to simple styling with few design details—let the fabric itself be the focal point. Limited seaming results in a non-bulky garment which handles well. Decide on closures early. Zippers and buttonholes are bulky. Far preferable are large hooks and eyes, or loops and buttons.

Fake fur fabric does have a nap, so be sure to buy enough fabric and use the "with nap layout" for directional cutting. Mark the back of the fabric with large chalk arrows in the direction of the nap. These arrows will be helpful when cutting out.

For short pile fabrics without heavy backing, use the "with nap" layout. Short pile fur fabric can be cut double and sewn with techniques used on regular fabrics. For short pile fur, use a size 90/14 needle, a straight stitch, sewing with 10 stitches to the inch.

If the fabric has a long pile, it is necessary to cut out the pattern through a single thickness of fabric. Place the fabric fur side down on the cutting table. The use of pattern weights instead of pins will prevent your pattern from tearing. Excess tissue should be cut away from the cutting line before you begin.

To cut, use sharp scissors with small precise cuts. Cut through only the fur back, not the fur itself. To keep the pieces in alignment while machine sewing, use an even feed, roller, or teflon foot on your machine. A long pile fur calls for a size 100/16 needle using a wide zigzag stitch and sewing 15 stitches to the inch. As you try a seam on a scrap, check for skipped stitches and thread breakage. Both of these problems can be corrected with an "NTW" leather needle which will pierce a heavy backing. Heavy-duty cotton thread is helpful as well. After the seams are sewn, pull the fur pile out of the seam from the right side with a blunt needle.

To enable the seams to lie flat on a long pile fur, shear the fur away from the seam allowances. This step can usually be eliminated on short pile furs. Cover the ironing board with a turkish towel. On the wrong side, press the seam open with the low setting on your iron. Do not use steam; kinky fur results. A higher setting will melt the backing. If the seam allowances refuse to lie flat, hand tack them to the backing or dot SOBO glue behind seam allowances and finger press in place.

For hems, catch stitch the top of the hem to the garment backing.

On long pile furs, buckling can be eliminated by shaving the fur from the hem allowance and gluing the hem in place with rubber cement. If the needle starts to skip stitches on backed fur, it may be due to gummy buildup on the needle from the backing of the fabric. Rub sewing machine oil or needle lube on the needle.

Rub oil or needle lube on the underside of the foot as well, so it will glide smoothly. If back is very gummy, rub a small amount of oil on the seamline to prevent the foot from sticking. Use only sewing machine oil.

See pages 160-161 for pelted fake furs.

The Velvet Touch

With the popularity of the dinner suit, this may be your season to sew with velvet, even if it is only on the upper collar. While most people are not intimidated by cotton velvet, since it can be pressed on the right side; silk, acetate and rayon velvets can be more scary.

Color varies with the direction of the pile. A garment may be cut in either direction (with or against the pile), but be consistent. All pattern pieces must be cut going In the same direction. Avoid marks by placing pins only in the seam allowances. Increase accuracy by cutting velvet one layer at a time when possible. Tailor's tacks are the most accurate and least damaging markings on velvet.

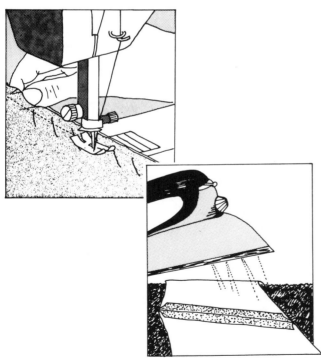

a. maeda

Before actual sewing on the garment, test stitch on velvet scraps. Use a new needle 70/10H. Either cotton or polyester thread is acceptable. Stitch at 10 to 12 stitches per inch. If possible, decrease pressure on the presserfoot. The use of a roller foot or even feed foot eliminates the need for holding the bottom layer of the seam taut as you sew.

Always stitch in the direction of the pile. If puckering occurs in your stitching sample, the top layer is shifting ahead. Try loosening thread tension. If this will not eliminate puckers, sew seam by holding the bottom layer taut as you sew.

Hand baste seams before sewing. Diagonal basting is most effective on velvet. Since it is almost impossible to sew an entire long seam without stopping, plan to stop the machine at regular intervals (every four inches). Stop the machine, leaving the needle in fabric. Lift up presserfoot and allow fabric to relax. Lower presserfoot and stitch another section. The stop and start technique on velvet controls the stretch of the top layer and prevents puckers.

If you do not own a velvet board, cover your ironing board with a fluffy towel. Lay the right side of the velvet against the towel. Pat surface slightly to work velvet into towel. Steam press on the wrong side, using steam from the iron. Finger press seams open. Never let the iron touch the velvet—right or wrong side.

Due to velvet's tendency to mark easily from the right side, do not even consider topstitching. Buttonholes should be worked by hand and zippers should be handpicked.

Velvet garments will keep their shape longer if stored flat with tissue paper between layers. Restore to perfect unwrinkled condition by putting garment on a hanger in a bathroom full of steam.

Noted for outrageous designs and exotic headgear, New Zealand designer Robert Gomack prides himself most on his unusual fabric combinations. Gomack won the prestigious 1989 Bensen and Hedges award with a body hugging shirred purple stretch velvet evening coat, worn over wide pleated culottes in metallic brocade. The headpiece featured brocade and fur entwined.

Metallics

A metallic fabric is any fabric which uses metal coated threads.

Metallic fabrics come in knits and wovens. One of the most popular is "lame," a shiny slinky fabric which "appears" all metallic. Of all the metallics, lame ravels and snags the easiest. Brocade with occasional metallic threads is probably the easiest to work with but all metallics require special considerations for the results to be as special as the fabric itself.

Although a pattern pretest is always a good idea, a project in metallics makes a pretest mandatory. Metallics mark easily. A previously sewn seam may be visible forever. Metallics have little or no give. Allow enough ease in the garment to prevent stress at the seams. Metallics are not strong and will ravel easily. Always lay out the pattern pieces directionally as you would velvet. Metallic threads catch the light differently from different angles. Place pins in the seam allowances only to avoid permanent marks later.

Let the beauty of the fabric be the focal point; avoid design details which may ravel and cause construction problems. Use a package of brand new sharp needles. Metallic threads will dull your needle and cause snags unless the needle is changed. Finish all raw edges with an overlock or overcast stitch before you begin construction.

Unfinished edges invite out-of-control raveling. Sew seams with a regular stitch length, holding fabric taut from front and back.

Depending on the machine, lame acts differently under the needle. Pucker-free seams may require some needle experimentation. Begin with a fine needle— 60/8 H or 70/10 H—in the left position and an even feed foot. Lame seams like moderate speed continuous stitching with no stops and starts in mid seam if possible. If you are not pleased with the results, experiment with a fine ballpoint needle or a troubleshooting needle such as "gold band."

Consider fully lining any garment made with metallic threads.

Metallics can be scratchy. Lining will add to the comfort of the garment as well as protect seams from raveling.

Use a warm iron with no steam. Dampness of any kind causes tarnishing. Press on the wrong side of the fabric, using a presscloth. Heat gives metallic threads a permanent memory. Try a sample using a presscloth. If your fabric is brocade with metallic threads and a raised design, cover ironing surface with a Turkish towel. Press brocade from the wrong side, allowing the design to sink into the towel, preventing flattening of the raised design.

Since metallic threads snag so easily, limit accessories to those with smooth surfaces. A charm bracelet will snag on the metallic and ruin its appearance.

a. maeda

Sequins

Every woman should own a sequin jacket. If you choose a classic simple style, the jacket will never go out of fashion. It is the perfect accessory to your special occasion wardrobe reserved for birthdays, anniversaries, Christmas Eve or any occasions where you want to look special. Don't worry about being out of place. Due to their light reflective quality, you add a little glamour to the occasion.

For the most versatility, choose black, copper or steel gray sequin fabric. Choose a simply styled pattern, eliminating all styling details. A simple collarless jacket is an excellent choice. Let the fabric make the statement, keeping the style simple. Avoid gathers, pleats, and pockets—the result is too bulky. If you prefer the jacket to button, use bias loops as fasteners. Machine buttonholes cannot be performed successfully without breaking the sequins. If you choose a style which features a zipper, such as a skirt, the zipper must be applied by hand. Facings should be cut in lining fabric for a smooth surface against the skin.

Sequin fabric does have a nap. Place all pieces on fabric with sequins going in the same direction—down, so that the sequins can be brushed down after wearing—especially important in a sequin skirt. Cutting the fabric with the sequins going down often means cutting the fabric crossgrain. Trim all excess tissue away from the cutting line on the pattern. Hold pattern pieces in place with pattern weights. Pins are useless here.

Don't try to cut through more than 1 fabric thickness—too much inaccuracy results. Sequins will dull and nick scissors. Do not use your best pair for this project. Cut garment with 1 inch seam allowances. Mark fabric with the only thing that will show up—tailor's tacks.

Handle cut pieces carefully. One of two methods must be used to control the loss of sequins as you construct the garment. The least time-consuming method involves wrapping all cut edges with Seams Great® a lightweight flexible binding. Buy Seams Great® in a width of about 1 to 1½ inches.

Place strip of Seams Great® against the sequin side of the fabric. Sew binding with a ⅜ inch seam. Wrap Seams Great® around the fabric raw edge. Sew binding in place from the right side of the fabric in the well of the seam.

WRAP 'SEAMS GREAT' AROUND RAW EDGE

■ Having the right needles and interfacing on hand can save you hours of sewing time.

■ Matte sequin fabric which combines the look of fish scales and the subtlety of leather is now available.

■ Avoid folding velvets, organzas and sequin fabric. Store on a roll until ready to use.

Sequins

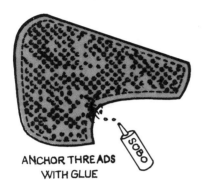

ANCHOR THREADS
WITH GLUE

The second method is more time-consuming but creates slightly flatter seam allowances. Create a fence or sequin loss by running a line of stitching 1½ inch away from cut edge around all edges of the cut piece. Pull sequins out of the seam allowance all around garment. Anchor threads with a dot of SOBO Glue or Fray Check. Try both methods on a sample to determine which one will be the best for your fabric. The second method is much more time-consuming.

Have a few size 16 sharp H needles on hand since sequins may break, dull and bend needles as you sew. If the sequins are rather thick and the needle continues to break, use a size 18 needle. Sew seams with a medium long stitch. Some sequins will break as you sew seams. After the garment is completed, replace "bald" spots by sewing on sequins by hand. Since a certain amount of sequins will fall off over time, keep extra sequins in your stockpile. Strengthen thread by running through beeswax.

Sequins melt under heat so the iron will not be involved in this project. Finger press the seam open. Hand whip the opened seam allowances to the back of the fabric to keep them flat and unbulky.

Eliminate facings whenever possible and use bias binding.

Necklines and armholes are flatter when finished with a binding of satin or silk charmeuse. Plan to line the sequin garment. It will preserve its life and make it much more comfortable to wear. Since hems and facings cannot be pressed flat, lining will run to the finished edges for crisp result. Always store sequin garments flat, wrapped in tissue, since the weight of the sequins will cause the garment to sag.

Special thanks to Pat Williams for her continual experimentation with a difficult fabric.

M. GRAYSMITH©

■ Test stitch fabric scraps before beginning a project. Problems and solutions can be worked out in advance. This method saves ripping time.

■ Most mistakes can be avoided by reading through pattern instructions before you begin, or substituting a more professional method if you know one. If you are confused, ask another sewer for help.

Pelted Fake Fur

Believe it or not, a fake fur coat can be sewn from start to finish in about two evenings for under $200.

Authentic looking fake furs are the ones with pelt lines, created in the manufacturing process by shearing. Pelt lines in a fur create a slenderizing effect by adding subtle vertical lines in the garment. Since pelt lines add height and subtract weight, why not take advantage of this feature when choosing a fake fur?

While all furs require simple styling to maximize the effect of the fabric itself, a pelted fur requires a pattern with nearly straight side seams to permit an even chevron effect.

It is of utmost importance that the pelt lines are straight and square on the finished coat. Since pattern pieces are placed on the wrong side of the coat, pelt lines (low pile lines) must be transferred from the fur side of the coat to the knit backing. With fabric right side up, place pins along pelt lines every five inches. Gently turn fabric to the wrong side. Using a ruler, draw lines between the pins with a soap sliver. You have now transferred the pelt lines from the right side of the fur to the wrong side of the fabric.

As you position your pattern, give some thought as to where pelt lines (low pile lines) should be positioned. The finished coat should contain as many full pelts (high fabric pile) as possible. On the back pattern piece, center either a pelt line or a full pelt at center back. If the pattern features a cut on facing on front, position facing fold line on a pelt line (low pile line) for an effective turn back (Illustration 1). Since pelt lines act as stripes, check positioning at side seams as well (Illustration 2). If the front seam falls on a partial pelt, position back piece so that back side seam will also fall on a partial pelt in the same location. After side seams are sewn, the two partial pelts at side seam will create a full pelt. On any pattern pieces in which a fold line is marked such as collar, cuffs or boa, center fold line of the pattern along pelt line (low pile line).

Since pelt fur is so thick, pattern pieces will be cut through a single thickness. With fur side against the table, position pattern pieces on the backing so that the nap runs down all the pieces.

Use weights instead of pins in layout stage. Cut seam allowances of ⅝ inch only at the neckline edge of the coat collar and facing. To reduce bulk ¼ seam allowances are cut everywhere else, including sleeve caps and armholes. Using a snip motion, cut through the knit backing of the fabric with the tips of the scissors. do not cut through pile. Forget about marking notches in the cut out stage. These are marked with a soap sliver or fabric marker later.

Keep a little vacuum cleaner handy. Although the fur sheds little, cut out pieces pick up every thing on the cutting table. By shaking or brushing each piece after you cut and quickly vacuuming the cutting table in between, mess is kept to a minimum.

Since fur pieces want to slip and slide during pinning, place a mark at 2 inch intervals along side seams, using a ruler with soap sliver or fabric marker (Illustration 3). Match these marks when pinning seams with extra long glass head pins, pinning across the seam.

Begin first stitches on samples using 80/14 HS or 100/16 needles and any good quality thread. Reduce presserfoot pressure to a minimum to allow fur to feed easily. Reduce needle tension. Sew in the direction of the nap. Seam techniques for pelt furs will simulate the stitch of a fur machine used by furriers. Sew ¼ inch seam with a long narrow zigzag stitch (3.5 length, 2 width). As you sew, allow needle to fall almost off the edge of the fabric, creating "hinged" seam used by furriers (Illustration 4). DO NOT PRESS.

Pin up hem allowances and adjust until hemline is equidistant from floor to hemline. The scalloped hem in a pelted fur occurs by simple turning up the hem. To finish hem with the satin finish used by furriers, only a one inch hem allowance is needed on the fur. Trim hem allowance accordingly. Measure the circumference of the coat and add two inches for error. From satin lining, cut eight inch strips of fabric on the bias or slightly off grain on the crossgrain. Strips can be pieced. Press under ⅜ inch along one long edge of satin strip. With right sides together, match raw edge of satin strip to fur hem edge, pinning on satin strip. Sew strip to fur with long narrow zigzag stitch. Pin up hem, placing pins in the fur portion of hem and at the top of the folded satin edge. Complete hem by sewing folded edge of satin strip to coat (Illustration 5).

Green pigsuede coat *is made fron a Burda pattern (see pages 180-184 for suede techniques). Contrast collar and cuffs are made from Guatemalan fabric interfaced with Whisper Weft (see page 25 for sleeve facing contrast technique). Large dolman sleeve shoulder pads are used. Wool gauge fabric custom pleated (see page 150) is used for skirt. Jade buttons with sterling silver bevels come from Paco Despacio - see Sources for address.*

Red ultraleather skirt is made from a Burda pattern (see page 192 for ultraleather tips). Skirt is particularly flattering on the body since shaping is built into the pattern. **Well cut top in puckered silk** (see page 163) is made fro Kwik Sew pattern - good source for great looking and fitting tops. Neck facing is eliminated using bias trim to finish neck (see page 210 in **Power Sewing**).

Plush wool velour jacket is made from a McCall's N.Y. N.Y. pattern and trimmed with a double layer of rayon braid (see technique on page 208) with hand beaded touches (see technique on page 202). Entire front and side front of jacket are fused with fusible knit tricot. Facing is interfaced with rayon and wool felt.

Amber button with sterling silver bevel comes from Paco Despacio - address in sources. Narrow rayon braid forms loop for button. Jacket is lined with "Ambiance," Bemberg rayon. Rayon rattail with gold threads forms decoration between facing and lining.

1. Double piping detailing on shawl collar (see page 210).

2. Multiple trim detailing with hand beaded touches (see pages 202 and 208).

Pelted Fake Fur

■ Fabulous Furs, owned by Donna Salyers, offers a wide variety of fake fur coat kits including suitable patterns, fur, lining, hooks, etc. which create outstanding results. See Sources.

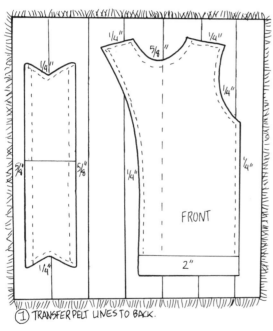

① TRANSFER PELT LINES TO BACK.

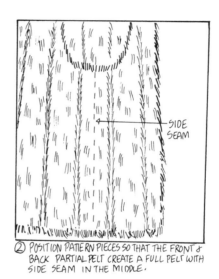

② POSITION PATTERN PIECES SO THAT THE FRONT & BACK PARTIAL PELT CREATE A FULL PELT WITH SIDE SEAM IN THE MIDDLE.

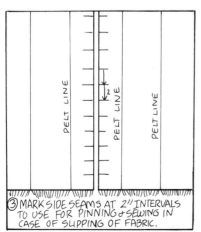

③ MARK SIDE SEAMS AT 2" INTERVALS TO USE FOR PINNING & SEWING IN CASE OF SLIPPING OF FABRIC.

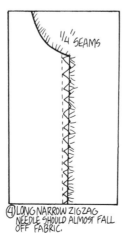

④ LONG NARROW ZIGZAG NEEDLE SHOULD ALMOST FALL OFF FABRIC.

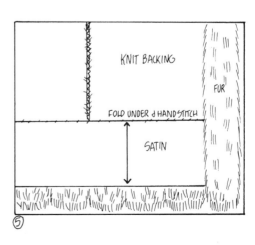

⑤

Puckered Fabrics

Puckered fabrics, while incredibly seductive on the bolt, often stay on the bolt. Most people feel intimidated by their uneven surface and four-way stretch, certain that a whole bevy of problems will surface as soon as the fabric gets near the needle. Such is not the case, says Delia Sanders, evening and bridal specialist at Fishman's Fabrics in Chicago. "Sewing on puckered fabrics is similar to sewing on Lycra: use a stretch stitch or zigzag with a fine sewing machine needle 60/8 H sharp, for near to invisible seaming."

Buoyed by Delia's encouragement, I bought my first piece of puckered silk, purchasing barely enough for the short sleeve top. Looking like normal width fabric on the bolt, the puckering process eats up much of the fabric width, leaving a narrower fabric, 22 inches wide, in the piece I purchased. You may need twice what pattern calls for under 44/45 inch requirements. Layout and cutting are a challenge with narrow fabric and limited length. Don't skimp—buy enough. Layout like this is simplified by cutting out additional pattern pieces to duplicate the ones in the pattern, supplying you with left and right pattern pieces which can be moved around jigsaw-style until you get a satisfactory layout. To avoid such frustration, measure fabric width and perhaps do a mini-layout in the fabric store.

Do not overlock garment pieces before seaming; this will stretch pieces and distort the shape. To seam, use an even feed foot, 60/8 H needle, medium-length stretch or zigzag stitch. Push fabric on both sides of the presser-foot into the needle as you sew. This technique, plus the even feed foot, cuts stretching to a minimum. After seaming, overlock each side of the seam allowance separately so that seams can be pressed open.

To prevent stretching and distortion at neck and shoulders, narrow strips of lining selvage or stay tape must be used. With the pattern as a guide, measure strips of stay tape the length of neckline and shoulders. Before staystitching, pin stabilizing strips in place, easing the puckered fabric evenly to the strip as you pin. Place pins on the tape side. Staystitch tape into place at both neckline and shoulders at 5/8 inch with tape side up. Feed dog will assist in easing the fabric to the tape. Stabilizing neck and shoulder seams cannot be stressed enough. My front neckline without stay tape stretched $1\frac{1}{2}$ inches while I was staystitching. Without a tape stabilizer, shoulder and neckline will be highly distorted.

Neckline should be faced with lightly interfaced lining fabric or companion, unpuckered fabric. Facings in puckered fabric are too bulky and prevent garment from lying close to the body.

Although pressing seams is hardly necessary after seaming puckered fabric, the garment can mold to the body better if seams are pressed open. To prevent puckers from flattening during pressing, cover pressing area with a fluffy Turkish towel. Iron temperature should not be higher than the silk setting or pressing will affect the elastic, providing the puckered effect.

Before hemming, overlock raw hem edge, pushing at the back of the foot to ease in extra fullness. Hand

Puckered Fabrics

hem, pausing every 3 inches to give the hem fabric a little pull, using slightly more thread in the hand hem. Knot at 3 inch intervals after pulling slightly, and continue.

Puckered fabrics make beautiful tops, short bolero jackets or sexy, body-clinging skirts and dresses. Although the fabric can be very body-revealing, if fitted snugly, this type of fit is not mandatory for the puckered fabric to look sensational. Puckered fabric provides incredible texture to an ensemble, quite striking if paired with a flat fabric within the outfit, such as velvet or wool jersey.

If a lining is desired, lycra is your best choice if you plan to take advantage of the fabric's four-way stretch. If not, China silk or Bemberg rayon make suitable linings for jackets.

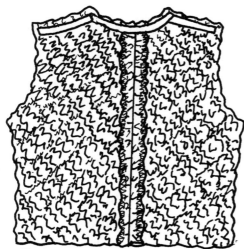

Stay tape on neck & shoulders, overlock seams.

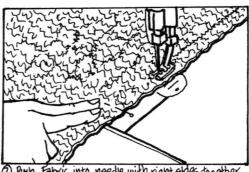

② Push fabric into needle with right sides together.

Microfibers

Even to the purist who prefers natural fibers, the seductive hand and drape of microfibers make these fabrics very attractive. Microfiber is a polyester fabric made with very fine threads—finer than a human hair. Polyesters of years past lacked the hand and drape of natural fibers. Such is not the case with microfibers. Logantex "silk gabardine" both drapes and feels like four-ply silk. Another high quality product imported from Madrid by Cadena, while slightly lighter in weight, makes an excellent lightweight wrinkle-proof raincoat. The advantages of microfiber over silk are; **care** —these fabrics require no ironing when hand washed; **cost**— the price per yard is half the price of a corresponding weight in silk; and **wrinkle resistance.**

While manufacturers claim that microfibers do breathe, they do not breathe as well as natural fibers. For loose pants and overblouses, heat retention is not a problem. If you live in a hot climate, avoid heat retention by not layering over a microfiber.

To avoid puckered seams in polyester fabric, it is recommended that crosswise or bias grainline is used. Puckered seams can be avoided in microfibers by cutting 10% or more off grain. If microfiber changes color directionally, cut all pieces in one direction against the pile. Sueded microfibers do have a nap. For best results use a fine needle, changing needle two to three times per garment. Needles dull fast when working with microfibers, so it is necessary to have a good stock of needles on hand.

While it is possible to sew microfibers with traditional seams and pressed open seam allowances, better results are possible by doing a one step seam process on the serger using four threads. Start project with a new needle in your serger. Reduce tension and experiment until seam is pucker-free without undulation. Due to the dense fine wave, reduce sewing speed somewhat to allow fabric penetration. Because microfiber is a high density fabric, needle holes from resewn seams will remain in the fabric. Think carefully before ripping out stitches.

On detailing or horizontal seaming, use a teflon or even feed foot. The teeth on the foot can mar the surface of the fabric on smooth-finish microfibers. If possible, reduce pressure on the presserfoot.

Press on the wrong side of the fabric or use a dry presscloth when pressing from the right side. Using a scrap, start iron temperature at the silk setting and increase temperature until you see adverse effect. While some microfibers melt at low temperatures, others do not.

Because microfiber is a polyester, it becomes a prime target for permanently pleated fabric.

Sueded Silks and Rayons

Surely you have noticed the craze for sueded fabrics. No wonder—these fabrics feel great, both to the hands and on the body. Faced with the decision in the fabric store of which sueded product to buy, sueded "washed silk" or sueded "washed rayon," consider the following:

Washed rayon has more weight to it making it suitable for full unconstructed styles such as full shorts, loose pants, uncomplicated tops, and tunics. Since straight grain rayon stretches much in the way a garment cut on the bias will stretch, avoid structured facings with buttonholes. The interfaced facing will hold its shape while the upper fabric stretches, making the facing pull taut and appear too small. Use self facings on vertical details. Since washed rayon seems reluctant to take a crease, avoid styling details which should lie flat such as pocket and plackets. Topstitching will help but not eliminate the slight puffiness. For price and drape, washed rayon gives good value if made in suitable styling. While washed rayon can be washed, the fabric does become "slightly" denser and thicker to the touch.

Washed silk, while more expensive, provides more options for garment choice. Washed silk presses well, permitting details to look sharp and crisp after pressing. Garments suitable for washed silk are the same as those for washed rayon but tailored shirts, anoraks, jackets, and dresses can be added since styling details do not present a problem.

Washed silks and rayons should not be machine washed and dried. Warm water hand washing in Ivory liquid or shampoo is best, followed by a cool water rinse in a basin after adding $\frac{1}{4}$ cup salt and $\frac{1}{4}$ cup white vinegar to prevent colors from fading. Air dry until damp, then press with a dry iron on the silk setting. Do not spray washed silk to dampen—water spotting results.

Use fine sharp pins when pinning pattern to fabric followed by sharp scissors for accurate cutting. To avoid slight color shading in certain lights, use "with nap" layout, cutting all pieces in one direction. For best results, interface with a layer of its own fabric, which can be fused with a heavier interfacing if stiff support is desired.

Do not sew seams with a serger; rippled seams result. Use the overlock to finish raw edges only. Machine sew conventional seams using a fine needle 60/8 H for washed silk and a 70/10 H needle for washed rayon using a medium-length stitch. For best control, switch needle to far left position. If fabric puckers slightly as you sew, pull fabric taut from front and back as it passes under the needle. Do not stretch fabric while doing "taut sewing" or wavy seams will result.

Quilted Fabrics

Not all quilted jackets look bulky. By varying the filler weight throughout the garment, you can obtain quilting results without the bulk.

Decide initially whether you plan to hand wash or dry clean the finished garment. If you plan to hand wash your quilted garment, choose a washable lining fabric not prone to wrinkling. Pretreat fabrics the way you will treat the finished garment, which means hand wash and air dry to preshrink; send to the cleaners if garment will be dry cleaned.

For quilted garments which will be hand washed, simple styling is recommended for ease in pressing later. For garments you plan to dry clean, more detailed styling—such as lapels—is possible since pressing problems will be handled by a professional. Hand-painted fabrics painted with "gutta resist" outlining may not be dry cleaned or lines will disappear. When quilting hand-painted fabrics, simple styling is advisable to gain the most from the fabric design as well as simplifying pressing problems later.

While a wide variety of batting is available, my favorite is a product put out by Hobbs Bonded Fibers called Thermore, a thin batting (⅛ to ¼ inch depth) especially designed for clothing. One bag of batting is sufficient for one quilted garment, providing it is not a full-length coat. Batting need not be preshrunk. For total luxury, silk batting in the form of "leaves" is available but difficult to find. Garments containing silk batting can be washed in mild soap. To use silk leaves, slash leaf up one side and spread out leaf smoothing out inconsistencies.

Cut out all garment pieces from fashion fabric, batting and lining with 1 inch seam allowances. Quilting eats fabric, so you need to compensate. To prevent bearding (the fluff from the batting coming through to the right side), sandwich a layer of lining fabric between fashion fabric and the batting.

Sandwich batting between layers of fashion fabric and lining. Hand-baste layers together diagonally, as well as around perimeter of the garment ½ inch from cut edge. Experiment with threads and stitch styles on a three-layered scrap (fashion fabric, batting and lining). Shiny rayon thread on top thread only, combined with a narrow, tight zigzag gives excellent results. Experiment with others; you are the designer.

If the fabric is hand-painted or has a pattern, quilting lines are predetermined. If you are quilting on plain fabric a quilting grid will have to be determined. A person with limited artistic talent, such as myself, has best results on patterned fabric. Good results are obtained if initial horizontal and vertical lines begin in the middle of the garment. Work from the center out in either direction. Don't stretch fabric as you quilt. Let feed dog feed in fabric.

■ To take advantage of the quilting craze without a folksy homespun look, quilt only parts of the garment, like flaps on a pocket, collar and cuffs.

Quilted Fabrics

If this is your first quilting project, I strongly advise quilting a 10 inch square sample before you begin on the garment itself. Problems such as top and bottom layer shifting can be eliminated by an even feed or roller foot. If top layer continues to move forward, lengthen stitch slightly or reduce presserfoot pressure.

After separately quilting each garment piece, re-pin pattern piece and cut along pattern cutting lines allowing for 5/8 inch seams. Since quilting reduces size, you may have little or none to trim off. To eliminate this step would be foolhardy. Every fabric quilts differently. Accurate cutting means getting the fit you want.

To eliminate bulk in sleeves or details such as collars, bands or pockets, consider quilting with a layer of preshrunk flannelette between fashion fabric and lining. Flannelette still gives a slightly quilted effect without the puffiness. In detailed areas where interfacing is desired, a press-on interfacing fused to the back of the preshrunk flannelette is very successful.

In order to give a finished look to the inside of the garments, use this technique when sewing seams. Cut crosswise or bias strips of lining fabric 1 1/2 inches wide. Press strips in half lengthwise. Place folded strips on top of the seam about to be sewn, lining up raw edges of strip with cut edge of seam allowance. Sew seam. Press open. Trim and grade seam to 3/8 inch. Pull seam allowances to one side allowing the folded strip to cover raw edges. Hand-sew folded strip in place.

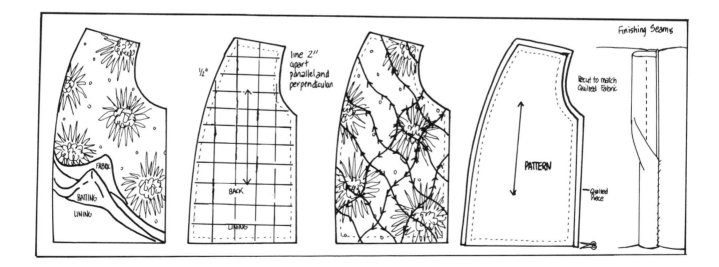

Quality Knits

GOOD RECOVERY   POOR RECOVERY

CROSSWISE

Turning out a knit top in less than 2 hours is not difficult, but good quality knit fabric is a must. Choose a first-class cotton knit, wool jersey or cashmere knit and the end result will be worthy of your talents. In addition, spend a few moments perfecting the patterns. Raising or lowering the neckline, tapering the body sleeve, arriving at the perfect length are pattern adjustments which make the difference between a top that you will make over again and one that hangs forlornly in the closet. I've purchased a top from ready-to-wear for the sole purpose of obtaining the perfect pattern. Correct fabric choice cannot be stressed enough.

While an imported cotton knit or rayon jersey might

be perfect for a wrap top or full circle skirt, this same fabric will be too clingy and revealing for many figures as well as for simple T-shirt type patterns. Recovery is a factor which must also be considered. Stretch 6 inches of fabric on the crosswise and see if it returns to 6 inches or remains stretched at 8 inches or more. Fabric without recovery power results in baggy, shapeless garments after a few wearings.

If you are using a cotton knit and truly want a wash-and-wear garment, buy an additional half yard per 3 yard length. put the fabric through washer and dryer cycles twice before cutting to insure against future shrinkage.

■ Polyester thread is best for lycra stretch fabrics due to its elasticity. Never use the 5-thread overlock when sewing knits, since it has no elasticity. The 4-thread overlock is the best choice because it is strong and can stretch.

■ To determine stretch factor on knits, fold fabrics on the crosswise grain perpendicular to selvages. Place two pins perpendicular to the fold, 4 inches apart. Stretch and match to stretch gage on pattern.

Knit Techniques

If you don't like to iron, cotton knits make a great alternative to linens but preshrinking is a must. If you happen to be lucky, you may even find a great piece of silk or rayon knit for real knit luxury.

Stretch can be accomplished in two ways: Combining fibers with lycra, or twisting yarns. Both techniques have been used to create stretch in denim, linen, cotton and wool.

Some fabrics have crosswise stretch only, while others stretch in all directions.

However, tactile interest and taming the fabric at the sewing machine are two different matters.

While some stretch needs to be built into the seam, you don't want the seam to grow 1 to 2 inches in the sewing process.

A slight stretch is built into the seam by using a medium stitch length with the tiniest zigzag possible, usually $1/2$ on a 0 to 4 range.

To prevent the fabric from stretching as it is sewn, use a combination of staystitch plus (pushing the fabric into the presserfoot from behind) and pushing the fabric into the presserfoot from the front.

This combination of pushing from both the front and behind controls the amount of stretch under the presserfoot. This is adequate for the vertical seams.

Depending on your sewing equipment, Kathy Ruddy, producer of *Generic Serger Video* suggests one of four methods when sewing on knits.

If your machine does nothing but straight stitch, you can still successfully sew knits by stretching the fabric slightly as you sew. With equal tension, stretch fabric from front and back as it is being passed under the needle. If the seam ripples after the fabric relaxes, you are stretching it too much. After the first seam has been completed, sew a second seam $1/8$ inch toward the seam allowance, parallel to the first. Trim seam allowance close to the second row of stitching.

If your machine sews only straight stitch or zigzag, use a narrow zigzag setting and do not stretch the fabric as you sew. After completing the first seam, use a wider zigzag to sew a second row of stitching close to the first within the seam allowance. Trim seam allowance close to the second row of stitching.

If your machine has built-in stretch stitches, use any of the stretch stitch settings recommended in your manual. Do not stretch fabric as you sew. Trim seam allowance close to outside edge of stretch stitch.

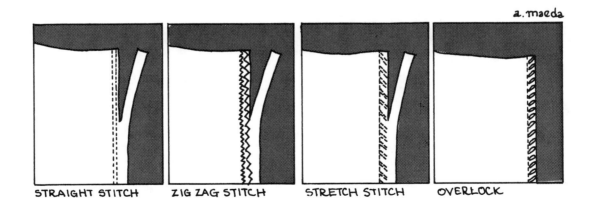

STRAIGHT STITCH   ZIG ZAG STITCH   STRETCH STITCH   OVERLOCK

a. maeda

Knit Techniques

Never be in a hurry when sewing with knits. Fast machine sewing often causes the top layer to stretch, say knit experts. Moderate to slow machine sewing ensures seams that are not stretched and wavy. If you are using a lightweight knit, a narrow zigzag (.5 width) is preferable to a knit stitch. Knit stitches with their back-and-forth motion put too much thread in the seam, resulting in bulky seams that do not lie flat.

Whenever one knit piece must be eased onto another—such as a sleeve—sew with the larger piece down. The feed dog will help to ease in the fabric. Since knits do not ravel, an overlocked seam gives a nice finish to the inside of the garment but is not mandatory. If you own a 5 thread overlock, the seam can be sewn and overlocked in one operation. The straight stitch on the 5 thread overlock gives the seam a higher quality look when pressed.

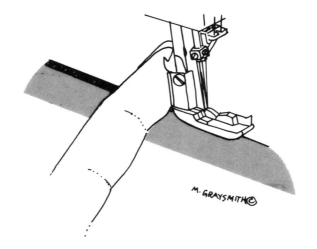

M. GRAYSMITH©

Even when using overlock, keep the machine speed moderate to prevent stretched and wavy seams. If you notice that, despite your best efforts, your knit is stretching, try placing your finger at the back of the presser-foot on the overlock to slow the fabric. This pressure, which causes slight easing on woven fabrics, merely controls stretching on an unstable knit.

The optimum machine for sewing knits is the serger (overlock), since it builds in stretch and simultaneously trims seams. If you sew with a lot of man-made fiber fabrics, your serger blade will need frequent sharpening or replacement. Most problems with sergers are caused by a dull blade. Before taking your machine in for repair, insert a new blade, and see if the problem disappears.

■ Stabilize shoulder or dolman sleeves with Seams Great® rather than twill tape. The result is a flexible seam with a memory.

■ To prevent hems from stretching when you topstitch with the double needle, interface hem with a lightweight fusible knit interfacing before stitching. Woolly lock nylon in the bobbin gives some stretch to the hem, eliminating top thread breakage.

Knit Techniques

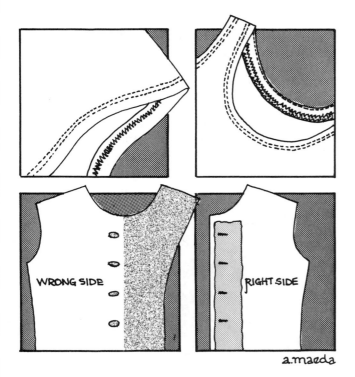

WRONG SIDE

RIGHT SIDE

a.maeda

Other seams, such as bodice, waistline, neckline, shoulder and even the long seams on a dolman sleeve, need additional stability for the garment to maintain its shape. Measure a length of twill tape or narrow selvage from the pattern. Pin the twill tape $1/2$ inch from the raw edge.

Force the stretchy fabric to conform to the length of the tape or selvage. This technique will force the garment to conform to the shape of the pattern in critical areas. Never stay tape vertical seams. Vertical seams must be able to relax with the weight of the knit.

Knitted ribbing makes an excellent finish for stretchy fabric, but the weight of ribbing or facing can stretch the long front edge by its mere weight.

Stabilize the seam allowance as mentioned above before ribbing or facing is applied.

Eliminate facings whenever possible in a knit. Neckline and armholes are finished by staystitchlng $1/2$ inch from raw edge. Press under a $5/8$ inch seam allowance using the staystitching line as a roll line. Topstitch into place with the wide spaced double needle. Do not stretch these areas as you topstitch.

Buttonholes can present problems in knits, forming stretched and wavy buttonholes much too large for the buttons. Stabilize entire facing with fusible knitted interfacing. Cut lengthwise grain of the interfacing in the same direction as the buttonhole. This will prevent the buttonhole from stretching. Cut a small oval larger than buttonhole from press-on interfacing. Press this oval behind the buttonhole placement on the garment itself, on the wrong side. Mark buttonholes.

Place a piece of Amazing Solvy available from Clotilde (see Sources) over the area of the buttonhole placement marking on the right side of the garment. Amazing Solvy is a see-through water soluble plastic that will prevent the presserfoot from stretching the knit as the buttonhole is made. If you don't have Solvy, waxed paper or a heavy plastic bag is a good substitute.

Make buttonholes through all layers. Tear away Solvy from finished buttonhole. Cut open buttonhole with a buttonhole chisel.

Hems, if not done correctly, can appear wary and stretched. Finish the raw edge of the hem with an overlock or zigzag stitch. The hem now may be sewn by hand or machine.

For every five hand stitches, slightly stretch fabric and thread and knot.

Knit Techniques

This technique builds a little stretch into the hand stitch, and prevents the hem stitching from popping as the garment is worn. This hem technique is excellent for any kind of fabric with elasticity.

If you prefer a machine hem, replace your traditional presserfoot with an even feed foot.

Machine hems using a double needle yield the most professional results on sleeve and garment hems. If your machine zigzags, it can accommodate a double needle (ZWI). Check the various widths available in double needles; you'll find the best selection in sewing machine stores.

Allowing for a 1¼ inch hem allowance, overlock raw edge at garment bottom. Press up 1¼ inch hem allowance. When using the double needle, you must topstitch the hem from the right side of the garment. I prefer the wide width (ZWI) double needle, since it creates an attractive ridge if the needles are positioned on either side of the overlocked raw edge. You can feel the raw edge of the hem while topstitching 1 to 1¼ inch from the finished hem on right side of the garment.

To give a slight stretch to the hem—important on knit garments—use a narrow zigzag while stitching with the double needle. Because the zigzag is so narrow, the two rows of topstitching actually look like straight parallel rows of stitching, but have slight elasticity as well.

Sew at a moderate speed, keeping your finger at the back of the presserfoot to prevent the fabric from flowing out too quickly. The combination of the slight zigzag, the double needle, and the pressure on the back of the foot results in an unstretched, unwavy hem with slight give, necessary to avoid popped stitches in a knit garment.

If you prefer a hem without a ridge effect-featuring two parallel rows of topstitching—use the same procedure described above, but sew rows of topstitching ¼ inch away from raw edge of the hem. Additionally, parallel rows of stitching at the neckline and armhole create an attractive solution for sharp decorated edges.

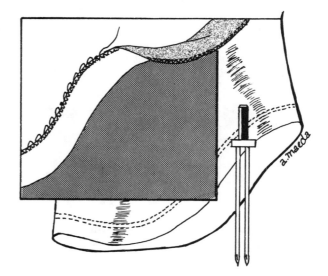

Ultra Stretch Fabrics

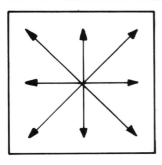

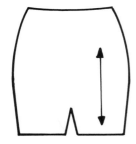

Ultra stretch fabrics are fabrics with stretch in all directions; crosswise, lengthwise and bias. Ultra stretch fabrics combine close fit with comfort. Familiar with wool and cotton knits, which stretch only crosswise, few sewers purchase or take advantage of the versatility of ultra stretch fabrics. Ultra stretch fabrics are fiber blends with lycra: the higher the lycra content, the greater the stretch.

Excellent recovery offered by these fabrics make them ideal choices for bodysuits, clingy tops and pants, bicycle shorts, and leotards. Traditional pattern sources offer limited pattern selection. For a wider choice check: Stretch and Sew, KwikSew, Prime Moves, Daisy Kingdom and Green Pepper. If these patterns are not available in your fabric store, see Sources. On patterns designed for multi-directional stretch, compare the stretch of your fabric to the stretch recommended on the pattern. These patterns are cut to measurements minus ease in both directions to take advantage of the fabric stretch and give a close fit. Make sure your fabric meets the stretch requirement on the pattern. If not, make additions in length and width to compensate. Buy patterns by your actual bust and hip size.

If you are using a conventional knit pattern designed for one way stretch, crosswise, going around the body and you want to take advantage of the up and down fabric stretch in your ultra stretch fabric, subtract 1 inch above the armhole, 2 inches below the armhole to the waist, and 2 inches above the crotch to the waist and 3 inches below the crotch for full length pants. Keep in mind that the results are a very close fit.

If you fall in love with a super stretch fabric, but don't feel that you have the figure for a close clingy fit, consider bodysuit patterns such as Vogue patterns by designer Donna Karan. Purchase the pattern one size smaller than you normally wear to take advantage of the multi-directional stretch in fabric. For a pair of pants which can fit snugly and never lose their shape, try a classic trouser in stretch wool crepe or stretch wool gabardine.

If you are making tight fitting pants such as bicycle shorts or tights, cut the fabric so that the greatest stretch goes up and down the leg. On all other garments, cut the ultra stretch fabric so that the greatest stretch goes around the body.

Ultra Stretch Fabrics

Due to its elasticity, your best thread choice is polyester. Do not wind the bobbin too fast to prevent thread stretching, resulting in puckered seams. Ultra stretch knits can be sewn on a conventional machine by using a stretch stitch and trimming seams to ¼ inch. A serged seam on the overlock gives the most stretch to the seam. If your overlock makes a straight stitch outside of the overlocked stitch, it will be necessary to stretch the fabric slightly as you sew or remove the needle responsible for the straight stitch.

For great tips on ultra stretch as well as elastic, see Gail Brown's article in "Serging Stretch Fabrics" (see Sources) are a great source of in depth up- to-date information.

■ Slow down a little when winding the bobbin with polyester thread. Too much speed causes the thread to stretch, resulting in puckered seams.

■ "If people allow patterns to control them, it takes away from their creativity." Credit to: Jo Anne Krause, producer of *Sew Like A Pro* video series (see Sources).

Tips with Ribs

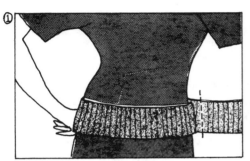
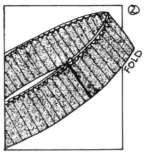
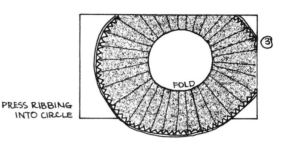

PRESS RIBBING INTO CIRCLE

FOLD

FOLD

a.maeda

Ribbing can add the ready-to-wear touch to a simply styled garment. Good quality ribbing is rarely easy to find. The best of it boasts 10 percent lycra content for good recovery stretch. Second best choice is 100 percent wool. Third best is 50 percent poly; 50 percent cotton ribbing. Last resort is 100 percent cotton which one might question using at all due to its poor recovery. If you simply cannot find suitable ribbing, consider making it on a knitting machine or by hand.

As the popularity of ribbing continues its growth in ready-to-wear, availability in a wide color range has finally reached the fabric stores. Don't limit our idea for ribbing to knits and sweater fabrics. Ribbing can be added to silk shirts, wool challis skirts, suede and leather jackets, as well as a multitude of other garments once you give your imagination free rein. If you can't find matching ribbing, any fabric with a 50 percent stretch can be substituted.

Kathy Ruddy, producer of *Generic Serger* video (see Sources), offers these tips on ribs. With a ruler, draw two lines perpendicular to the rib in the knit, 6 inches apart, cutting a 6 inch wide strip of ribbing. Cut on one rib to open tube into a flat strip. Ribbing has its greatest stretch and recovery on the crosswise grain

For hem bands at the waist or hip, fold ribs in half lengthwise and stretch folded strip around body snugly at the place you want the garment to rest. Ribbing will stretch slightly as it is sewn, so measure for a snug fit (Illustration 1). Allow an additional ½ inch for joining two ¼ inch seams. Join ends of ribbing to form a circle (Illustration 2). If ribbing is unstable, zigzag or overlock raw edges together.

Tips with Ribs

For wristbands, stretch folded lengthwise strip around wrist a little less snugly. Shorter, the wristband will not stretch as much as it is sewn. Allow an additional ½ inch for joining two ¼ inch seams. Join ends of ribbing to form a circle.

To determine the length of ribbing needed for a neckband, stretch a length of ribbing snugly around head. Pin into place. Pull band down over face and check fit at neck. If the band seems too big, pin a bit smaller but check to be certain circle will fit over the head. Add a seam allowance at each end before cutting off excess ribbing. Press-form the neckband in a circle before application (Illustration 3). After the side seams are sewn in the garment, attach the tube of ribbing in this manner.

To ensure that the fullness in the garment is evenly distributed on the ribbing, divide both ribbing and gar-ment in quarters. Pin (Illustration 4). Attach ribbing to garment by sewing with ribbed side down and garment facing you. Stretch ribbing to fit garment as you sew.

Do not attempt to attach bands with the serger. Stretching fabric while sewing with the serger can bend or break the loopers. Machine sew both raw edges of ribbing to the garment with your regular sewing machine first. When attaching ribbing, do not use a smaller stitch than 9 stitches per inch. A smaller stitch puts too much thread in the seam and the seam cannot recover to its original size after sewn. Try on; make sure ribbing rides on your body as you had hoped, and has the correct amount of snugness. As the final step, serger over initial machine stitching, trimming seam allowance and adding stretch in one step (Illustration 5).

PIN EVENLY, THEN SEW RIBBING. OVERLOCK

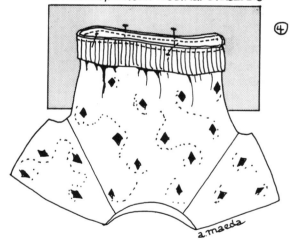

④

a. maeda

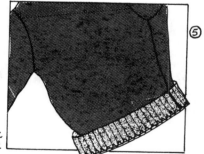

⑤

ZIG ZAG OR OVERLOCK
ALL EDGES TOGETHER

■ Instead of making shoulderpads for every garment, make two sets and use them in all your garments. Make two styles, one for a set-in sleeve and one for a raglan. For the smoothest look, cover the pad with lingerie jersey. Sew a Velcro strip on the top of the pad. Sew a mated Velcro strip at the shoulder seam in your garments. Pads can easily be removed and transferred.

Ribbing as a Facing Substitute

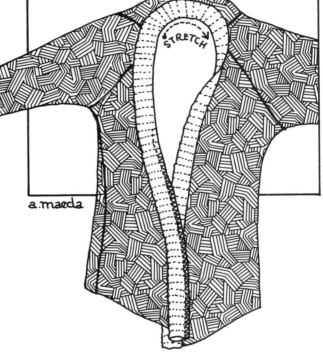

a. maeda

Ribbing is being applied to a variety of fabrics and styles, from knit sportswear to silk crepe de chine bomber jackets. Since it is often difficult to find a wide color selection, consider the use of ribbing as contrasting style detail.

Consider substituting ribbing for the pattern suggested facing. In addition to creating a more ready-to-wear look, the ribbing fills in the gap from the finished edge to the neckline.

Cotton ribbing has greatest recovery when the fabric content boasts lycra. Wool ribbing is adequate in its pure form. It is not advisable to preshrink ribbing as the preshrinking process makes layout and cutting more difficult. If the correct length of ribbing is used, the fabric can absorb any minimal shrinkage that might occur. Ribbing has its greatest stretch and recovery crosswise, letting you stretch the ribbing during application. Because ribbing is used crosswise rather than lengthwise, a minimal amount of ribbing is needed for the garment. To determine cut width of ribbing, double the desired finished width and add two seam allowances. For a finished 3 inch rib on a cardigan, cut ribbing 7¼ inches wide. To determine ribbing length, measure the seamline to which the ribbing will be applied by standing the tape measure on edge.

Cut length of ribbing smaller in a 2 to 3 ratio or ⅔ ribbing to one part back garment neck from shoulder to shoulder across the back of the neck. For example, If the neck measures 6 inches from shoulder seam to shoulder seam in back, use 4 inches of ribbing in this area.

The purpose of using a shorter length of ribbing across the back neckline is to allow the ribbing to hug the back of the neck rather than stand away from it.

Measure distance from shoulder to hemline. Add seam allowance at bottom. Subtract 1 inch from this measurement. This prevents the front from sagging with the weight of the ribbing.

To apply ribbing to a cardigan, hem the cardigan before ribbing application. Finish the ends of the ribbing by seaming with right sides together, then turning right side out. Press and pound with a clapper. Sew the raw edges of ribbing to garment with right sides together, stretching ribbing in a 2 to 3 ratio along back neckline and very slightly from hem to shoulder to ease in extra 1 inch on garment to ribbing.

For best control sew with ribbing side up. Sew seam with a medium-length stitch and a very narrow .5 zigzag. Overlock seam if desired for final finish.

Ribbed V-Necklines

A ribbed V-neck can be an excellent solution to an unflattering jewel neckline. Trace new neckline onto garment from a pattern featuring a V-neck. Cut V-neckline 1 inch deeper than pattern since 1 inch ribbing will be used to fill in the neck. Measure neckline along seamline. Cut crosswise length of ribbing 2 inches longer than neck measurement and $2\frac{1}{2}$ inches wide for a 1 inch finished ribbing width.

Staystitch neckline along seamline. Trim seam allowance to $\frac{1}{4}$ inch for easier neckline application. At the point of the V-neck, clip seam allowance to within one stitch of the point of the staystitching. Fold ribbing in half lengthwise. Press ribbing—without stretching—on the right side of the garment. Place raw edges of ribbing against one side of the neckline, extending ribbing 1 inch beyond V in front. Pin ribbing from the point of the V to the shoulder, stretching ribbing 1 inch between these points. Stretch ribbing from shoulder to within 2 inches of V point on opposite side of neckline, once again stretching ribbing slightly, 1 inch of stretch between these points.

Begin sewing at the exact point of the V neckline. Sew neckline seam with a very small width zigzag (.5) and medium-length stitch. Sew with ribbing side up, stretching ribbing between key points as you sew. Stop stitching 2 inches from point of V neckline on opposite side. Turn ribbing to inside of garment, allowing unsewn side of ribbing to lap behind sewn side. Place a pin through all layers at the point of the V neckline. From the wrong side of the garment, stitch remaining seam closed through both layers of ribbing, continuing seam again around the other side of the point for 1 inch. Trim excess ribbing close to stitching.

For a fine finish, overlock raw edges. Press with steam and pound flat with a tailor's clapper.

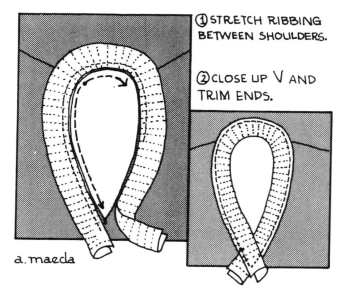

① STRETCH RIBBING BETWEEN SHOULDERS.

② CLOSE UP V AND TRIM ENDS.

a. maeda

■ Don't point out the mistakes you made." Jo Anne Krause, lecturer and sewing video producer.

LEATHER AND SUEDE SKINS–THE REAL THING

The Leather Process

A great choice for a leather or suede garment might be a pattern favorite you have made once or twice before. Making it in suede or leather will give it a totally different look and eliminate the possibility of re-sewing seams for the fit you want. Don't try to make a pattern in suede or leather without pretesting it in another fabric. Needle marks leave a memory that seldom can be disguised. If your pattern favorite has a lot of detailing, consider simplifying the pattern a bit.

Always make a pretest out of the pattern in a fabric of similar weight to the skin—denim and heavy muslin are good choices. Suede tears easily, so be sure to allow enough ease for sitting. On the other hand, smooth leather pants stretch and should be cut without ease so that they can grow 2 inches in the first wearing and still look good. A flat pattern measurement to fit a 36 inch hip should measure 36 inches.

Sources for leather vary depending on your area. Look under "Leather Goods," in your telephone book to see what can be found locally. Tandy Leather Company has 350 stores nationwide, as well as mail order. Prairie Collection offers a wide sample of skin swatches for $3. Horizon Leather Corporation offers a wide selection of domestic and imported skins. Cinema Leathers offers good swatch selection and often has attractive offerings on lambsuede (see Sources).

Probably your most important decision in leather is your choice of skins. Lambskin tanned in England, Spain or Japan feels softest. Many mail order sources will send samples. When you request these, ask for leather with a gauge of 1 to 1½ ounces in thickness. This leather weight is flattering on the figure and can be sewn on the home sewing machine with the help of a teflon foot and a leather needle (NTW).

Ask for leather which is drum-dyed rather than spray-dyed; it will be the same color throughout. Spray dyeing makes the leather stiffer and less flattering. You will need 4 to 5 small skins to make a pair of pants

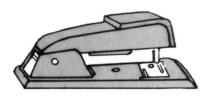

HOUSEHOLD STAPLER

WALLPAPER SEAM ROLLER

CHALK MARKING PENCIL

TEFLON PRESSER FOOT
(TEFLON COATED BOTTOM)

The Leather Process

with a seam at the knee. Unless you are experienced in leather cutting, the fifth skin is usually necessary. If you are disappointed in the skins when they arrive, send them back with a note describing precisely what you don't like about them.

What kind of leather is compatible with a home sewing machine? Fortunately, the soft leathers and suedes, which happen to be the most flattering on the body are easy to sew on the home sewing machine. For best results, choose one of these three leather products: Cabretta, because it is a hybrid of haresheep and lamb, the smooth skin leather combines the sturdiness of the goatskin with the softness of the lambskin. The only drawback of Cabretta is that it has a tendency to stretch and should not be used in a fitted pant in which a fitted shape is important. All leather products stretch slightly and should be fitted with this in mind.

Plonge, a wonderful thin cowhide with a beautiful drape. This yields the most professional smooth leather results.

Lambsuede, a soft drapey suede skin makes the finest suede clothing.

Pigsuede is an attractive alternative to the above choices because of its affordable price and the large size of the skins, making piecing often unnecessary. Some pigsuede skins are stiff and thick—both of these factors make the product difficult to sew on the home machine—causing skipped stitches. *IF* with capital letters; *IF* the skin is soft and drapey, pigsuede is then a viable alternative. Most pigskins are suitable for straight skirts but too stiff for pants.

If you have a choice of skins, check each skin carefully. Some dye lots are stiffer than others. This is the result of overdying leftover skins from another dye lot or dying of skins which were rather thick to begin with.

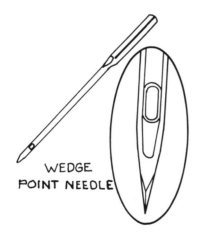

WEDGE
POINT NEEDLE

RIBBED ELASTIC

■ Pretest pattern intended for leather in denim. You will quickly see if this pattern is flattering enough for your beautiful skins.

The Leather Process

Unlike fabric or manmade leather or suede, real leather and suede are sold by the square foot. Most Cabretta, Plonge and Lambsuede run about 5 to 6 square feet per skin. For a traditional straight leg pair of pants, you will need at least 24 square feet. If the style is fuller, more is required. To make a matching blouson jacket, you will need an additional 30 square feet, and a straight skirt needs between 18 to 20 square feet. Until you become adept at manipulating and piecing the skins, purchase of an additional skin is not a bad idea. You can always make a belt or small purse with the leftover.

Debra Prinzing wrote an article for *Sew News* which gave an excellent formula for determining the amount of square feet needed per garment. An excerpt:

"Hides are sold by the square foot, and a full hide is usually required for minimum purchase. Pigskin hides range from 10 to 12 square feet. Cabretta ranges from 6 to 8 square feet. Lambskins range from 6 to 7 square feet. To calculate the amount of leather or suede you'll need, use the following formula: Check the pattern's fabric requirements for 36 inch wide fabric. Multiply this number by 9 and add 15%. For example, if the pattern requires 3 yards of fabric, multiply 3 by 9 equals 27 square feet. Add 15% of 27 ($4\frac{1}{4}$ square feet) totaling 31 1/4 square feet of leather or suede. (Round to the next quarter to allow for flaws in the hide.)"

Always interface behind pockets with press-on Pellon or a sew-in interfacing. Do not use steam on leather or suede; steam burns and shrinks the skins. Use a high dry iron setting and a presscloth when pressing on the right side.

Since skins are seldom large enough to accommodate full pattern pieces, skin piecing is often necessary. Plan where seamlines would be the most flattering and draw in a style line on the pattern. Mark an X on either side of the style line before cutting the pattern apart. The X will remind you to add seam allowances when cutting out. The most natural place for a seam on a pair of pants is at the knee. Seaming at the knee also gives reinforcement. Seams can be

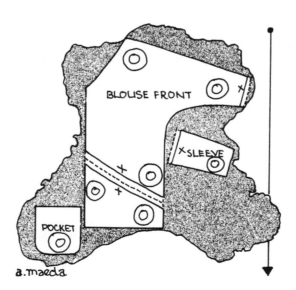

a.maeda

The Leather Process

placed straight across the knee or at a diagonal from high on the side seam to lower on the inner leg seam crossing the knee on the front leg. Seams must match at inner and outer leg seams. Measure seam placement from the bottom of the leg pattern on both front and back pant pieces.

Examine skins for imperfections and uneven thickness. Hold skins up to the light to show weak spots. Use the thicker part of the skin for the areas which will receive the most stress and will need the most support, such as knees and fanny. The thinner parts of the skin should be placed under pleats in front. If the entire skin seems thin or stretchy consider underlining with Skinner's Bemberg rayon. Circle with chalk any holes or skin imperfections, so that they can be avoided or placed in an inconspicuous place during cutting. Imperfections can often be camouflaged with shoe polish or felt tip pen. Examine each skin individually and carefully before cutting.

Avoid pin holes by using pattern weights in the layout. Sharp scissors or a rotary cutter are mandatory.

Holding garment pieces together for sewing is best accomplished by stapling ¼ inch from the cut edges. An alternate method for holding is with paper clips. Pinning leather or suede is difficult and often leaves holes.

The ideal choice of machine needle is a 80/12 H needle. This is the same needle used for a medium weight woven. Many machines do not have enough power to sew on skins without skipped stitches with this needle. If you find this to be the case, switch to a leather needle 90/14 NTW. Since the leather needle cuts into the skin slightly, the seam is not quite as strong. This is not an issue except for a very tight pair of pants, where a strong seam is mandatory. If you are sewing on pigsuede and cannot get rid of the skipped stitches, even with a leather needle, try sewing the seam with a strip of paper or Tear Away® under the seam. Keep in mind that some home machines are incompatible with pigsuede.

Polyester or bonded nylon are the best thread choices. If cotton thread is used, it will rot over time due to its

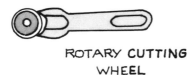

ROTARY CUTTING
WHEEL

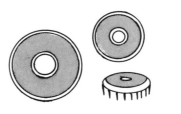

PATTERN WEIGHTS

M. GRAYSMITH ©

The Leather Process

reaction with one of the oils used in the tanning. Because the top layer of the skin tends to move ahead as you sew, much in the way velvet does, use of an even feed (walking) foot or teflon is a great help. Certain parts of the skin stretch more than others. Hold skins together firmly at front and back as you sew. Due to the thickness of the skins, use a stitch length slightly smaller than a basting stitch (8 to 10) stitches per inch. Small stitches in a seam cause a seam to pucker slightly and tear. Do not topstitch side seams. Topstitching makes altering difficult and can makes seams wiry. Stretch underarm and crotch curves as you sew. Secure threads at ends of seam with a drop of glue.

Try a sample of each skin before you press on it. Each skin reacts differently to heat. Iron skin from the suede side. If the skin has been vegetable dyed, it can usually be pressed from the smooth side. Iron should be a dry iron on medium setting. Be careful when pressing embossed or crinkled leathers. Heat will remove some of the design since it was heat processed. Press interfacing on wrong side of these fancy leathers. Reposition pattern and trim to size.

For interfacing, iron-on Pellon or fusible weft make good choices in waistbands, collars, and under buttonholes. If elastic is used at the waistline, use vertically ribbed elastic, since this variety is capable of a stronger pull.

Hems and seams are pressed open and glued in place with rubber cement. Leave the top off the rubber cement for 24 hours before using. This will let some of the water in the glue evaporate and eliminate "soak through" to the right side. Never glue all the way to the edge of the leather. Start glue $\frac{1}{4}$ inch back from the edge to avoid glue stains. For a glue with some elasticity, try Barge Cement. To flatten areas which have been glued, roll flat with a wallpaper roller (small wooden one) or pound flat with a padded hammer.

There has been some controversy about whether to put a separate lining in leather and suede pants. Leather sportswear manufacturers agree that a separate lining shifts within the pant and doesn't always signify a quality leather garment. Be sure to allow 2 inches ease when cutting the lining. Although the leather will stretch in the first wearing, the lining will not. After the first wearing, the leather pant and the lining will be the same size. Cut pant lining 1 inch shorter than leather pant. Attach lining at zipper and waistband only.

Fly Front Leather Pants

If you don't own a pair of leather pants, you may wonder why every fall season features some version of the black leather pant. If you do own a pair, you know not only how comfortable they are, but how versatile they are In the fashion picture. A well fitting pair of black leather pants can be a Jeans substitute, worn with loose overshirt or tight sweater tucked in by day and transformed into knock out evening attire with high heels, eye catching accessories and Chanel styled Jacket.

If the only thing stopping you from makIng a pair of leather pants is the fry front zipper, don't let this stop you. Making a fly front in leather pants is simple if you follow the following formula for success. Cut fly extensions on both sides of the pant fronts, Just as you would for any other fly front opening pants. For extensions, cut 1½ inch extensions past the center front seamline on pant fronts.

Cut a fly facing from a leather scrap, 8 inches long and 4 inches wide. If you are short of leather, this can be cut from a firm cotton, which has been interfaced with fusible interfacing to give it some body. A leather facing is what you will find in a pair of leather pants from ready to wear. Shape the fly facing at bottom to imitate the fly front curve. (Illustration I).

On the outside of the right front, place the right side of the zipper against the outside of the right front, lining up the zipper tape with the edge of the cut on fly

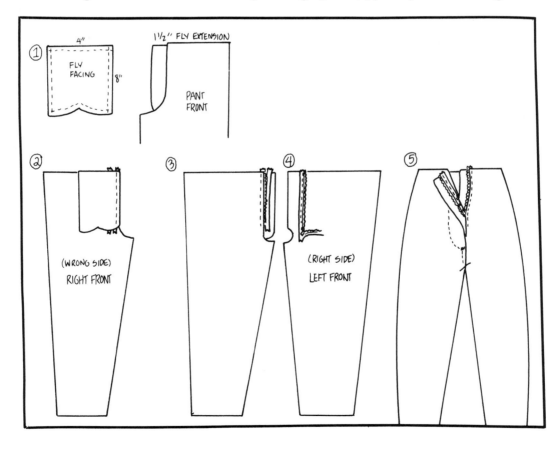

Fly Front Leather Pants

extension. Now overlay the right side of the fly facing over the zipper and the right front, sandwiching the zipper between the right pant front and the fly facing. Using a zipper foot, seam the 3 thicknesses, sewing close to the zipper teeth.(Illustration 2)

On the wrong side of the unsewn half of the zipper facing, paint rubber cement, if you are using a leather facing, Fold the applied fly facing in half with wrong sides together. The glue will hold it into position. Let glue dry for a few minutes, to avoid glue residue on the needle. If you are using a woven fabric for a fly facing, secure the fly facing in half with an overlock stitch. Now topstitch the zipper into position, sewing close to the zipper teeth. (Illustration 3) The topstitching goes through the right pant front, the zipper and both thicknesses of the fly facing.

Now sew the inner leg seams, Joining each back leg to each front leg separately Sew crotch seam together, from back to front. Stop stitching at the bottom of the fly extension. Finger press the left fly extension into place, using the center front seamline as a guide for your fold. Pound in place with a padded clapper or padded hammer. Mark crease with a snip at the top and chalk on the creaseline on the wrong side of the pant. Close zipper. Position left pant front over right front, the way it will lie in its finished position. Determine position of remaining half of the zipper on soon to be folded back fly extension. Mark zipper teeth placement with soap sliver. Move fly facing out of the way. Open zipper. Race the remaining side of the zipper, right side down against the left fly extension, positioning teeth on soap slivered marked placement. (Illustration 4) Sew zipper tape to left fly extension only. Paint a thin strip of glue on crease on wrong side of left fly extension. Fold extension back into place.

Pull zipper up and allow pant fronts to lie in their finished position. Mark topstitching line on left pant front $1\frac{1}{4}$ inches away from fold. Unzip zipper and move fly facing out of the way again. Starting at the top of the pants topstitch into place until you have sewn about a half inch around curve. Fold fly facing back into place and continue topstitching to end of curve. This will catch fly facing in stitching at bottom of curve and anchor into place. Pull clipped seam allowances to the left side and continue topstitching on crotch curve.(Illustration 5) Bar tack if desired at bottom of crotch curve.

■ Seams on leather, velvet, satin, and chiffon simply cannot be ripped out if you make a mistake. Stitched holes leave a memory from the seam. Hand baste seams. Try on garment with hand-basted seams before machine stitching.

Pockets
in Leather

While pockets are optional, most likely all of your favorite pants have pockets. If the pants you are making are leather, patch pockets are too bulky. Welt pockets are attractive, but if the pants are tight, they tend to gap open. If your pattern has a separate side front piece, so that a pocket can easily be inserted, this is an excellent option, especially if you will take the time to pipe the curved edge.

The following is another pocket option which can either be put in the side seam or the seam between the waistband and the pant front in the center of each front panel. If the pocket is put between the waist-band and the pant front, a smaller pocket of 4 inches is appropriate.

Since the traditional pocket has a 6 inch opening, cut two strips of leather 2 inches wide by 8 inches long, which will give you an inch at either end of the pocket opening for pocket finishing. Cut pocket lining, best in a firm cotton, rather than lining fabric for longer wear, 8 inches long and 12 inches wide. Seam a leather strip on each end of the lining piece, along the 8 inch sides. (Illustration 1)

Mark pocket placement at side seam of pant front, usually 2 inches down from the waistline seamline.

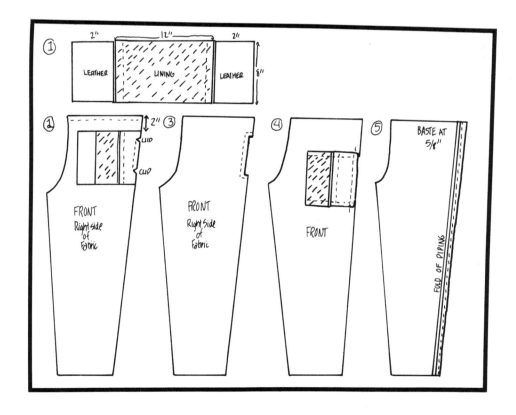

Pockets in Leather

Place the right side of one leather strip against the pant front at desired pocket placement, lining up raw edges of pant front and leather strip. Sew seam ⅝ inch away from raw edge, starting and stopping seam 1 inch from each side of leather strip. Clip at each end of the stitching, almost to the stitching line. (Illustration 2) Turn pocket piece to the wrong side of the pant front. Topstitch all around pocket opening, including ends (Illustration 3). Ends of opening were not previously sewn, to avoid bulk these raw ends will not be visible after side seam is sewn.

Bring the other half of the pocket up, so that the raw edge of the leather strip on the other end of the pocket lining matches with the cut edge of the pant front on both ends of the pocket opening. (Illustration 4)

Make snip a bottom folded edge of lining fabric close up sides of pocket by machine. Baste pocket into position along seamline. When pant front and back are sewn together at side seam, pocket opening will remain free.

Contrasting piping in a side seam on leather or suede pants is optional, but definitely slimming, since it provides a vertical seamline accent. Most women need as many vertical accents as possible to keep the eye moving up and down rather than across the body, which is why horizontal seaming is seldom accented with piping.

If you want to pipe a side seam in your leather pants, cut a strip of leather 1¾ inch wide. This will result in a piping strip of ¼ inch standard width. Paint rubber cement on the wrong side of the leather strip. Fold strip in half lengthwise. Finger press flat. Pound flap with a padded clapper or padded hammer. Cording is not used in leather piping, because it becomes too bulky.

Sew piping to pant back at side seam placement, placing right sides together. The decorative fold part of the piping will extend ¼ inch into the body of the pant (Illustration 5). Join front and back pants at side seam, placing right sides together. Use previous line of stitching, which joined the piping to the back pant as guide for new seamline be careful not to catch pocket opening as you sew side seam.

■ Whereas leather is often used as trim on fabric, the reverse can be attractive as well. New Zealand designer Maria Scully and Kim Fraser won the Leather Industry Award in 1989 with a Napoleon jacket in brown aviator cowhide trimmed in Denim.

Piped Leather Buttonholes

1

2

3

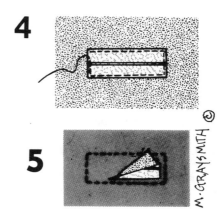

4

5

M. GRAYSMITH ©

Once you make these buttonholes, you will be reluctant to make any other kind. This piped buttonhole is easy, non-bulky, and is suitable for any man-made or genuine suede or leather garment, using suede or leather strips.

Depending on the number of buttonholes you want, cut a long 1 inch wide strip of suede or leather. Paint rubber cement on the wrong side of the strip. Fold strip in half lengthwise, pressing wrong sides together. Pound strip flat. Cut folded strip down to a width of ³⁄₈ inch. A rotary cutter gives the cleanest cut, but this is not necessary.

Buttonhole placement should be visible from the right side of the garment with interfacing on wrong side as a stabilizer. On outside of garment, place newly cut edge of suede strip against buttonhole placement marking. Extend strip ¹⁄₂ inch on either end of buttonhole length. Hold strip in place with tape on ends. Mark beginning and end of buttonhole in center of strip. Sew in the middle of strip, through strip and garment, between placement markings. Sew once, leave needle in last stitch, turn around and sew again—the line of stitching is doubly reinforced without backstitching. Butt cut edge of second strip against cut edge of first sewn strip. Repeat process, sewing in the

Piped Leather Buttonholes

middle of the second strip twice between buttonhole markings. Remove placement tape (Illustration 1 on page 189).

On garment wrong side, cut opening for turning strips. Cut garment only, not strips. Form long triangles at ends of opening, clipping in close (within one stitch) to corners (Illustration 2). On wrong side of garment, paint rubber cement over stitching lines along length of buttonhole, no glue on triangles. Turn strips through buttonhole opening. Butt folded edges together. Glue will hold buttonhole in place. On wrong side, tape ends of strips together with a small piece of tape. Anchor triangles to ends of butted strips with stitching (Illustration 3). Pound buttonhole flat with padded hammer.

Attach facing to garment. After facing has been pressed and pounded into final position, place garment with right side facing you. On the outside of the garment, stitch a rectangle inside of the buttonhole box along the edges where the buttonhole joins the garment. Stitching will join the garment with the facing (Illustration 4). On the back side of the facing, trim away suede from inside buttonhole box of the facing (Illustration 5). Buttonhole is now complete.

■ Seam imprints can be avoided by pressing with the point of the iron in the well of the seam. Never rest the weight of the iron on an open seam.

■ Time not spent on needed pattern alterations translates into unworn garments.

FABULOUS FAKES IN LEATHER AND SUEDE

■ If you can't decide whether a style will work well in leather, make a pretest from scrap upholstery fabric to see if the style is flattering.

Synthetic Leather

If you want your synthetic leather to look like the real thing, use construction techniques for genuine leather. For starters, do something with your fake leather that would never be possible with real leather. Throw it into the washing machine and dryer. The knit backing shrinks slightly in the first washing, and this prewash helps eliminate skipped stitches and later fitting surprises.

If you are trying to make a genuine look-alike, choose a pattern with small pieces or create seams in large pieces. Most leather and suede skins are small and oddly shaped; therefore, seams are planned in large pattern pieces. Pants are pieced at the knee. Skirts are pieced within panels. The most successful garments in both synthetic leather or suede seem to have a controlled shape to the pattern. Boxy shapes add weight because they do not conform to the shape of the body. Duplicate all pattern pieces so that you can have left and right sides for all pattern pieces. Since leather does not have grain, more economical use can be made of the material.

Darts can be sewn in a conventional method, but they should be cut open at wide end for flattering results. To remove excess fullness in hems, deepen seems in hem allowance. Extra fullness is removed without the tell-tale signs of "ease" on the wrong side.

Since the fabric has stretch in all directions, grainline considerations can be forgotten. Fit pattern pieces on the synthetic leather just as you would on a genuine-leather skin, any way they will fit. This advantage means you will use less fabric than the pattern calls for. Do a quickie layout at the store or use leftover fabric for accessories. Since this fabric tends to resist pins, use pattern weights to hold pattern pieces in place while you cut.

Since the fabric doesn't ravel and leaves a clean edge between cuts, serger seam finishes can be eliminated. What is necessary is use of a walking or even feed presserfoot. This foot eliminates the problem of "pushing top layer ahead". If your machine cannot accommodate this foot, substitute a Teflon presserfoot, which is capable of gliding over the fabric. Synthetic leather is not particular about thread and is happy to gobble up any provided. Skipped-stitch problems can be eliminated on all machines, if the fabric has been prewashed, with an 80/12 HS machine needle.

For an authentic leather-looking garment, treat seams as follows: No glue stick necessary! Sew seams with a slightly longer stitch length. Trim one side of the seam allowance to $1/8$ inch, usually the one facing the front of the garment. Lay the untrimmed seam allowance over the trimmed one. Do not turn under. Topstitch seam allowances into position at $1/4$ inch. Trimming one seam allowance makes the seam much more flexible than leaving both seam allowances the same width.

Synthetic leather CAN BE PRESSED but never without a PRESSCLOTH and with no higher than medium on your iron. Pressing without a presscloth will melt the fabric's finish; pressing with a presscloth allows you to get crisp detailing and hem folds.

While hem on synthetic leather can be glued, why glue when machine stitching and hand stitching look professional and eliminate re-gluing after subsequent washings? Several rows of topstitching, $1/4$ inch apart from the right side, give a tailored effect. Synthetic leather can also be hand-stitcher by attaching hem to one or two threads on the synthetic leather knit backing.

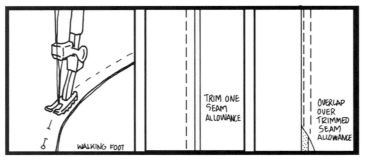

WALKING FOOT

TRIM ONE SEAM ALLOWANCE

OVERLAP OVER TRIMMED SEAM ALLOWANCE

Synthetic Suede

Facile™ and Caress™ react very similar under the needle and in care to Ultrasuede™, but drape better on the body.

Although a pretest in a similar weight fabric is always advisable before taking on a synthetic suede project, memory of former stitches can be erased when a seam is let out by washing the garment and brushing the nap with a toothbrush in the affected area.

Don't forget to make identical alterations on lining pieces, cutting the lining from a no-iron washable polyester.

Skipped stitches can be avoided by washing and drying the fabric before cutting. This method removes resins from the fabric which are the chief culprit of skipped stitches. If skipped stitches are a problem on synthetic suedes or leathers, moisten the thread slightly with Sewer's Aid™. Put drops of Sewer's Aid™ on finger and run around the spool of thread occasionally. Skipped stitches can be eliminated on most machines by using a size 80/12 HS (ballpoint needle). For even feeding, use a teflon, roller, or even feed foot with slight pull on fabric from front and back (taut sewing). To eliminate bent pins, pattern weights are recommended for layout. Although synthetic suede does not have an obvious one way direction, slight shading can be seen in some lights when the synthetic suede is not cut directionally. Cut pattern using with-nap layout.

■ Since topstitching on hems can produce a somewhat wiry result, Stitch Witchery® is your best bet. Cut Stitch Witchery® the width of the hem minus ¼ inch. Soft invisible hems result. Credit to: Hazel Boyd, author of *Silks and Satins* and *Couture Action Knits* (see Sources).

Synthetic Suede

Whisper Weft is the most compatible interfacing for synthetic suede. Don't forget to interface elbows, since this is the first place an Ultrasuede™ jacket shows wear. Fusible interfacing of the jacket back inhibits movement. Use a woven interfacing cut on the bias for greater flexibility. Since synthetic suedes make sleeve easing difficult, remove 1 inch of ease from sleeve cap by folding out a ½ inch horizontal tuck above the notches, in the cap of the sleeve. This procedure reduces sleeve ease from 2 inches to 1 inch. If the pattern you are using is designed for synthetic suede or leather, this sleeve alteration is not necessary.

Stabilize both facing and garment front behind buttonholes with interfacing. Use glue stick between facing and jacket layers under buttonholes to keep the facing from shifting during the buttonhole process.

A synthetic suede garment may be spot cleaned with soap and water since it will not water spot. If the garment seams pucker after machine washing and drying, the garment was left too long in the dryer (overdried). Puckered seams can be removed with a damp presscloth and a steam iron. Never iron directly onto the synthetic suede; always use a presscloth.

Credit to: Harriett Baskett

■ Underlining dart area in soft lining fabric will eliminate dart pucker on man-made suedes.

Pressing Tips
for the Master

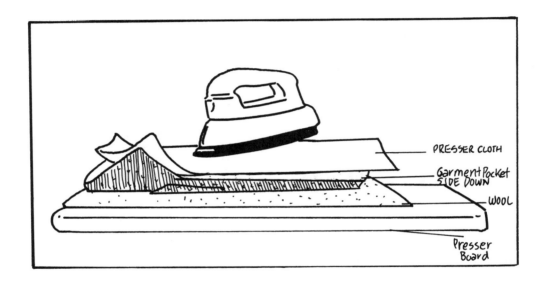

PRESSER CLOTH

Garment Pocket
SIDE DOWN

WOOL

Presser
Board

■ Eliminate "pressing shine" on design details by covering the pressing surface with a wool scrap before positioning detail. Then place detail down against the pressing surface. Cover with presscloth. Steam well and pound with a tailor's clapper.

Pressing Tips

"Never sew across an unpressed seam." Good advice but not quite enough to result in a quality looking garment. On many fabrics certain precautions must be taken to avoid creating seam imprints on the outside of the garment. "Oh no, not brown bag strips again." Strips of brown bag do work when placed between the seam allowance and the garment but seam imprint can be avoided more easily by alternate methods.

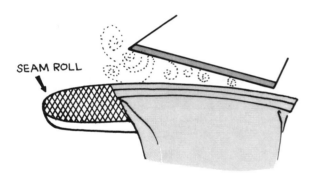

SEAM ROLL

Pressing seams open on a seam roll eliminates seam imprint since the curve of the roll allows the edge of the seam to follow the roll while pressure is applied flattening the seam $1/4$ inch on either side of the seam itself. Pressing seams open on the straight edge of a point turner works as well to eliminate seam imprint, because the straight edge is only $1/2$ inch wide. By centering the seam over the straight edge, the seam may be pressed open with pressure $1/4$ inch on either side of the seam itself. No matter how much pressure is exerted, the edge of the seam allowance is not in contact with the pressure of the iron. The second method using the edge of a point turner is extremely helpful when pressing fabrics which are difficult to flatten, twill weaves such as wool gabardine and manmade suede, such as Ultrasuede®.

All seams should be pressed as stitched from both sides to flatten the fabric and relax the threads. Seam pucker is eliminated in this step. If pressing the seam flat does not eliminate seam pucker, try pulling the fabric taut from front and back as you sew. Let the feed dog move the fabric under the needle. If this does not eliminate the problem, perhaps your needle is incorrect or your thread too heavy.

"When grading seams before pressing, many people become confused as to which layer should be trimmed closest to the stitching. Remember that the stitched edge will always fall toward the seam allowance that has been trimmed closest to the stitching. For example, since you want the seam to roll slightly to the underside of a collar, trim the seam allowance on the undercollar side by the greatest amount."—June Tailor in her book, *The June Tailor Method of Custom Detail Pressing* and her video, *Pressing Matters* (see Sources).

When pressing up a hem or a miter, cushion the garment against an imprint of the hem or the miter with an envelope. Press darts or curved seams over a tailor's ham to build in shape. Do not press front darts on a skirt or pants over the ham. Pressing this area over the ham will build in a rounded shape to fit over the tummy, emphasizing an area most of us do not wish to draw attention to.

Get in the habit of using a presscloth. Pressing directly on the right side of the garment without one

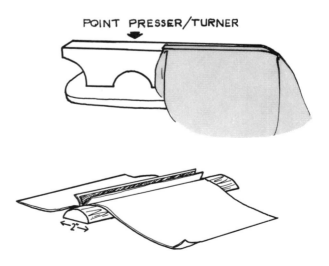

POINT PRESSER/TURNER

Pressing Tips

should be an exception rather than the rule. Cotton drill cloth is excellent because it enables you to raise the temperature of the iron for difficult to press fabrics without scorching the garment. Cheesecloth makes an excellent presscloth when moisture is needed for molding or setting a crease. To turn out professional-looking garments, capable pressing equipment is a must. For years, professional dressmakers swore by the Sussman gravity feed iron. Loyalty to the Sussman has now switched to Naimoto HYS-5, a gravity feed iron without maintenance problems. The steam from this $400 iron cannot be equalled. If you don't have a local source for this iron, see Sewing Machine Exchange in Sources.

If you lack the space for a gravity feed iron, the Bernina iron and the Rowenta heavyweight model, are the best on the market for weight and steam. Other Rowenta models with the removable water tank have had leakage problems, the Rowenta cordless doesn't stay hot enough, but the Rowenta DE 82 is terrific.

For setting creases, fusing interfacing, flattening lapels, the Elnapress or a similar large press can't be beat. After you own one you may find you use it more than your iron. Because of the large soleplate, pressing is flat and uniform. In addition, the 100 pounds of pressure is unbeatable for flattening lapels.

Try this technique for flattening seams during pressing. Pressing over hardwood prevents the steam from escaping the fabric quickly. The combination of steam and pressure can tame and shape a fabric. Try pressing over a 3 foot by 2 inch dowel which has been cut lengthwise. lay the flat side of the dowel on the table. Position seam on rounded side of dowel. Pressing on a rounded surface such as a dowel or a seam roll prevents seam imprint from the right side. One inch seam allowances press flatter than 5/8 inch. Use a presscloth, steam and clapper to flatten seams from wrong side. let fabric dry completely before moving off the pressing surface.

To remove shine from the right side of fabric, place dampened cheesecloth on fabric. Hold a dry iron 1/2 inch above the surface of the cheesecloth covered fabric. Remove cheesecloth. Brush fabric to raise nap.

■ "You can skip lots of steps if you know how to press. Pressing can be like basting. It can make or break what you're doing," says designer Isaac Mizrahi in an interview by Diane Sustendal for *Sew News* magazine (see Sources).

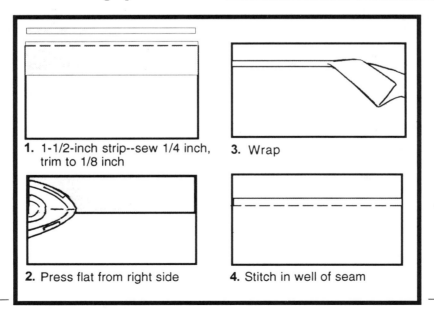

1. 1-1/2-inch strip--sew 1/4 inch, trim to 1/8 inch

2. Press flat from right side

3. Wrap

4. Stitch in well of seam

Hand-Picked Detailing

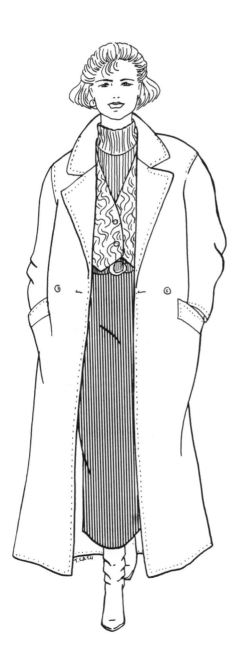

■ To duplicate hand-picked detailing found in ready-to-wear, a more substantial thread is needed which will not sink into the fabric and disappear from visibility. Madiera and Sulky produce shiny rayon threads which produce a pleasing contrast against matte finish fabric. Buttonhole twist thread can also substitute for hand-picking. Either single or double thread is used depending on desired visibility. Strengthen thread and eliminate knotting by running thread through beeswax before stitching. Hand-picking is a hand stitch which slides from stitch to stitch between fabric layers, surfaces for a small hand stitch on the top, disappearing once again between layers. Hand-picking on coats appears $\frac{1}{2}$ inch from finished edge with stitches $\frac{1}{2}$ inch apart. Spacing on jackets appears $\frac{1}{4}$ inch from finished edge with stitches $\frac{1}{4}$ inch apart. Spacing on blouses appears $\frac{1}{8}$ inch from finished edge with stitches $\frac{1}{8}$ inch apart.

Saddle Stitch

Western and Santa Fe style clothing is often finished with saddle stitch. Saddle stitching replaces topstitching and is designed to be visible. When saddle stitching is done on leather, holes must be punched with a leather punch. At half-inch intervals, narrow strips of leather lacing overcast edges, giving a "made solely by hand" appearance.

Saddle stitch can appear on the outside edge of a shawl collar made from Navajo-inspired fabric, coat sleeve cuffs, outside edges of a vest, or outside edges of a wrap skirt in ethnic fabric or suede.

While seam to be decorated should be sewn, trimmed and well pressed, access to seam allowances is necessary to hide knots in decorative thread. Perhaps the nicest saddle stitch is made from two strands of Madeira Silk Embroidery Floss. This thread combines good weight, twist, and sheen. Cotton Floche thread or buttonhole twist can also be used with good results. Use all of these threads double, reinforced by running through beeswax and threaded through a "Glover's" needle, commonly used on leather.

Saddle stitching is positioned $\frac{1}{2}$ inch from seamed edge at $\frac{1}{2}$ inch intervals. For professional looking results, mark outside edge with tailor's chalk at $\frac{1}{2}$ inch intervals. Begin by hiding knot in seam allowance. Bring the needle out on the front side of the fabric. Wrap thread around seam, inserting needle $\frac{1}{2}$ inch lower on the backside of the fabric. Needle is now brought straight through to topside. This wraps the stitching at a slight angle. Saddle stitching continues wrapping seam and going into backside $\frac{1}{2}$ inch lower than position where thread comes out on the topside. Try to keep the same tension from stitch to stitch, not pulling thread too tight. Plan ahead where to knot off since each knot must be hidden in seam. Double knot thread in seam, or dot with fabric glue to secure.

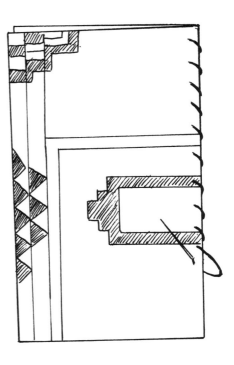

Embellish with Beads

To covet a designer beaded scarf is one thing, to shell out $4,500 is quite another. With a few simple skills, you can undertake a beading project of your own. Beading is very much like knitting in that it is portable, time consuming, and somewhat mindless, yielding results that are quite spectacular.

Beading can be done on any fabric: chiffon, organza, rayon crepe being the most popular. Since dry cleaning a beaded garment is inadvisable, choose a washable fabric such as a silk chiffon for a scarf or a dark colored dry-cleanable fabric which can be spot cleaned or sponged off for a garment. A beaded scarf is an excellent first project because you can get an idea of the time involved for embellishment without being overwhelmed.

To keep the fabric from bunching up as you work, stretch fabric over an embroidery hoop for small areas or a quilt frame for large areas. Since both the hoop and the frame can be moved as you work, neither needs to be as large as the piece you are working on. Cover the hoop or frame with ribbon to prevent snagging the fabric. If you plan to bead a garment, cut each pattern piece with $1\frac{1}{2}$ seams. "Keep stitches short on the back of the fabric to control shrinkage," says couturier beader Blossom Jenab. The process of beading consumes fabric. To support the weight of a fully beaded piece, such as a velvet jacket, garment pieces should be interfaced before beading with a medium weight interfacing. For very fine garments on silk chiffon, interface with two layers of silk organza. Re-cut the garment piece accurately from the pattern piece after beading to the seamline. If scarf fabric is fragile, consider beading through 2 thicknesses to eliminate interfacing.

■ To sew bugle beads in a straight line, put a long string of bugles on the thread. Anchor at beginning and end on fabric. Go back and sew through each bead with a separate stitch to anchor to the fabric.

Embellish with Beads

If a large selection of beads is not available in your area, an extensive mail order catalogue with bead swatch cards is available from Garden of Beadin. Additional bead sources can be found in the magazine *Ornament* (see Sources).

Sequins, beads, and pearls can be dyed. For best results, leave in a dye solution for an hour. Beads are usually sold by weight. If you plan to bead a large area, it is important to have enough beads on hand to complete the project. A closely beaded dress may weigh 40 pounds or more. Bead one square inch of fabric on a scrap. Count the beads.

Multiply the number of beads needed in the sample square inch times the number of square inches for the entire project.

Needlepoint transfers, comics, and design books are excellent sources for pattern inspiration. Perhaps most inspiring are the actual bead work garments themselves which are color photographed in the oversize book called *Haute Couture Embroidery (The Art of Lesage)* by Palmer White.

Now transfer designs to fabric with Clo chalk, a disappearing chalk, Mark Be/Gone, a disappearing mark tracing paper, or colored pencils.

Beading authorities differ on the kind of thread used. Cotton thread was used in vintage garments. In time, some beads fell off because the thread had rotted. Cotton wrapped polyester and silk thread are recommended for the longest life. Metallic threads give an interesting texture and will pass through most beads as well. For most beads, a size ten beading needle is used. If you are working with antique or very fine beads, make sure the size ten needle goes through the bead. If not, a finer needle will be necessary. Unless you have a very steady hand and good eyesight, invest in a needle threader.

To prevent design distortion or shifting in the fabric, bead the piece from the center out right and left. On fine fabrics, use a single thread for beading. On heavier fabric or for beaded fringe or heavy beads, use double thread for the beading stitches. Avoid beading on stretchy fabrics or interface behind the fabric with medium weight interfacing.

BEAD TERMINOLOGY
* Seed Beads—Small round bead of various sizes.
* Bugle Beads—Tubular shaped beads.
* H-Beads—Six sided beads.
* Roundels—Flat donut shaped beads.
* Faceted Beads—Beads with numerous facets.
* Drops—Pear shaped beads or ornaments.
* Fancy—Various shaped ornaments.
* Sequins—Shiny metallic or plastic decorations.

TYPES OF SEQUINS
* Spangles—Flat discs with center holes.
* Cups—Dome shaped discs with center holes.
* Pailettes—Flat discs with side holes.
* Fancy—Unusual shaped sequins.

■ If a hole in a bead or an ornament is not in a place you desire, make a new hole by heating a needle over a flame and piercing.

Beaded Stitches

Careful examination of beaded garments will reveal beads that attach individually or up to six at a time. Complexity of design will determine how many beads can be attached in one stitch. To eliminate knotting, use thread no longer than 24 inches. After stringing bead on the thread, let bead drop down and touch the fabric before pushing the thread to the back of the fabric. Three basic stitches will cover most of your bead-

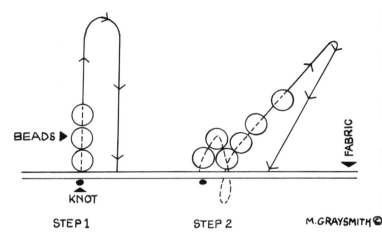

STEP 1   STEP 2   M. GRAYSMITH ©

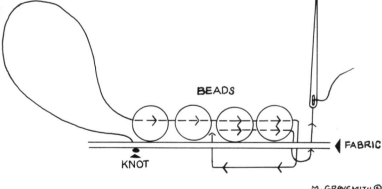

M. GRAYSMITH ©

ing needs. For the basic bead stitch, start with a knot on the back of the fabric, bring the thread up and string on one to six beads. At the end of the space needed for these beads to lie flat and not be cramped, put needle back into the fabric, bringing the thread to the back of the fabric. Back up half the number of beads you used on top in this stitch and bring the needle up in between them. Go through the last half of the beads again, bringing out the needle at the end of the last bead and taking the thread to the back of the fabric. Bring the needle out right next to where you last went in and repeat the process again.

Beaded edges are an attractive way to embellish necklines, armholes, hems and scarfs. Beaded edges are formed by sewing three beads in a space large enough for two beads. The middle bead floats on the top. After knotting thread on the back of the fabric, bring thread to the front of the fabric. String on three beads. Push the needle back through the fabric at a distance which will accommodate two beads. Move back a few threads on the back of the fabric and bring the thread up through the last bead of your set of three. String on two more beads bringing the needle down in a space which will accommodate two of the three beads. Repeat the edge stitch all around the edges.

Beaded Stitches

Beaded fringe, although time-consuming is a spectacular finish for the ends of a scarf. Fringe is usually spaced at $\frac{1}{8}$ to $\frac{1}{4}$ inch intervals. Beaded fringe can be any length but shorter than two inches will not drape as well as the longer fringe. Beaded fringe is a great place to intersperse beads and bugle beads for length. Start the fringe close to the edge of the fabric, with a knot on the wrong side of the fabric. Number of beads strung varies with the length of the beaded fringe you want to use. Try a sample. For example, string on five round beads and five bugle beads alternating. Form a beaded loop at the end of the fringe by stringing on six round beads. Pass the needle back through the original five round beads and five bugle beads which were alternated. Bring the needle back through the original hole where the fringe began. Monofilament fishing (17 pound) line can be used to give strength to very long beaded fringe. Secure knots with 5 minute epoxy glue.

Place fabric glue or clear nail polish over all knots after the beading process is complete. For more beading stitches and detailed beading instruction send for the well illustrated book by Therese Spears entitled *Beaded Clothing Techniques* (see Sources).

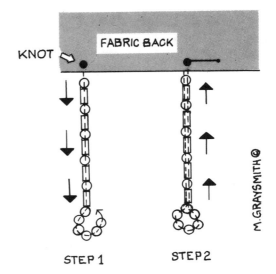

STEP 1   STEP 2

■ A fishing tackle box makes great storage for beads.

Beading by Machine

If you closely examine an elaborately beaded and/or embroidered piece, you will usually find a combination of both hand and machine beading. The ability to machine bead part of the garment cuts down considerably on the time spent on heavily embellished work.

Believe it or not, it is possible to machine sew a string of pearls or numerous other small strung beads so invisibly that machine sewing will not be suspected. Machine beading is made possible with a knit edge foot or pearls 'n piping foot, a foot with a fairly deep tunnel, originally designed as a foot with an ability to take loft when sewing bulky sweaters together. The wide tunnel under the foot allows the foot to ride over the

strung beads. The secret to truly invisible machine stitches in this process is use of an invisible thread. This thread is not wiry see-through nylon thread, but a transparent thread almost as fine as a strand of hair. The best thread is available from Treadleart (see Sources), and called Invisible Wonder Thread, available in clear for sewing on light colors and smoke for sewing on dark colors. Before you begin, it is necessary to re-string the beads by hand onto nylon beading thread. Most beads are pre-strung on poor quality cotton thread, unlikely to hold up long-term.

Invisible Wonder Thread is used on the top, regular thread on the bobbin. Strung beads will be machine

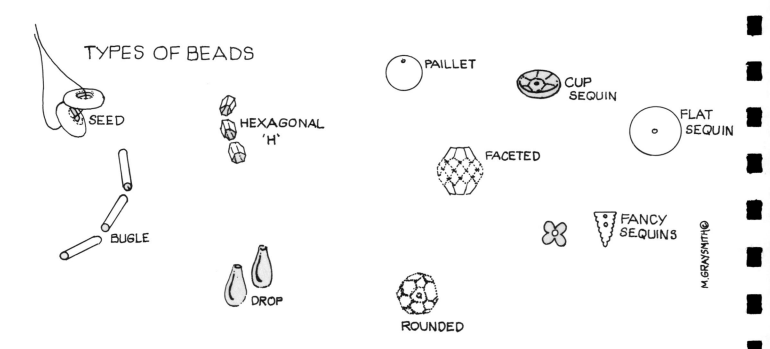

TYPES OF BEADS

SEED

HEXAGONAL 'H'

BUGLE

DROP

PAILLET

CUP SEQUIN

FLAT SEQUIN

FACETED

FANCY SEQUINS

ROUNDED

M. GRAYSMITH©

Demonstrated on *Power Sewing* Video #8: *Embellishment.*

Beading by Machine

sewn with a 80/12 needle (H for wovens; HS for knits) and a knit edge foot or pearls 'n piping foot, also available from Treadleart (see Sources).

If your machine can be switched to *sew slow*, do so. If your machine can be switched to *needle down* when stopping, do so; needle down will hold your place as you arrange the string of beads for work. Neither of these special machine capabilities are necessary; both merely make work easier.

Using a zigzag stitch, adjust zigzag to a fairly wide width (4 on a 0 to 6 scale) and medium to long length (long enough to go to the next bead). Adjust length and width on a scrap with a sample length of beading before beginning on actual project.

Begin first stitch on the side of one bead. Feed string of beads into foot, sewing fairly slow. Allow the machine to zigzag over string of beads. If you break a needle more than once, switch to a larger size 90/14.

Strung sequins and rattail cord can be sewn on technique.

Credit to: Mary Glardon and Peggy Trimble, Pfaff, Educators.

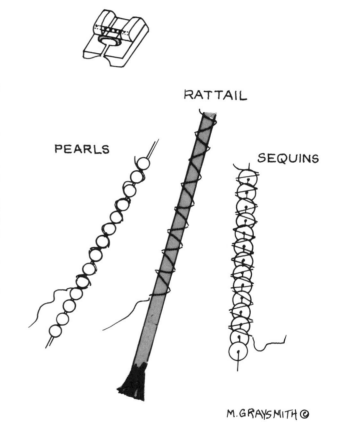

RATTAIL

PEARLS

SEQUINS

M. GRAYSMITH ©

■ Round beads provide points of light and color. Since they do not flash with movement, they are more subtle. Flat surface such as sequins create glitter because they provide flashes of light with movement.

Grosgrain Framed Lapels

Lapels framed in piping add a subtle touch; lapels framed in grosgrain or satin ribbon make a statement. Black grosgrain or flat rayon trim often trims and frames lapels on red or white jackets. Black satin, moire ribbon frames lapels on black gabardine giving a tuxedo touch. If you are looking for a way to make a jacket special or give a facelift to a jacket you already own, this is it. This decorative touch can be applied after the garment is completed.

Make sure you purchase 4 inches more trim than you think you need. This is not a place to skimp; corners need to be mitered. You might even consider framing the sleeve with a row or two of the same trim.

While most ribbon frame trim is applied by machine in ready-to-wear, results are more professional, as well as giving you more control over the finished outcome, if the trim is applied by hand.

On the lapel, trim begins in line with the finished edge of the collar. This does not go into a seam. To prevent ribbon or trim from fraying, sew a row of smaller machine stitches through a single thickness of ribbon. Push trim into the needle or pull trim from side to side under the needle to prevent trim from widening as you machine sew. Trim ribbon end close to the stitching. Now, go to the iron and press under $1/8$ inch to $1/8$ inch, the smallest fold you can make on the end of the trim.

Begin with folded edge in line with the finished edge of the top collar. Align the outside edge of the trim with the finished edge of the lapel. Within a few inches, the ribbon must turn a corner at the lapel point. This is accomplished by mitering the corner (see *Power Sewing* page 205). The miter can be sewn by machine or hand. Trim out bulk under miter if it seems bulky. Continue down lapel. Ribbon trim should not be stopped at the lapel turn but continued all the way to the hem. After the trim leaves the lapel and trims the inside of the jacket on the facing, move the trim 1/8 inch in, slightly away from the jacket edge to prevent trim edge from showing on the outside. At the bottom of the jacket, the trim is finished the same way it started with folded edge turned under.

On the collar, the end of the ribbon goes into the seam where the collar and lapel join. Before you begin, cut enough ribbon plus a little extra to go around the outside edge of the collar. Fold ribbon length in half. Begin work at center back, moving toward collar points; miter continues around the point. Align edge of trim with edge of collar. On the collar the end of ribbon goes into seam where the collar and lapel join. If jacket is being constructed, ribbon can be applied to collar before collar is attached to lapel. If lapel is completed, merely open seam gently with a ripper the width of the trim only. Slip $1/2$ inch on the end of the trim into the seam. Invisibly close seam opening with a hand stitch. Pocket flaps on jacket may be embellished in the same manner.

■ Ribbon which features a tiny scallop on the edge has the ability to mold while straight-edge ribbon does not.

Grosgrain Lapels

If jacket is not yet constructed, an alternative technique can be used which eliminates hand stitching.

Choose ribbon ⅝ inch wider than desired on the finished product. After collar and lapels have been interfaced, overlay ribbon onto top collar and lapel separately. Corners must still be mitered. Machine stitch ribbon to collar and lapel along both sides of ribbon. Dots of fabric glue or strips of fusible web can hold ribbon into position for machine stitching. Construct collar and lapel including one edge of ribbon in ⅝ inch seam. Press, trim, press and pound with a tailor's clapper.

While this technique is faster than the hand stitching method first described, the ribbon does make seams bulky and more difficult to press flat. For this reason, I prefer the hand sewing technique.

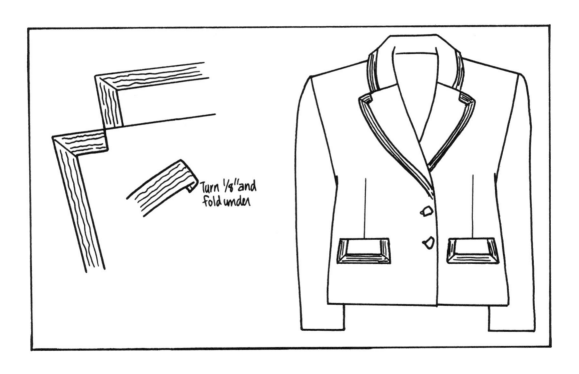

Turn ⅛" and fold under

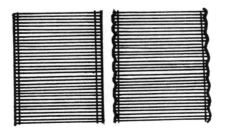

Trim as Embellishment

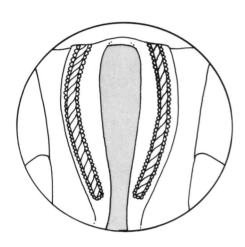

DECORATIVE TRIM

No matter how many times I find myself browsing in the trim department, this question always comes to mind... what do people do with this stuff? Not until I saw the work of San Francisco one of a kind designer, Kenneth King, did I ever become inspired. I am convinced that if one of King's pieces were on display for a month in Britex in San Francisco, the trim shelves would be bare.

King often uses two to four compatible trims in one piece, decorating a lapel, cuff or hat. King even stacks trims on top of each other for a more three dimensional effect. For trims to be stacked, the trims must not only be visually compatible but possess repeats which match. If the repeat is off slightly, the repeat can be adjusted by stretching or compressing with steam. To determine yardage, measure the length needed to decorate the desired area. Add 8 inches to allow for finishing on each end. If trim will be applied to a curve, make sure trim is not too rigid to go around curve.

Determine placement of trim and mark with tailor's tacks or chalk. Pin trim to well interfaced garment piece. If trim is to go around shawl collar, interface collar pieces, join at center back and mark for trim placement. If trim is to go over shoulder seam, join front and back bodice, interface behind intended trim area

FREE UP ALL ELEMENTS. SOME THICKER ELEMENTS MAY NEED TO BE SEPARATED.

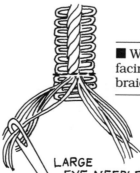

LARGE EYE NEEDLE

■ Wool felt, when you can find it, makes great interfacing for a collar which will be supporting rows of braid or beads.

Demonstrated on *Power Sewing* Video #8: *Embellishment.*

Trim as Embellishment

and mark for trim placement. Pin trim in place, leaving 4 inches on each end for finishing.

Run double thread through beeswax to strengthen. Sew trim on by hand with a stab stitch in a zigzag pattern on either side of the trim. Do not pull thread too tightly or fabric will buckle beneath the trim.

Trim which ends in a seam poses no problem in finishing. What is most outstanding in King's work is his ability to end trim anywhere with absolutely no visible fray or raw edges. The trim just seems to disappear.

King's secret is the following: Decide where you want the trim to end. Backstitch three to four times along the chain stitches holding trims together, above where you want the trim to end. Clip the chain stitching holding the trim elements together. Unravel chain stitching, freeing up all elements. Determine a pleasing pattern to end each element. Using a carpet needle (large eye, blunt point), pull trim elements through to the underside of the garment. If an element is composed of thick yarn, the element may have to be separated to allow it to pass through the eye of the needle. After all elements are brought through to the underside, hand stitch behind the hand sewn trim in a zigzag pattern to secure. Dot with SOBO glue.

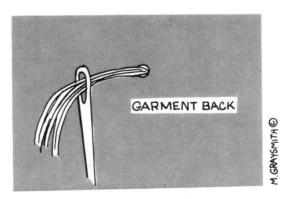

GARMENT BACK

M. GRAYSMITH ©

PULL THROUGH TO
UNDERSIDE

■ Before preshrinking fabric which is likely to ravel, wrinkle, and twist, such as Guatemalan cottons, machine baste lengthwise edges together. Fabric is easier to flatten for layout; machine basting is cut off when garment is cut out. Credit to: Helen Snell, Fairfax, California.

■ Before sewing braid to garment, preshrink in lukewarm water and air dry. Braid which Is not preshrunk will cause puckers at the first dry cleaning. Sewing braid or trim on curves is easier if it is shaped first with an iron.

Double and Triple Piping

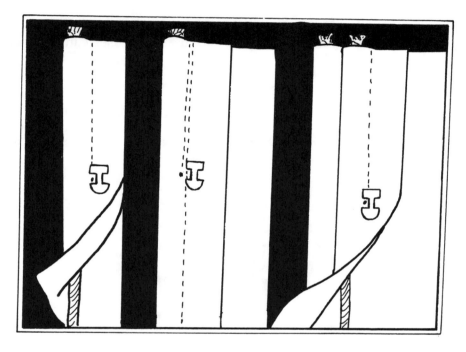

An outstanding jacket or vest can be the element that pulls an outfit together. A shawl collar becomes a real focal point when framed with double piping. Since piping thickens the seam and makes it less flexible, a piped seam within the interior of the garment such as a princess seam is seldom successful due to its rigidity unless the fabric itself has quite a bit of body. Piping an outside seam such as a collar is far less of a problem.

Piping a seam so that no stitches are visible even when pulling finished piping apart is possible when using a technique executed by one-of-a-kind designer Kenneth King, whose double piped bead embellished vests sell for $1,800, jackets for $3,500. Seem outrageous? Examine his work at Maxfield's in Los Angeles and you might change your mind.

Most seamstresses are familiar with $\frac{1}{4}$ inch polyester cording as filler for corded seams. In King's work,

he prefers to use rattail, a rounded rayon satin cord available in different colors and diameters in a well stocked trim department. King prefers rattail because it is flexible, has more body and will not crush. Rattail can be used "as is" in dry cleanable garments. In washable garments or if rattail is unavailable, polyester cording makes a suitable substitute. Preshrink cording in warm water and air dry if it is being used in a machine washable/dryable garment.

Covering your own cording gives unlimited options for varying effects. Solid color knits cut crossgrain offer the flexibility of a bias woven, using very little fabric. Striped knit strips, cut across the stripe, yield a checkerboard effect when used as piping. Satin lining strips cut on the bias give subtle shine against a flat weave. Silk charmeuse and silk crepe de chine strips when cut slightly off grain can offer almost the flexibility of bias without using nearly as much fabric. While bias

210

Double and Triple Piping

strips are always preferable for covering cording, cross-grain and off grain strips can work equally well if fabric is not rigid. Cut strips 3 inches wide for single and double piping, one inch wider for each additional piping row.

In a garment, piping will be required to go around curves and angles. While single or double piping can accomplish this, additional rows of piping can make the piping strip more rigid, depending on piping fabric, limiting its flexibility. While additional rows of piping can be quite attractive on straight edges, double piping offers more flexibility. Accordingly to Kenneth King, the secret to invisibly stitched piping lies in using two different placements of the needle.

Switch standard presser foot to a zipper foot. How close the needle is to the edge of the zipper foot is determined by using an adjustable zipper foot or varying the needle placement on a fixed zipper foot. Begin with the needle on the left side of the zipper foot. Adjust the zipper foot or the needle itself so that the needle is as close as possible to the inside curve of the zipper foot (Position #1).

Select fabric strip for the first piping which you want on the outer edge. A second piping will be closest to the garment itself. Sandwich the first piece of cording between the fabric strip. Cover the cord by sewing with the needle in Position #1, close to the inside of the zipper foot. The next step attaches the second strip of fabric to the first covered piping. Lay the piping you just covered in the center of the second piping strip, right sides together, the cord itself centered on the strip. Switch needle position so that needle is now away from the inside of the zipper foot, closer to the outside edge of the zipper foot (Position #2). Sew covered piping strip to second strip of fabric. Since you have switched needle position away from the inside of the zipper foot, you are now sewing a line of stitching closer to the pip-

ing than the first row of stitching which encased the piping.

To complete the second row of piping, sandwich cord between the wrong sides of the second piping strip, (which is already joined to the first covered piping). Switch the needle back to the inside curve of the zipper foot (Position #1). The second row of piping is now formed by sewing a line of stitching with needle in Position #1. If you are planning to use double piping on your garment, stop at this step. If you would like to join additional rows of piping, continue as above, always using the needle in Position #1 when wrapping the cording and using Position #2 when joining a new piece of fabric.

After the desired number of piping rows are com-

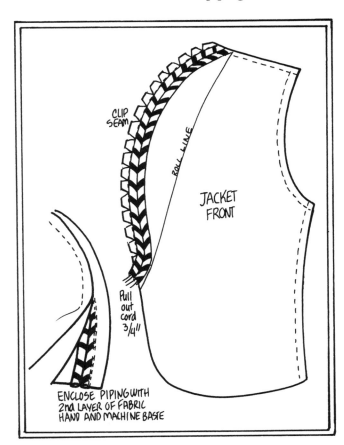

Double and Triple Piping

pleted, trim all excess seam allowances to ⅝ inch from the last row of stitching to the raw edges of the strips. Open the two outside seam allowances and trim the inside seam allowances to ¼ inch and ⅜ inch graded. The outside seam allowances remain at ⅝ inch. To give flexibility to seams, clip piping seam allowance at 1 inch intervals, clipping almost to the stitching line.

Pin piping to garment, right sides together, raw edges together. To prevent garment from curling, clip piping seam allowances every ¼ inch around curves and to within one thread of seam at corners. Keep in mind that piping on an outside edge needs to be larger to go around the edge smoothly without cupping. Push in slightly more piping than garment as you attach piping to garment.

To prevent piping from shortening seam, hand baste piping to garment. Machine stitching shortens seam with too much thread in the seam. Hand baste along last stitching line sewn to piping. Piping created in the King manner has a right and wrong side to it, therefore when used on a lapel, piping must leave the seam at the roll line, decorating the lapel and collar, not the lower part of the jacket. To accomplish this, lead the piping out into the seam allowance where the roll line intercepts the seamline. Cut off the piping at the end

of the seam allowance, where it is led out of the seam. To reduce bulk at the seam, pull cording out of the piping for ¾ inch at each piping end. Cut off cording. Piping will look corded to the end, but bulk will be eliminated where cording goes out of the seam.

To complete the piped seam, place the right side of the facing against the right side of the garment. Piping is sandwiched between the two layers. Pin with the garment side up so that you can see basting line. Still using the zipper foot, adjust the needle so that it is in Position #2, giving you the ability to sew closer to the piping than the hand basting which attached the piping to the garment. Using a slightly longer machine stitch to prevent the seam from shortening, sew seam slightly deeper than your hand stitching indicates, sewing closer to the piping.

Clip and grade all seams. Turn right side out. Press well but refrain from using a clapper on piped seams to prevent seam allowance imprint from showing on the right side.

Note—On a Chanel-inspired type jacket, all edges may be decorated with multiple piping by using facings all around the jacket including the hem.

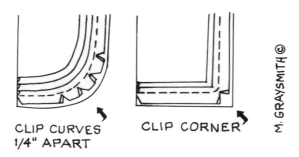

CLIP CURVES 1/4" APART   CLIP CORNER   M. GRAYSMITH ©

■ "Moire taffeta bias strip makes beautiful piping," says Barbara Kelly from the Sewing Workshop.

Fabric Painting

Even if you do not consider yourself artistic, you may surprise yourself with not only the results of a fabric painting project but the fun you will have doing it. Fabric paints have come a long way from "fabric dyes," and "puff paints," of years past. Permanent fabric paints now come in small containers, about the size of craft paints and need no additives to make the paints permanent. Some paints are permanent when dry, others require a few minutes heat set from the iron.

If you do not consider yourself an "artist," you may have better luck controlling the result with either a calligraphy pen or fabric paint markers. These new markers come in superfine, fine and broad points. The color is permanent when dry.

My very first project was the front of a white tuxedo shirt for my husband, decorated with a series of small ¼ inch geometric designs (circles, squares, triangles, and rectangles) spaced at random on the front pleats. Secondhand stores are a great source for tuxedo shirts. The small designs were accomplished by dipping a cal-

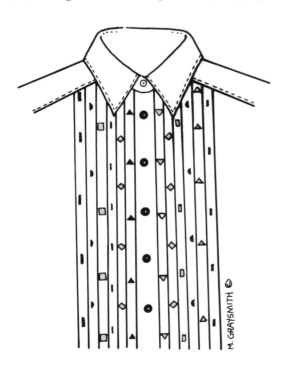

ligraphy pen with a medium point into small jars of DEKA fabric paints. After the paints are thoroughly dry, heat set the paint by covering the area with a presscloth and pressing with a medium high dry iron for about ten seconds. This tuxedo shirt goes with the other white shirts to the laundry and the designs remain sharp and clear.

All sizing must be removed from anything you are planning to paint. For washable items, merely run the item through the washer cycle with detergent. Place waxed paper or foil behind the layer you are painting. This prevents the paint from soaking through to other layers. Get inspiration for designs from children's coloring books, comics, stencils and quilt design books. Simplify designs as much as possible for the first project. Before beginning, it might not be a bad idea to practice on a man's handkerchief. Determine design placement by scattering colored paper clips or push pins on the garment. Consider painting only certain sections—like the yoke, collar and cuffs on a shirt.

If you feel timid in drawing, outline intended shapes with an air erasable pen. If you really want the shapes to stand out, outline all areas to be painted with a black fine point fabric marker. This was quite successful for a white linen shirt I decorated in Sante Fe motifs. After outlining small ½ inch size cactus, chili peppers, cowboy boots, mini mountains and cattle skulls, I filled in the outlines with a calligraphy pen and fabric paint. Start your first outlines in the least visible place on the garment. Gain confidence as you go along.

Let paints dry completely—overnight at least before pressing. Check instructions on paint containers to see whether air drying or heat set makes them permanent. Since I often combine the two, I heat set everything. You can now wear the garment. Some paints

Fabric Painting

recommend allowing the paints to set a week before washing.

Children love to fabric paint. All ages from 4 to 20 want to get in on the project. Purchase Fruit of the Loom, Sears or Penney's white short sleeve crew necks in a package of 3 for about $9. Since the T-shirts shrink a lot and kids like them BIG, size large seems the most popular. I buy a dozen at a time. They make great night shirts if nothing else.

Glitter paints are another option for a fun T-shirt or dressing up a simple cotton knit or wool jersey for a holiday occasion. These fabric paints are available in flat, glossy and neon. Glitter has been added to the paint to make it sparkle. These paints can be applied directly from the container since they come with a nozzle on the end. Sequins and small beads can be added to paint when wet as well. Children love these because they are easy to apply, give flashy results and instant gratification. Keep in mind that these paints sit on top of the fabric and are slightly stiffer soaking in and becoming part of the cloth like the earlier paints discussed.

To find fabric paints, check the notions departments, craft stores and art supply houses. Dharma Trading Company has a large selection (see Sources).

■ Turn fabric painted garment inside out to wash. Dryer okay for T-shirts.

THE BRIDAL
CHALLENGE

M. GRAYSMITH ©

The Wedding Dress

Every bride who has looked through bridal magazines or tried on wedding dresses has dreams of what she wants, but seldom are all of the features in one dress. Making your own wedding dress is one way to get exactly what you want.

Tackling a wedding dress can be intimidating until you have made one. Then you are a pro. According to wedding gown specialist Cheryl Gregg, If you can make a dress, you can make a wedding dress. "Think of a wedding gown like making a dress and putting lace on it."

Just looking at bridal fabrics can make a designer out of you. The selection is tremendous, whether you are on a tight budget or whether the sky is the limit. Let's start with one basic. No matter how elaborate the dress is, a base dress must be made upon which embellishment can be added. If you must have natural fabrics, then your base dress will be made of silk taffeta at $18 per yard or silk peau de soie. Peau de soie combines a dull satin finish with a beautiful luster, costing $20 to $40 per yard for fabric which is 45 inches wide. Check fabric requirement on your pattern since some patterns require 60 inch wide fabric for a very full skirt. Price per yard is usually a consideration since the average wedding dress calls for between 8 and 12 yards. If the style you have chosen is a plain one upon which little embellishment and simplicity make the statement, peau de soie makes an excellent choice since the fabric itself is so beautiful.

If you plan a more ornate style with an overskirt in lace or considerable lace embellishment, polyester satin or acetate satin might be your best choice price-wise. There will be little difference in the overall look of the dress, since the embellishment will get the attention. Polyester satin has a pearly luster, resists wrinkling and comes in 60 inch width—a requirement for some full designs. Polyester satin ranges between $13 per yard for single sided satin and $17 per yard for double sided satin. Polyester satin has a tendency to wrinkle and water spot. Once again these two factors might not be a drawback if you plan to use a fair amount of embellishment over the entire dress.

For a summer wedding, you might decide to use an embroidered Shiffli lace, which retails at about $30 per yard. This lace can be recognized because it is embroidered on very fine net and is bordered on one side. Since the yardage is already decorated with a border on one side, it is suitable for a dress with straight panels but not one with a train or curved skirt panels.

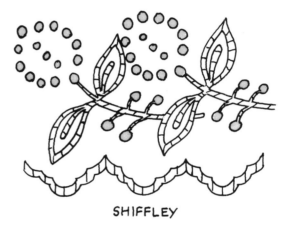

SHIFFLEY

The embroidered organzas are laces embroidered on organza with or without cut work. The yarn used has some sheen. Beaded and unbeaded varieties are available from $60 to $120 per yard for 60 inch wide fabric. These laces can be used as yardage for a bodice or cut apart and used as appliques on various parts of the dress such as sleeves, cuffs, bodice and skirt for decoration. If an embroidered organza is used on the bodice, underlining one of the base fabrics mentioned is appropriate. The sleeve can be underlined in organdy if a puffy sleeve is desired. To give the skirt a fuller appearance, lining is preferred to underlining. Perhaps the most traditional bridal fabric is the imported Alencon lace, which is lace that has been reembroidered over cording to give the pattern definition and depth. The yarn used is cotton and has little or no sheen. Alencon lace comes in varying widths: 4 inch, 9 inch, 12 inch, 18 inch and 36 inch. If you are using the Alencon lace over the bodice and sleeve, the 36 inch width is appropriate for this area.

The Wedding Dress

Narrower matching lace is usually available, and can be used as a border around the skirt or cut apart and used as appliques over the dress. If the piece you choose has a border on both lengthwise sides, you will only need yardage half the skirt width since the fabric can be cut apart to take advantage of the border on each side. The lace in the middle can be used for applique decoration. If you want a great deal of applique decoration over the dress, use a wider width Alencon lace so that the center can be used for appliques. Alencon lace comes in beaded and unbeaded varieties. Since the beading is done by hand, the beaded laces usually cost about twice as much as the unbeaded varieties. If you want only certain portions beaded, consider hand beading these yourself, using double thread which has been run through beeswax and a fine needle.

If you love Alencon lace and want to cover the entire dress with it, consider the domestic Alencon lace, unbeaded, 60 inches wide, retailing for $56 per yard. This is a good value for width and price.

ALENÇON

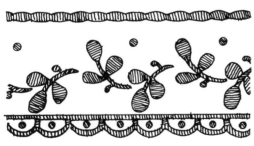

EMBROIDERED

"Good quality laces have a variety of textures, net designs, and motifs which can be clipped to make borders, panels, and individual motifs. In comparison, inexpensive laces have a flat, monotonous look," says Claire Shaeffer in *Fabric Sewing Guide*.

Many laces are available and worth serious consideration. Fabric shopping in person is worth a day's travel to a good source. If this is not possible, mail order is your next best bet.

Popular Bridal Laces

Re-embroidered Lace—any lace with designs outlined and emphasized with embroidery stitches. Alencon lace is often re-embroidered.

Venice—a heavy needlepoint lace with a floral design worked in high relief. Design is usually connected by picot edgings.

Alencon (ah-len-sun)—a solid floral design outlined by a heavy cord on a ground of fine net.

Chantilly—a delicate pattern of floral sprays or scrolls outlined by a fine untwisted thread.

Cluny—a heavy lace often made from thick cotton or man-made fibers. Motifs are usually paddles, wheels or poinsettias.

The Wedding Dress

Consider substituting many tiny buttons in place of a zipper.

Pearl buttons come with plastic and metal backing. Choose plastic backed pearl buttons for the dress. And guess what?

Little button loops come on a strip—now what could be better!?!

How much do you save by making your own wedding dress—about ¾ if you make it yourself or ½ if you use a dressmaker.

Depending on your taste, you may save hundreds or thousands of dollars. A point to remember is—PLAN AHEAD. When you use a dressmaker or sew the gown yourself, plan 3 to 6 months in advance.

The fabric of your dreams may need to be special ordered, if there is not enough on the bolt. This takes time. If you feel too pressed for time to take the project on yourself, use a dressmaker. By using a dressmaker, you can still get exactly what you want, while saving money as well. Ask a fabric store with a good selection of bridal fabrics for the names of bridal gown specialists. See examples of her work. Make sure she is equipped with good fitting skills as well as fabric technical skills. Make sure that she is able to work within your time table. Call references. Consider this time well spent—after all—this is YOUR WEDDING DRESS.

Whether you make the dress yourself or have it made, save the large fabric scraps. These make a beautiful christening dress or bride's ensemble for a doll.

■ An iron in perfect condition is essential when working on bridal fabrics. This hint from Claire Shaeffer's *Fabric & Sewing Guide* is worth its weight in gold. "If the iron is clogged and doesn't steam properly, clean the water reservoir. Fill it with ¼ cup white vinegar and ¼ cup water; allow it to heat for 3-5 minutes. Unplug and adjust to steam setting. Place the iron flat on a rack in the sink and allow the solution to drip for half an hour. Rinse several times. Repeat if necessary."

The Wedding Dress

Before you cut into your fabric, pattern alterations are a must and a pretest of the bodice and one sleeve is advisable. An hour or so spent at this stage saves hours later. Your biggest fear in a wedding dress is cutting into the lace. Lace does not ravel, so it can be cut like any other fabric.

Experiment with needle size, using size 12 and 14 sharps. Use the smaller size if you can do so without skipped stitches. Both polyester and cotton thread work equally well. Purchase good quality thread to eliminate thread breakage. Hold fabric firmly from front and back as you sew. If you are using lace embellished with beads and sequins, use a size 14 sharp needle for machine sewing. The sewing machine is able to sew through sequins but not beads. Remove beads on the path of the needle. After the seam is stitched, if any gaps in the embellishment appear, a few beads can be sewn on by hand from the outside.

Cutting and sewing bridal fabrics are really no different than working with other fabrics. Keep this in mind before you make your first cut. If you can sew a dress, you can sew a bridal dress. Keep your hands and machine clean. Cover the floor under your sewing area with a sheet to keep the cloth clean as it falls away from the sewing surface.

Many pattern instructions call for enclosed seams in the wedding dress. Wedding specialist, Cheryl Gregg, advises finishing seams with an overlock stitch or binding seams with a Hong Kong finish. Enclosed seams make alterations difficult.

Darts can be sewn by one of three methods: (1) Traditional dart method—good for plain fabrics; (2) Dart width cut out from the center of dart, following pattern design, butting newly cut edges together; (3) Dart sewn in traditional method, then hand appliqued over dart to disguise existence.

Never use a fusible interfacing on a bridal dress. Opt for organza, voile or a stiffer nonfusible interfacing in an area which needs a great deal of support

Undergarments may be worn under the wedding dress or built into the dress itself. Soft bra cups designed for wedding garments are available. Line up the dart in the bra cup with the dart in the dress. The point of the cup lines up with the apex of the dart. Underslips may be purchased or constructed. In either case, a

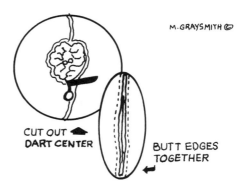

M. GRAYSMITH ©

CUT OUT ← DART CENTER

BUTT EDGES TOGETHER

smoother line in the dress is possible if the slip is attached to the dress itself. Half slips are made by sandwiching a layer of net between two layers of taffeta. The net gives support and the taffeta prevents the dress from catching on the net or scratching against the legs. Do not make a slip which is too full for the dress, or the dress will tend to ride up on the slip. Determine placement of the slip in the fitting process. Attach to lining or underlining at the side seams.

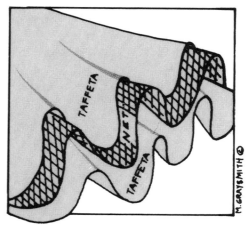

A LAYER OF NET BETWEEN 2 LAYERS OF TAFFETA FOR BRIDAL SLIP

The Wedding Dress

Horsehair interfacing in the hem gives the hem a nice roll as well as added body. Cut horsehair 1 inch wider than hem. Width of hem is determined by garment fabric. A lightweight fabric such as taffeta looks well with a ½ inch hem. A heavy fabric such as a satin needs a deep 4 inch hem. Butt the edge of the horsehair against the crease of the hem shaping the horsehair with your hands to follow the curve in the hem. Do not try to shape the horsehair by pressing, since pressing directly on the horsehair causes the horsehair to lose some of its body. Attach horsehair by machine to the top of the hem. The horsehair will extend 1 inch past the raw edge of the hem. Hand stitch hem in place with a short fine needle, stitching ¼ inch to ½ inch apart. If the skirt is underlined or lined, attach hem to lining or underlining only, making all hem stitches invisible. If you desire slight transparency in certain sections of the bodice, the entire dress may have to be attached to the netting.

To support the weight of the dress, a strong but soft netting is essential. Although a wide variety of netting is available, cotton English netting is the strongest to support weight. At $17 per yard and 72 inches wide, English netting is your best investment.

Tracking down information on bridal dresses isn't easy. Claire Shaeffer's book *Fabric Sewing Guide* is an excellent reference as well as having hard core information on sewing with laces. *How To Make Your Own Wedding Gown* by Claudia Ein gives the most information (devotes a whole book to it, in fact) but is out of print. A well stocked library, used bookstore, or design student resource center is your best bet for this one.

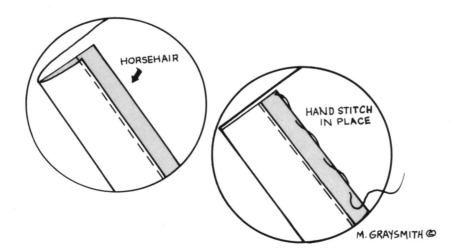

HORSEHAIR

HAND STITCH IN PLACE

M. GRAYSMITH ©

The Wedding Dress

Think of appliques as the icing on the cake, applied last after the dress is fitted, construction finished, and hem completed. Do not be afraid to cut lace apart for appliques or shaping at hemline. Simply cut the net or organza—holding the lace patterns together, away from the lace. Sharp embroidery scissors will allow you to trim close. No further finishing is necessary.

Keep in mind that laces with large motifs are more difficult to position. If you fall in love with a lace with a large motif, determine yardage by positioning bodice and sleeve pieces on the lace itself.

Appliques should look as though they float on the surface of the garment. Machine stitching is unable to achieve this result; therefore, appliques should be sewn on to the garment by hand with a fine needle and double thread, which has been run through beeswax. Attach appliques with a loose backstitch at ½ inch or so intervals. Too many hand stitches take away from the applique float appearance.

HAND SEW APPLIQUE TO DRESS

MAGAZINES HAVE GREAT IDEAS

M. GRAYSMITH ©

CUT OUT APPLIQUE

Bridal magazines are a great source for inspiration in placement of lace applique work. Sleeves, hemlines and necklines are naturals. If you would like to frame the entire neckline with lacework, pin front and back bodice pattern pieces together at shoulder seams. Position cut apart lace appliques around the neckline, outside of the seam allowances, within the bodice itself. Determine where the appliques will join each other and join them by hand. After the dress is complete, the joined applique work shaped to fit the neckline can be overlaid onto the bodice. Pin into place. Hand stitch applique neckline onto bodice.

Bridal Veils and Headpieces

Making a bridal veil and headpiece is an opportunity for a fast rewarding project with good money savings. A bridal headpiece and veil combination costing $120, can be made for $30, more than a ¾ savings. Continue the same feeling of the gown into the headpiece. A simple gown calls for a simple headpiece. An elaborately embellished gown calls for a well embellished headpiece.

Veil length and dress length must be compatible. Gown specialist, Cheryl Gregg, speaking from a wealth of experience recommends these lengths. The fingertip veil is perhaps the most versatile since it works with most gowns, and especially well with an ankle length gown or a floor length gown. The fingertip veil requires 2 yards of 72 inch width netting. A floor length gown works better with a fuller veil of the same length, calling for 2 yards of 108 inch width netting. Chapel length veiling to the floor can also be worn with the floor length gown in a three tiered veil needing 4 yards of 108 inch width netting. Tiered veils are always layered with the long veil on top. Shorter veils of different lengths are used to support the long veil and give more "poof." A cathedral length gown with a train can use a cathedral length three tiered veil using 6 yards of 144 inch width netting. If your gown has a great deal of back detailing, try not to cover it up with too much veiling.

Veils are shaped In four basic shapes: U-shaped, oval, circular, and blusher. Extra layers (poof) may be added under top layers for fullness. Since netting does not ravel, veil finishing on edges is not mandatory. If edging is desired, edge veil before gathering. Using a grooved presserfoot and the widest zigzag, machine stitch over a topstitching thread, pulling slightly on netting from behind the foot. Veil decoration is done before the veil is gathered to the headpiece. Glue lace, appliques, pearls, sequins, or rhinestones onto veil if desired. A wide variety of headpiece forms are available ranging in price from $4-$7. Glue ribbon or appliques over headpiece with a hot glue gun or milliners glue. Do not use water soluble glue or the form will soften.

To attach veil to headpiece, machine gather netting to size.

Hand stitch veil to headpiece with double thread run through beeswax. Glue or sew elasticized bridal loops into headpiece at center front and center back and sides so that combs or bobby pins can be positioned where needed.

BALLERINA LENGTH FINGER-TIP LENGTH FULL-FASHIONED FINGER-TIP LENGTH CHAPEL LENGTH CATHEDRAL LENGTH

Bridal Accessories

Accessories to the bridal ensemble are important as a finishing touch. Accessory choice is important to create harmony.

When choosing shoes, look for ones which mirror detailing in the dress. If you can't find or afford the perfect ones, decorate a plain pair by simply gluing on one or two lace appliques, beads, or other detailing from the dress.

Comfortable shoes on your wedding day are a must. You will be standing for long periods of time. If the heel is too high, not only will your feet hurt, your walk will appear awkward, maybe even causing you to trip on the many layers you are wearing. A medium heel pump is always a good choice for a long dress. If your dress is shorter, consider an open-backed shoe. Dress length should be determined with you wearing the shoe for that day.

Even though your shoes are white, they will probably need to be dyed slightly to match the color of your dress. Take a fabric swatch with you to the shoemaker. Shoe color appears different under artificial light. Let the shoe dyer know whether the shoes will be worn primarily inside or outside.

Make sure that you have everything with you when you give your dress a final fitting, including the bra and slip. This is a good opportunity to give your dress a trial run. Check for wandering straps, smooth hems and anything that is uncomfortable or could detract from the ensemble. Check in natural light to make sure all colors are compatible.

Purchase an extra pair of hose, good insurance for last minute runs. While gloves are optional, they can be quite beautiful with a wedding dress. Weather dictates fabric content for gloves. While warm weather options are open crochet or cotton, cool weather fabrics include soft leather, taffeta and stretch satin.

Don't let your choice of earrings detract from your headpiece. If your veil is well decorated, a simple button earring is the most compatible. The headdress and earrings should not compete for the eye's attention. Whereas if the headdress and hairstyle are simple, an eye-catching drop earring can draw attention to the face.

If the sleeve is long, forget a bracelet, but if the arm is bare, a beautiful pearl bracelet can be stunning.

All of the little things count, adding up to a complete, beautiful ensemble.

"A couple of weeks ago, I was looking in on one of our sewing classes and started noticing the broad range of women in the class: two black women, one Jewish woman, two Irish women, and one I'm not sure. The thing that struck me was how they were working together, toward one common goal, each separate but more than willing to help each other.

"For those two hours, color, religion, or looks meant nothing to these women. They were learning and doing something they loved."

Harvey Federman who owns Sew Right Sewing Machines in Bayside, New York, continues:

"I started to think of all the women in all the sewing guilds, quilting clubs, and homemaker groups who get together to do charitable sewing for AIDS babies and children's hospitals. It occurred to me that of all the reasons I'm aware of that women get together for sewing could be the biggest and truest of them all. Sewing has nothing to do with meeting men, losing weight, the Republican Party, drunk driving or other groups. Sewing is about women getting together with other women to enjoy each other and the craft they love. And it occurs to me for a moment, what a great business I'm in."

■ A strip of interfacing behind the zippers will prevent the seam from stretching during zipper application, making the zipper seem higher on the waistline.

Dolman sleeve jacket *is made from a Stretch and Sew pattern from two large (45 inch square) Nicole Miller scarves. Entire jacket is underlined in flannelette (see page 7). Flannelette on front, front placket and facing are interfaced with fusible knit tricot. Double piping (see page 210) is used on shawl collar (see page 14). Contrast collar and cuffs (see page 25) are made from textured polyester. Fimo buttons are used as accents.*

Black raw silk double breasted jacket is made from a Burda pattern. Front and side front are fused with fusible tricot, facing fused with Whisper Weft (see pages 8-9). Shawl collar is double piped with a bias satin strip and striped knit strip cut at right angles to stripe (see pages 210-211). Buttonhole welt pocket (see **Power Sewing** page 180) uses interfaced stripe knit cut on bias for pocket welt strips. Antique buttons are used with hand worked buttonholes (see **Power Sewing** 152 for technique).

1. This double silk chiffon oblong scarf with mitered silk charmeuse binding (see page 227 for technique) is a copy of the one seen in New York for $440.

2. Attractive scarves can be made (see page 226) from polyester, rayon and silk chiffon (listed consecutively) if the fabric drapes adequately. All three scarves are oblong. Off white scarf has occasional pearl embellishment.

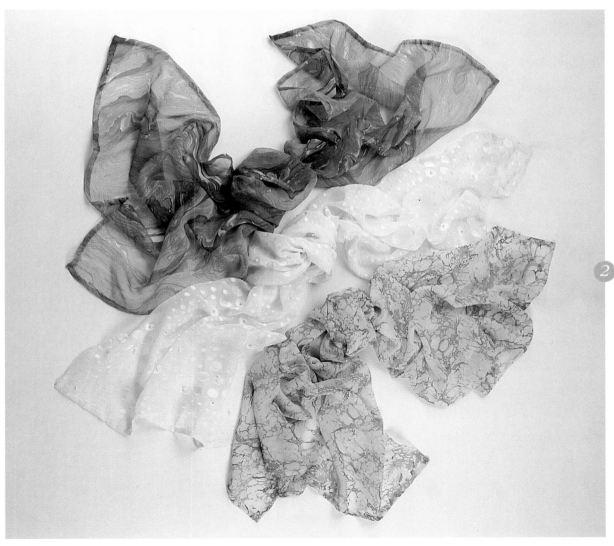

1. **Both vests, made from a man's vest pattern from Burda,** are constructed using vest technique (see page 232). Black vest fabric was created by joining rows of elastic using lapover technique. Shawl collar is double piped (see pages 210-211). Vest is embellished with antique Japanese sequins—from General Bead in San Francisco—no mail order—(see pages 200-203 for technique). Grey vest is made from metallic silk organza on one side and mesh fishnet on the other.

2. **Fun weekend look in checked wool walking shorts** is possible from a Burda pattern, white blouse (purchased) and simple Burda man's vest. Pleats are constructed to stay closed over tummy (see pages 69 and 101). **Black cotton tapestry vest** is trimmed with striped cotton knit strips cut at right angles to the stripe using the same techniques used for leather trim (see page 211 in Power Sewing). Foolproof flap pocket completes detailing (for technique see page 76).

Luxury
Unessentials

■ When you find a pattern you love, preserve its life by fusing to Pellon. Use dry iron to fuse.

Hand Rolled Scarf

The importance of scarves and shawls is here to stay. One doesn't have to be an excellent seamstress to make a scarf. Dimensions are important as well as finishing techniques.

A piece of fabric 2 yards long will make two well-proportioned oblong scarves by cutting the fabric in half lengthwise. If you are short, a fabric length of 1¾ yards is more in proportion.

Beautiful scarves are not seamed, so don't even think of buying one yard, cutting in half and seaming. Make one scarf for you and one for a gift. If you want a large shawl, use a 2 yard length of fabric 45 inches to 60 inches—its full width, perfect in a fabric such as wool jersey. If you want a small scarf to decorate a ponytail, a half yard of 36 inch fabric makes a great hair tie, perfect in chiffon or silk crepe de chine.

Square scarves can be made from 1¼ yard of 45 inch width fabric or 1⅝ yard of 60 inch fabric. Wool crepe, rayon challis and silk crepe de chine make beautiful square scarves.

A scarf with a hand-rolled hem can be an heirloom, worth the time spent hand sewing. To make the hand sewing process easier, machine sew around all edges a half inch from the edge of the fabric with an "even feed" foot. This foot will prevent puckering. Do not try to sew closer to the edge than ½ inch or the needle will push the fine fabric into the bobbin opening.

Trim close to machine stitching with rotary blade or small sharp scissors. Go to the pressing surface. Create tension on the end of the machine stitching; pull gently letting the raw edges roll under. Press into position. Pin periodically.

Hand stitch with a fine needle and silk thread using a running stitch or a blind stitch.

This information was the result of a collaboration of Marci Tilton and myself one summer afternoon at my summer house in Westport, California.

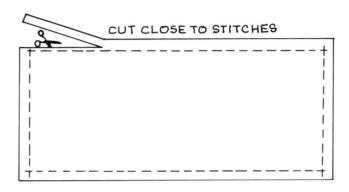

CUT CLOSE TO STITCHES

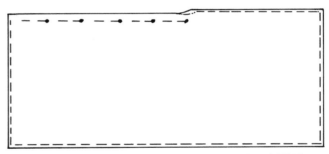

PULL STITCHES TO CREATE ROLLED HEM
PIN IN PLACE

FINISH WITH RUNNING STITCH OR BLIND
STITCH HEM

M. GRAYSMITH ©

Chiffon Scarf with Double Mitered Satin Binding

One of the most alluring examples of the double miter is the 72 inch long silk chiffon scarf with 2 inch wide contrasting color silk charmeuse binding. To make this scarf you will need 2 yards of silk chiffon and $1\frac{1}{4}$ yards of silk charmeuse. If you would like the contrasting strip to be one continuous strip without seaming you will need $5\frac{1}{8}$ yards (this is not necessary or practical fabric-wise unless you are making several scarves.) These scarves retailed in the Fall of '88 for $400.

The width of the binding can vary for personal taste. The formula for cut-binding is two times the desired finish width plus $\frac{1}{2}$ inch. Cut length of binding, desired width to go around the entire chiffon piece plus 4

inches. Fold binding strip in half with right sides out and press. Mark $1\frac{3}{4}$ inches away from the raw edge all around the chiffon scarf with chalk.

Start in the middle of one long scarf side, with one thickness of satin binding starting $\frac{1}{2}$ inch from the raw edge of the binding. Place right side of the binding against the wrong side of the scarf. Since chiffon does not really have a right and wrong side, in this case it makes no difference. Bring the raw edge of the binding $\frac{1}{4}$ inch past the $1\frac{3}{4}$ inch chalk marking on the scarf. Therefore the raw edge of the binding is $1\frac{1}{2}$ inches away from the raw edge of the scarf. Join bind-

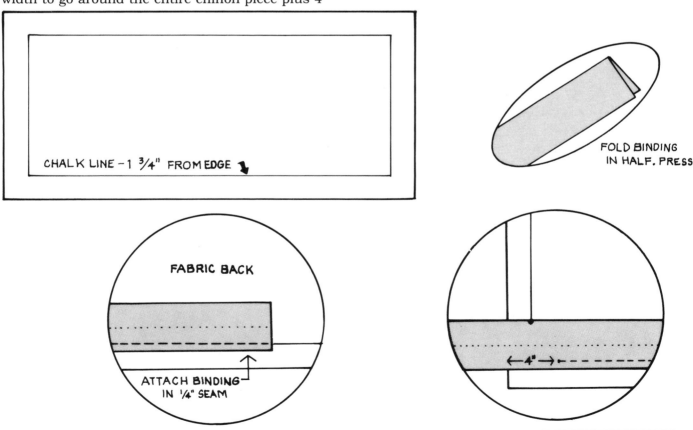

CHALK LINE – $1\frac{3}{4}$" FROM EDGE

FOLD BINDING IN HALF. PRESS

FABRIC BACK

ATTACH BINDING IN $\frac{1}{4}$" SEAM

←4"→

Chiffon Scarf with Double Mitered Satin Binding

ing to scarf in a ½ inch seam. Continue joining binding to the scarf in this manner until 4 inches from the scarf corner. Take work out of the machine.

With binding folded in half lay binding against the scarf. On both halves of the right side of the satin binding, mark with chalk where the two chalk mark lines on the scarf intersect at the corner. From this mark, measure down on the binding toward the unsewn end, twice the width of the desired finished binding (in this case 4 inches). Mark both halves of the binding, on the right side with chalk.

With right sides together and binding open to full width match chalk markings, begin angular stitching ¼ inch from raw edge of binding. Sew from chalk mark to point, marked by depressed crease in the binding. At point, hand walk one stitch horizontally and turn stitching line to angle up to the other half of the binding. Stop stitching ¼ inch from the cut edge of the binding. All angular stitching is done through binding alone; none on the scarf. Reposition satin binding on chiffon, bringing raw edge of the binding ¼ inch past the 1¾ inch chalk marking on the scarf. Continue stitching down lengthwise side and one stitch into the

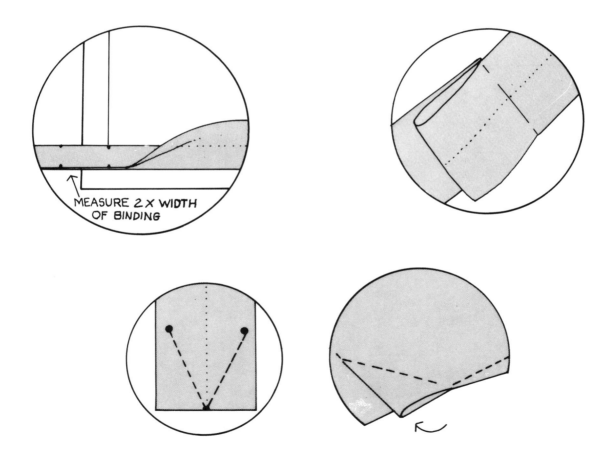

MEASURE 2 X WIDTH OF BINDING

Chiffon Scarf with Double Mitered Satin Binding

corner, pivot and continue stitching across crosswise end of the scarf. After each miter, turn binding right side out to make sure you positioned corner correctly. Four inches from the next corner, miter the next corner as you've just done with the first.

After all corners are mitered around the scarf and the ends of the binding are joined, you are ready to complete the satin charmeuse binding on the right side of the scarf. Trim excess fabric from the inside corners of the sewn miters. Fold in ¼ inch on the silk charmeuse binding and pin into position just covering the original line of stitching. Topstitch or hand stitch in place. Press and pound binding flat with the clapper.

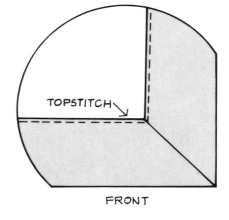

FRONT

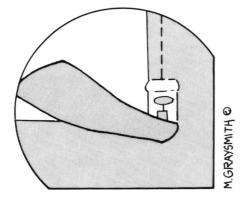

M. GRAYSMITH ©

■ Don't feel guilty about updating your sewing equipment. Think of how much you save on psychiatry.

Classy Clutch

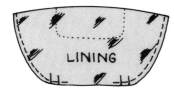

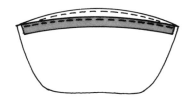

JOIN LINING TO PURSE

Why spend a bundle on a purse when in three hours you have exactly what you want? Shopping for the right purse can take three hours itself, especially for a special event purse. Ghee's (see Sources) puts out a large assortment of purse patterns as well as frames, fasteners and other findings needed to make the purse a class act. I became particularly motivated when I spotted a pony skin clutch purse in a New York catalogue for $360 which closely resembled Ghee's Classic Elegance purse pattern.

If you are making the large clutch without straps, you will need ½ yard of 45 inch fabric (check out the latest in imported fake furs—using Schmetz 90/14 H needle), ½ yard of polyester fleece, 1½ yards of fusible web, ¾ yard of lining, 1 yard of fusible interfacing, and one 12 inch tubular aluminum frame (see Sources).

Fuse polyester fleece to fashion fabric with a layer of fusible web. Fuse fleece to wrong side of frame covering strips. Fuse interfacing to wrong side of lining pieces. An inside pocket is a real plus. Shorten pattern pocket piece by 2 inches; cut out of lining and interface with fusible interfacing.

Form bottom tucks on each purse and lining piece. To make the purse more like a ready-to-wear one, cut 3 inch strips shaped to the upper purse of lightweight real or man-made leather or suede. Topstitch leather strips to lining on bottom leather edge. Topstitch pocket onto lining.

With right sides together, join two layers of outer purse fabric. With right sides together, join two layers

Classy Clutch

of lining fabric, leaving a 4 inch hole in the bottom for turning.

Turn in 1/2 inch on each end of frame covering strips. If fabric is too heavy, eliminate this step but do not trim off 1/2 inch turnunder. Fold strips in half lengthwise, with right sides out. Place double layered strip against right side of the top edge of the purse, 1/4 inch from each seam on the purse end. Sew with 1/4 inch seam.

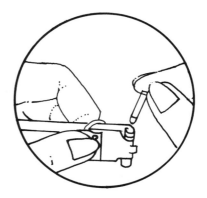

Join lining to purse at upper edge by placing right side of purse against right side of purse lining. Sew 1/4 inch seam. Turn purse right side out through 4 inch unsewn seam in bottom of purse lining. Close opening with a slip stitch.

Slide frame through casing matching opposite ends of frame. Press ends together to align holes. You may need pliers and a strong arm. Slide rivets through holes.

If your fabric was heavy and therefore too bulky to turn under when making frame covering strips, cover ends with a 1x2 inch piece of leather. Machine or hand sew with a leather needle.

M.G.

Vest from Start to Finish

The vest is almost more of an accessory than a piece of clothing. Some form of the vest is always in fashion. If you like your vest oversized, choose a man's vest pattern. Most fitted women's vests appear skimpy unless you like very close fitting clothes. A loose man's vest can be worn over a blouse or a sweater, often providing a final touch to an ensemble. A vest can be casual or dressy depending upon the fabric and how elaborately it is embellished.

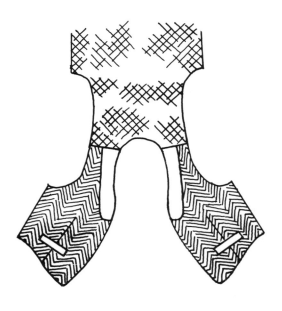

Most vests are cut with a fashion fabric front and a lighter weight lining fabric back. If the fashion fabric is not too heavy, the vest is a perfect candidate for eliminating the front facing and cutting the front double. If you plan to pipe the outside edges of the vest, facings can be eliminated since the piping will protect the garment from lining roll out at garment edges. Whatever you decide, two separate vests will be constructed at shoulder seams. The vests will then be joined where one will become the vest lining. Complete darts or princess seaming in vest and vest lining. Interface. Complete designer details such as collar, back belting, and welt pockets. Join detailing to outer vest pieces. Join outer vest front and back pieces at shoulder seams. Join vest lining front and back pieces at shoulder seams. Press seams open.

If piping is planned, pipe outside edges of outer vest. In accordance with the turn of the cloth principle, trim 1/8 inch away from vest lining at armholes and all outside vest edges. Do not trim side seams.

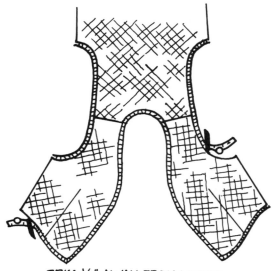

Place outer vest joined at shoulder seams on table with right sides up (side seams are not sewn). On top of this, place vest lining joined at shoulder seams, wrong side up. Place the right side of the lining vest against the right side of the outer vest. Pin the two vests together at armholes and vest front edges. Begin pinning 3 inches from side seam along lower front edge. Pin up one side of the front, around the neckline and down the other side of the front, stopping 3 inches from the side seam on the opposite front. Pin vest together with lining side up so that the feed dog can assist you in easing the outer vest to the slightly smaller lining vest (turn of the cloth principle).

Sew vest areas just pinned at 5/8 inch. Clip curved seams. Press seams open. Grade and trim seams. Side seams on outer and lining vest are not yet sewn. Turn

TRIM 1/8" AWAY FROM LINING. DO NOT TRIM SIDE SEAMS.

Vest from Start to Finish

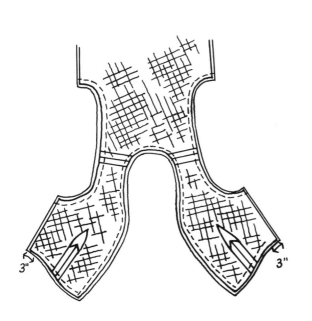

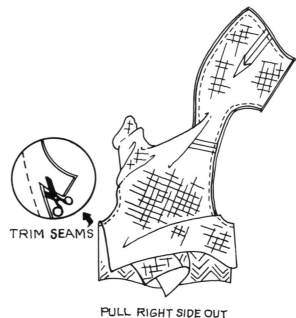

TRIM SEAMS

PULL RIGHT SIDE OUT
THROUGH SHOULDER

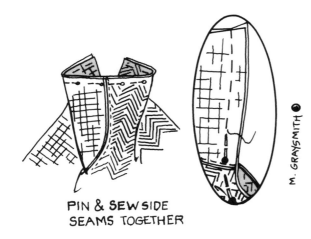

PIN & SEW SIDE
SEAMS TOGETHER

M. GRAYSMITH

vest right side out by reaching from back to front through the shoulder seam. Pull each front out separately through the shoulder.

Press and pound all sewn areas flat with a tailor's clapper. To close side seams, pin outer vest front and back side seams together. Match armhole seams well. Continue pinning front and back side seams of lining together. Sew each side seam continuously from outer vest to lining vest. Press seams open. Trim triangle of bulk from underarm seam joint.

The bottom of the vest can now be closed by a hand stitch or partially machine sewn by turning each side back on itself.

Press and pound well all outside edges. The vest makes a great canvas for embellishment. See beading and trim sections for ideas. Choose buttons carefully and to scale.

KNOW THYSELF

NO

YES

Shoulder Emphasis

a.maeda

■ New Zealand designer Rosaria Hall gives shoulder seams distinction without shoulderpads by initially sewing shoulder seams at ¼ inch with right sides together. On outside of the garment, all thicknesses are pinched together and sewn again at ⅜ inch, creating an elevated ridge along the shoulder line. A more pronounced ridge can be created by allowing for a 1 inch shoulder seam. Sew initial seam at ⅜ inch. Pinch ⅝ inch to the outside and sew again.

Pear Shaped Silhouette

Don't feel you're alone with the pear shaped figure. Your figure type is in the majority. With a few key tips, you can give the illusion of top and bottom halves in perfect balance. Since the bottom half of the body is not your favorite, keep the eye emphasis from the waist up. Accessories are great friends to the pear shape. Large earrings. interesting necklaces, and beautiful scarves are excellent tools to lift the eye up to your "better half." Interesting bodice styling such as wrap and asymmetrical are also effective tools for directing the eye upward. Shoulderpads are a must; they are the easiest way to take off ten pounds and give balance to the lower half of the body. Try these other tips for successful pear shape dressing:

Never overfit the bottom half of the body; this only draws attention to the hips. Full pleated or gathered trousers are better than straight leg, stirrup, legging, or jean cuts.

Loose, man-type shirts, tunics, and long loose sweaters can hide a multitude of sins. Pair these with tight fitting pants or straight skirts and the full hip is hidden under the loose top.

Semi-fitted or full cut jackets and coats are best bets for the pear shape. Overly fitting merely outlines the natural silhouette which we are balancing with other tricks.

Avoid hip and seat pockets on skirts and pants. Keep the styling simple on the bottom half.

Skirts with controlled fullness are your best bet; A-line, circle, and gored skirts make great choices. Drapey fabrics are a must.

If your waist is small, good belts with important buckles are also an asset.

If you love shoes (who doesn't?), a shoe color repeated in the bodice is a great way to focus the eye away from "problem area." Match hose color to skirt or pant to elongate the silhouette.

Don't forget makeup and an attractive hairstyle. A great face keeps the eye from wandering anywhere else.

■ Keep only pieces which make you feel great in your closet. If you don't feel good in an item, get rid of it. Life is too short not to enjoy the moment.

Inverted Triangular Silhouette

The inverted triangle, sometimes described as "the wedge," is characterized by broad shoulders and small hips.

These women have the least style difficulty since this figure type is the one designers love. Correct fit in the shoulder and neckline area is crucial.

Watch for gaping necklines and horizontal stress lines across the shoulder and upper sleeves which may be too tight. Avoid boat necks and yokes. Both raglan and dolman sleeves are flattering. Consider tapering out some of the fullness under the arm if a dolman sleeve starts at the waist.

Pattern necklines to look for are V-necks, with or without lapels, scoop neck, cowl or funnel necks. Look for detailing and diagonal lines. Full circle skirts and fanny wraps give balance and are worn well by the inverted triangle figure. The most flattering silhouette for this figure is a full bodice with a straight skirt.

Straight chemise or float dresses that hang from the shoulders are good as is almost any garment that hangs from the shoulder. Dropped waistline styles are also flattering. Best jacket/coat lengths for the wedge are: High hip, ¾, ⅞, or full length.

Very broad shoulders look better by slightly narrowing the shoulder line on extended shoulders or puffed sleeves.

Broad shouldered short/stocky women should avoid puffed sleeve and extended shoulder treatments.

Long jewelry, scarves, and shawls create a good diagonal line. Fanny wraps are a good trick to try for balance.

Full or skinny pants with plenty of style detailing are for you. Take advantage of it while giving your figure balance as well.

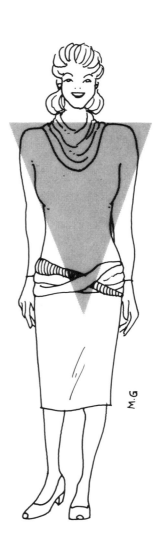

■ "All garments have both inside and outside lines. The outside lines are the silhouette or shape that the garment gives your body, what you look like from a distance. The inside lines form the design details of a garment within the silhouette. They can be formed by seams, braid, contrasting inserts, a line of buttons, a ruffle..." says Clare Revelli, author of *Style & You*.

Hourglass Silhouette

The hourglass figure is characterized by a full bust and full hips with obvious waist definition. Look for patterns with diagonal seams, asymmetrical and wrapped stylings.

Choose slightly tapered jackets with as many seams as possible. To avoid the sausage effect, jackets should never be too tight. Peplums or jackets with a slight flare under the waist flatter the hourglass figure. Narrow lapels and shawl collars narrow the figure with vertical style lines. Avoid patch pockets on bust hip or seat, as well as bulky or balloon style sweaters. Cardigan styling is excellent in jackets, vests or sweater. Sweaters which end at the hipbone or full hip are best.

Lightly taper body skimming jackets or coats, but never too tight. Add a center back seam on jackets and coats.

The best jacket length is high hip.

The short waisted, heavy hourglass figure looks slimmer in A-line and princess styles. Cardigan and tailored jackets are best at high hip length. Slim skirts without a waistband, overblouses and tunic tops create a longer silhouette. Avoid gathered skirts and patch pockets, fussy details and large collars.

The hourglass figure is enhanced by longer than knee-length skirts; the sweep of a long skirt makes the waist seem smaller, person taller.

Try skirts with flare, gores, soft, controlled fullness, unpressed pleats, in fabrics with drape such as wool jersey, crepe, double knits, suede and matte jersey.

Handkerchief hems and asymmetrical draped, sarong styles on skirts are good as well.

Pants should be straight legged or tapered (take in pant at knee), with pleats or soft gathers. If you are round in the high hip, use gathers in back.

Soft pants and a top with a peplum effect (belted) are a good look for taller figures.

Choose one color or close value color schemes in tops and bottoms.

V necklines are best; create this effect with jewelry, scarves, shirts worn open at the neck. Wear jackets and blouses with the collar up, sleeves rolled up.

■ You will accomplish a great deal if you can get rid of anything in your closet you don't love.

Rectangular Silhouette

The rectangular shaped figure is characterized by straight up and down proportions with little waist definition. Any belting or seaming at the waist will be a disappointment because the waist will not appear small. Loose belts at high hip or fanny wraps are much more flattering. Important buckles are eye-catching and detract from large waist.

Shoulder detailing and fullness at skirt hem help define the waist and make it appear smaller.

Create a long, lean look with straight skirts and long sweaters or tunic tops, belted closely or not at all. Chemise or dropped waist patterns are flattering on this figure since there is no attempt at waist emphasis. Raglan and dolman are the most flattering sleeve styles for the rectangular figure.

Emphasize the long, lean look with long scarves, opera length beads. Keep the eye going in a vertical direction.

Fitted jackets should be avoided. Give preference to straight hip length jackets with shawl collars or low lapels if long waisted. Bias cut skirts are flattering as long as they are smooth at the waist, with no detailing. Use yokes rather than waist gathers and pleats.

The rectangular figure type is often accompanied by a small bottom. Avoid fitted pants patterns in favor of full pants styles in drapey fabric to camouflage the small seat.

A close fitting pant can be worn with a loose long sweater, tunic, or overblouse loosely belted—anything which is able to camouflage the comparison of the small bottom with the tummy, which seems large in comparison.

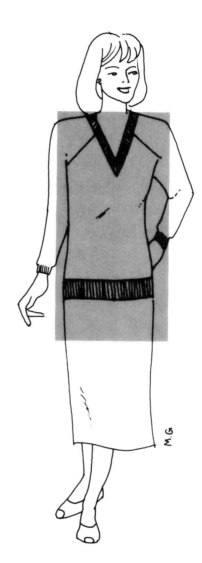

■ If you have limited closet space, purge twice a year.

Cylindrical Silhouette

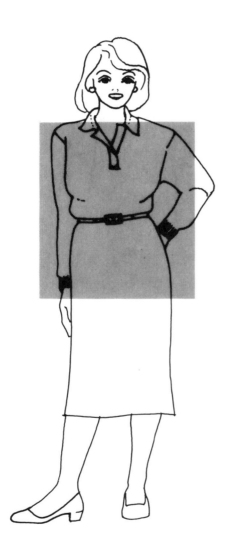

Many women feel they don't fit into any of the four figure type categories: hourglass, pear, inverted triangle, or rectangle. For those women, we will add a fifth category—"the cylinder." This is the large size figure. Like any figure type, the cylinder has assets to accent and liabilities to camouflage.

Large women usually make two mistakes: Wearing clothes that are too tight or wearing clothes that are too large. A combination of full and narrow reads slimmer. Pants that taper to narrow at the ankle are much more flattering to a large figure than pants that are too wide. Watch pant length—pants should cover the heel of the shoe in back and break slightly in front. To appear taller, avoid color blocking—wearing one color on top and one color on the bottom. Related colors or dark neutrals are interesting and will look better.

With regard to fabric choice, Leona Rocha, Vogue patterns fashion consultant says, "The large woman can take advantage of strong prints that would overwhelm a smaller sized figure. Count on bright colors for day and more subdued shades for night."

Don't be afraid to use large scale fabric designs or bright colors; both can change a so-so outfit into a spectacular one. One color outfits create a longer look than color blocking top and bottom.

If you want an additional accent of color on the outfit, try it at the collar or cuffs. Accessories—a great necklace or bold earrings—are another way to get a shot of color as well as direct the interest toward the face. Avoid fabrics that are overly textural; those add weight.

Fabrics should be soft and drapey. Wool jersey, cotton knit, rayon challis, and wool crepe are excellent choices.

Remember to wear hose that are color related to skirt or pants. Feminine shoes are flattering, whereas clunky shoes make the foot appear wide and heavy. Mid-calf is the best skirt length for the cylinder shape, giving length to the silhouette.

In styling, avoid wide waistbands, midriff inserts or peplums. Instead, go for elasticized waistbands, faced waistlines, and blouson styling. A straight skirt with a long straight tunic will always be a great look. Avoid

Cylindrical Silhouette

yokes, which cut the body in half, and high necks. V-necklines and scoops are more flattering, as well as more comfortable.

The bodice should be well fitted from the armhole to the neck. Raglan sleeves often do better than set-in sleeves. Use proper buttonhole placement over the bust area to avoid pulling and gaps. The large figure often has sloping shoulders; this can be corrected by wearing shoulderpads, which also give balance to the large hip. Avoid sleeveless or short sleeves, opting for $\frac{3}{4}$ length or rolled up sleeves. The longer sleeve length draws attention to the forearm which is attractive on almost all women.

"Fit is crucial to comfort," Rocha adds, "Armholes should be an extra $1\frac{1}{2}$ inches deep." For sleeve comfort, try cutting the sleeve on the bias. Of course, that will not work with plaids and stripes.

A bias cut sleeve often allows the large figure comfort with a smaller sleeve, and eliminates the need to add extra fabric at the side seam to ease in a larger sleeve. For the fuller arm, ease the entire sleeve cap from underarm seam to underarm seam. Do not limit the ease between the notches. More comfort is accomplished by ease well distributed around the entire armhole.

Always direct the attention toward the face with necklines or open collars. Larger accessories, including watches, are more in proportion to the large figure than smaller, insignificant pieces. Bold earrings, one-of-a-kind necklaces, or beautiful scarves are effective ways of drawing the eye toward your assets and away from your liabilities.

■ To instantly upgrade a moderately priced ready-to-wear garment, just change the buttons.

■ "The kind of fibers (wool, silk, cotton, etc.) and the pattern in which the fibers are woven (twill, crepe, broadcloth, etc.) determine how the fabric feels and falls," says Clare Revelli in *Style & You.*

■ Silk crepe de chine is available in 2-ply, 3-ply, and 4-ply. For top quality silk evening pants, 4-ply gives the weight and drape you desire.

Petite Style

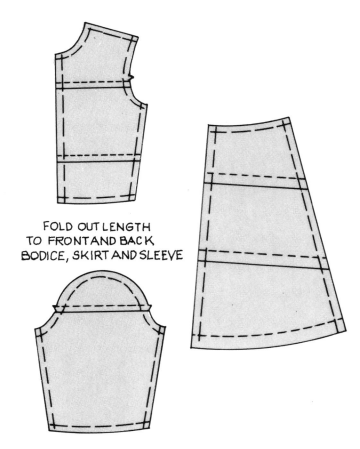

FOLD OUT LENGTH
TO FRONT AND BACK
BODICE, SKIRT AND SLEEVE

"A petite woman can be chic and stylish if she rejects cutesy clothes, juvenile prints, ruffles and wholesome 'Alice in Wonderland' hairstyles. Don't settle for the cute little girl image," says Susan Ludwig, author of *Petite Style*. Dressing for the petite woman is often a chore, dictated by long-standing axioms such as: "Never wear big prints; always wear high heels; never wear cuffs; scale down jewelry." *Petite Style* challenges the reader to reexamine those beliefs and develop her own personal style. *Petite Style* is well photographed and presented in an easy-to-read format.

Ludwig doesn't ignore all of the rules for petites, she merely advises when and how to break them so that petites don't feel so limited in their wardrobe options. "Earrings the size of a quarter are not large enough," Ludwig advises. "Bring the eye up to the most expressive part of your body, your face. Wear significant accessories.

Petites often believe that by wearing one color they will appear taller. This axiom may be extremely limiting when choosing separates. To achieve a lengthening effect, "Wear colors of the same intensity, such as a mint green skirt and peach jacket. Wear a blouse in a contrasting color under a jacket or cardigan in the same color as skirt or trousers. Wear different colors in accessories, carrying the color from head to toe.

Petites can wear any skirt length, simply "don't end a skirt at the widest point of the calf," Ludwig advises. Petites do not always have to match hose to shoes. Try matching skirt and hose, introducing a new color in the shoe.

Repositioning buttons, shortening sleeves and hems, shortening elastic, tapering the torso, and repositioning pockets are just a few of the alterations Ludwig addresses. In addition, she advises petites on choice of fabrics: "Keep prints in proportion to your figure, no larger than your hand. Select plaids with dominant vertical lines. Avoid stiff bulky fabrics which reflect light," she says.

If you are 5-feet-3-inches or less, a total scaling down of the pattern will be necessary in order to make the style look in proportion to you. If the pattern is described as "very loose fitting," buy one size smaller than you normally purchase to scale down the designer ease more to your proportions.

Petite Style

Most patterns for women 5-feet-3-inches or under will need to be shortened above the waist—not just in one place, but in two. Scale down the pattern between the shoulder and the armhole as well as the armhole and the waist.

You might want to pay a dressmaker to determine all the alterations needed on a very fitted style. Pay her to fit a basic to your figure and then to transfer all the adjustments to the tissue pattern. Stabilize the tissue pattern with press-on interfacing and write the alterations in different color felt tip pens for additions and subtractions. Use the pattern pieces as reference for alterations on other patterns.

If you under 5-feet-3-inches, try these adjustments for scaling down the bodice. Fold out $\frac{1}{4}$ to $\frac{1}{2}$ inch horizontally at the notch point in the armholes, front and back. Fold out the corresponding amount $\frac{1}{4}$ to $\frac{1}{2}$ inch in the sleeve at the notch point. These alterations will shorten the distance between the shoulder and armhole, preventing gaping necklines and bulging lapels. Now, shorten the distance between the armhole and the waistline at the "lengthen-shorten line" as indicated on the pattern. Shorten between $\frac{1}{2}$ to $1\frac{1}{2}$ inches on front and back bodice depending upon how short-waisted you are. These adjustments are important for proper shaping even if a waistline seam is not involved.

On the figure 5-feet-3-inches and under, skirt shortening is always necessary. To maintain the style of the skirt, never cut more than 2 inches off the bottom. Shorten the 2 inches at intervals throughout the body of the skirt.

■ An underlining adds opaqueness and depth to light-colored fabrics, preventing seam allowances and inner construction from showing through to the right side of the garment.

■ Make less but make only things you love.

■ Taping the roll line is mandatory on all tailored and shawl collared garments to prevent the garment from standing away from the body in this area.

THE FINER POINTS

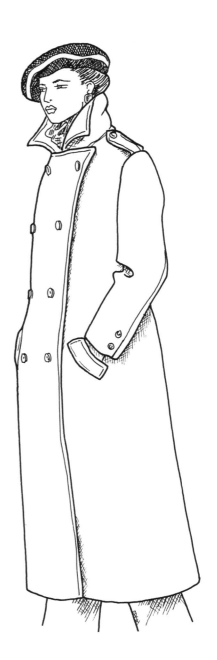

AMERICAN SEWING GUILD

If you would like to connect with other sewers in your area, the American Sewing Guild is a nonprofit organization which provides sewing information through lectures, classes and newsletters. To find the chapter nearest you contact: ASG, National Headquarters, P.O. Box 8476, Medford, OR 97504, (503) 772-4059.

■ Never machine baste underlining to garment pieces. Hand basting prevents the puckered seam resulting from too much machine stitching

Knowing
When to Stop

I was 40 years old before I realized that a truly chic look was not possible by making every item in the outfit. To be specific, until this time, I made the skirt, the leather belt, knitted the sweater, and restrung the beads to create one-of-a-kind necklaces. I even considered taking a class in making shoes! In retrospect, every item was so unusual, so interesting, so textural, that the final result screamed "homemade."

Being craft-oriented and always trying to save money, the home sewer may attempt, as I did, to make everything. Unfortunately, she is often disappointed with her "look" because it lacks the sophistication and polish of her "off-the-rack" friends.

Guilt is the first hurdle the home sewer must overcome toward the goal of chic dressing. Just because you are good with your hands does not mean you have to make everything. If a friend is visibly disappointed when you answer, "No, I bought it, isn't it wonderful?"—this is her problem—not yours. Give yourself permission to buy that great belt or fabulous necklace that will pull the whole outfit together. Unless your specialty is accessories, aren't you always a little disappointed in your homemade purses and belts?

If money is a problem, stop making so many outfits and concentrate on putting one great one together. Consider starting with the accessories. I am often inspired by a great pair of shoes or a belt. Due to the wide range of available fabrics, it is often easier to match the fabric to the accessory than the reverse. If you find a fabulous sweater, build a whole look around it. Take the sweater with you when you pick out the fabric for a skirt and a jacket. Give the sweater more mileage by making a pair of pants as well.

Unless you have unlimited funds, never purchase an accessory which goes with only one outfit. A well chosen accessory will go with many things in your wardrobe. If you think of an accessory as a friend, you will never purchase an accessory you do not love. Never buy impulsively. Visit the item in the store several times before you give it a home.

If you follow this advice, people will stop saying, "Did you make it?" and start saying, "You look fantastic."

■ European women shop with a specific need in mind. American women often shop for recreation, giving little or no thought to where the item will fit into their wardrobe. This practice leads to bad choices.

Texture and Color Create Pizazz

Despite being well put together, many outfits lack interest or a certain pizazz which makes the outfit complete as well as exciting. Perhaps you have fallen into a rut with monochromatic dressing which, although flattering, may be quite boring. A touch of unexpected color in a scarf, belt, or shoe may add just the interest the garment needs. If you like black or white as neutrals but find neither color your best friend, add a flattering color near your face with a scarf, blouse or sweater.

Both French and Italian women have developed a reputation for being both well dressed and original. For starters, the European woman buys far less than the American woman, bringing into her wardrobe only the items which will coordinate with others she already owns. Clothes are considered an investment, one which is not taken lightly. French and Italian women also tend to be more daring, combining unusual fabric and color combinations. Fabric textures are mixed—nubby with smooth, matte with shiny. If your wardrobe lacks excitement, separate your closet into colors and begin combining items which you have not tried before.

How about a satin shirt with denim pants, a tweed jacket with velvet pants, a linen blouse with lightweight wool flannel? Mixing pieces keeps your look from becoming so predictable, making dressing more fun, too.

In addition to texture, excitement can be created with interesting color combinations. Look for these when perusing fashion magazines and decorating books.

Experiment with different color combinations in your own wardrobe; try blending soft pastels which have the same color intensity, or mix vibrant colors to create a whole new look. Blend unexpected neutrals such as black with brown, red with brown, brown with burgundy. Accent with metallic tones.

Every season has its fashion colors. Give your wardrobe an instant update with one of the season's new colors in a scarf, shirt, shawl, belt, purse, stockings, socks or shoes.

■ Some pieces of clothing become friends, worn years after their original purchase. Analyze these pieces and you will find elements of your personal style.

Confessions of a Personal Shopper

Have you dreamed of a personal shopper who could weed out those duds and fill your wardrobe with exciting separates, which could be mixed and matched for a hundred different looks? Take a few tips from Lynne Ferris Associates, based in San Francisco to whip your wardrobe in shape.

Do not buy on impulse. Shop with a definite plan and shopping list based on solid fashion trends (not fads) to update your wardrobe, combined with what you already have. Include special events as part of your wardrobe plan. Buy the best you can afford.

Limit your wardrobe to a few basic colors (based on colors flattering to you), using complimentary colors as accents. Until you have built a solid basic wardrobe, buy (or make) clothing in units—jacket, skirt, pants and top in the same color. For best selection, shop for Spring in the beginning of March, Fall in the beginning of September. Do not be afraid to try new looks.

Always keep your eyes open for unusual accessories which work with your personal style. Always accessorize what you have before buying another outfit.

Bring swatches or clothing you wish to match when you shop. Shop alone or with a consultant—not a friend. Do not shop when extremely stressed or hurried. This results in poor decisions. Arrive early in the day. Do not shop until you drop. Take short breaks. Know when to quit.

No matter how much you spend on clothes (or fabric), if your hair or makeup are ignored, clothes do not matter.

If your wardrobe needs a face lift and the task seems overwhelming, maybe you should consult a personal shopper. Most individuals who use personal shoppers actually save not only time but money, since the items they do purchase are worn, not just hung in the closet.

Secrets
of a Traveler

As spokesman for the Sewing Fashion Council, I find myself rethinking travel wardrobes as I go from city to city appearing on local television talk shows. This is what works for me. To begin with, get yourself a lightweight yet durable suitcase preferably one that can be considered a carry-on. A few trips in and out of an airport will make you resent the extra weight involved in

a. maeda

leather luggage. Invest in a large but lightweight soft tote that can accommodate cosmetics, a book, magazines, snacks and structured leather box for your jewelry.

Since terrific accessories are hard to find and expensive, don't risk their disappearance in a checked suitcase. In fact, anything you can't live without for 24 hours should be inside this tote.

For the wardrobe itself, check the weather forecast before you pack. I once arrived in St. Louis in a snowstorm without a coat. Travel light and think layers; lightweight clothes can be layered for warmth. All clothes should be color related so that pieces can be interchanged. One primary color scheme requires only two pairs of shoes: The casual ones you wear on the flight and another dressier but comfortable pair. Shoes are heavy—take as few as you dare. Take one primary color scheme which also works with your small soft purse and your giant tote, so you can look put together at all times.

Travel is hard on hose—take two to three extra pairs of color matched hose. Take a slip. Nothing is worse than looking in the full length mirror at the hotel and discovering you need the slip you left at home. Pack an extra pair of shoulderpads in case you lose one.

Separates in knits are my favorite way to travel: Cotton knits for warm weather, wool jersey for cold weather. No matter how wrinkled a knit can get in a crammed suitcase, wrinkles can be removed by hanging the garment in the bathroom.

Layered, unstructured coats are my secret to warmth, rain, and versatility. Make three such coats from the same pattern: One in the same fabric as the knit separates to finish and dress up the look. One in a tweedy fabric coordinating with the first that can be layered for warmth or worn on the plane (doesn't show the dirt). One in a wrinkled nylon or rib stock that can be stuffed in the tote ready for an unexpected rainstorm.

If you take a lot of anything, it should be scarves, pins, and earrings. Accessories can dress your separates up or down and provide a focal point for your outfit.

Inspiration

Where do successful designers get their inspiration? Designers get ideas from many sources: Street fashion, vintage clothing, architectural design, sculptural forms or simply by fabric experimentation on the human body. Few home sewers have either the time or the talent to be inspired in these ways. Let's explore some creative ideas which might work for you.

Spectacular outfits rarely start with a piece of fabric. Although we have been told, "Let the fabric tell you what to do," often the fabric refuses to speak. If you collect unique jewelry, consider creating a garment as a backdrop to show off an art piece. For example, knowing the length and shape of a necklace enables you to choose a compatible neckline. An unusual pin might inspire a jacket where the pin becomes the focal point. An outstanding belt demands a pattern with design emphasis on the waistline.

Working from accessories to fabric also has the advantage of being able to match color hues. Do you remember making a spectacular dress or suit and being unable to find any color compatible shoes or hose? Wide color range is seldom available. Every season may feature a green and a brown but each season the tones or color values will be different. Color matching will always be easier working from accessories to a fabric rather than the reverse. This process also enables you to build a wardrobe around a color family. A great pair of boots can go with everything you make.

Since coat construction is time-consuming and expensive, choose a coat fabric which works with numerous outfits. A muted tweed in your favorite colors can work with everything you own. Buy 1/8 yard samples of fabric possibilities. Run these sample choices through your closet. Choose the most versatile fabric.

Inspiration

When you find a pattern which works for your figure and life-style, make it in a series of fabric for different variations, perhaps once in a knit, once in a soft drapey woven and finally in suede. A great outfit is one that you never get tired of and always feel good in.

If you own a piece of fabric which you love but which fails to inspire you, find another compatible fabric which might make it more interesting. Companion fabric might be used for contrasting piping, welt pockets, neckband under collar or cuffs. For a challenge, combine two or three fabrics in the same garment. If the available fabric seems less than exciting, buy fabric paints from a craft shop and paint your own.

Keep a running list taped to the inside of your closet door of items you wish you owned. These can be mates to items you already have. Cut from magazines pictures of garments you can see yourself in. Look for similar silhouettes in the pattern books. For style and fabric compatibility, take note of what fabrics are being used in the industry.

■ "Coats infused with the spirit of the wind." Issey Miyake, describing his wind coats collection.

■ Double-faced basting tape can prevent shifting when sewing on plaids

Tricks to Look Thinner

Forget dieting after your holiday indulgence—get some optical illusions working in your favor. Try these tricks.

The outside silhouette is created by you, but the inside silhouette is created by styling details which cut the width of the silhouette into smaller sections, making you appear longer and thinner.

Piped seams are not just a great way to show off your sewing skill and creativity; they also add vertical lines. Dig into that button collection and line up rows of contrasting color buttons for another vertical line. Choose piping or buttons; both might be overkill.

Color blocking is not for you. Dress in one-color schemes. Sounds boring, but it doesn't have to be. Several shades of dark green or burgundy can be dramatic. Forget black; everybody trying to look thin wears black—but do they really look thin? If you have great legs and the height to carry it off, you could risk a contrasting color band at the hem, but never at the waist.

Avoid nubby, puffy, textured or thick fabrics such as melton. They add unneeded pounds. Go for the flat weaves in fabrics which drape close to the body. Several layers of drapey wool jersey or wool crepe will be far more flattering than a suit in wool gabardine.

High-waisted skirts and pants add length to the legs but can also attention to the tummy. High-waisted styles can work if they fit loosely over tummy and hip.

No one with a waistline larger than 33 inches should be belting at the waist unless the belt is worn inside a jacket where only the buckle shows. Terrific buckles keep the eye off the circumference.

Match hose and shoes to the color of your skirt to appear taller. Avoid clunky shoes. Choose feminine styles but avoid ankle straps; visually, they cut the length of the leg.

If you have a round face and a round body, avoid repeating roundness with curved jacket edges and curved patch pockets. Look for angular detailing such as welt pockets on a slant, pointed rather than rounded lapels and squared-off jacket bottoms.

Spend a fortune on great earrings, important necklaces, beautiful scarves. These accessories direct the attention to the face, which looks relatively unwrinkled since it is usually filled out a bit like the rest of the body.

Belts for the Thick Waisted

For most women, middle age brings not only a few more wrinkles, but a few more pounds as well, which seem determined to stay right under the belt regardless of good intentions and exercise.

Belt-lovers, beware. You may have to rethink this issue. Eye-catching belts are rarely flattering when the waist is larger than 33 inches. This does not mean you can't wear a belt, but your choice of belts is different.

A belt will be more flattering if the color is matched to both the skirt and bodice. A buckle that attracts the eye is terrific because it draws attention away from the circumference. Belting loose over the hip is another option, more flattering than the cinched-in look. Try flexible links in gold or silver, belted loosely at a slight angle.

Now for the problem of tummy camouflage. An oversized man's vest worn unbuttoned does the trick. Yoked waistlines are out of the question. High waisted pants worn loose can be very flattering. Tight waistbands only emphasize the problem.

This season's chemise, a waistless dress, gives a terrific silhouette to the wide-waisted figure. The straight line between the bust and the hip gives only the illusion of a waist. A loose, but not baggy, fit skims the hip, giving a taller, more sleek silhouette. Straight, chemise-shaped, long sweaters worn with slim pants or straight skirts can also be a friend to the thick waist.

Short jackets and fitted shapes are not sympathetic to this figure. Longer, straighter shapes will add height and hide the problem. If you love fitted clothing, full peplums and large shoulderpads will create better waist definition.

Three-quarter length sleeves, created by rolling up a cuff on a jacket, give focus to smooth forearms, which can be adorned with beautiful bracelets.

Perhaps most important is not to spend any more energy wishing your middle were smaller. Fashion is based on optical illusion. Eventually you will just forget about your large waist and accept it as part of you.

Closet Revamp

Spring is coming and it's time to tackle the closet again. Get the discard bag ready. To begin with, take out anything which doesn't fit, is uncomfortable, or unflattering in either color or style. These garments will never be worn. Next, pick out the separates that have nothing to go with them. Try them on. Are they worth making a mate for? If so, hang them on the closet door. If not, discard.

Organize your closet one of two ways—either by color or by separates. Color organization often increases the options of what goes with what. Review outfits which get continuous wear. What makes them favorites? Perhaps a similar outfit in another color would be just as popular.

My favorites seem to be simple dresses in architectural shapes in wool or cotton knit which can be dressed up or down depending on the way they are accessorized, My favorite pair of pants is black suede, in a classic style, which never wrinkles and has an elastic waist.

Perhaps you need a jacket to pull some of these outfits together. Make a jacket which will work with all styles. To accomplish this, the pattern must have a deep armhole to accommodate set-in, dolman, and raglan sleeves. A wool tweed is a good choice for fall, a silk tweed good for spring.

What garments did you wish for last spring? Perhaps a black linen jacket, a white flannel skirt or white linen tailored trousers? Get a jump on the season and make these classics right now.

Check out your shoe inventory. Get your favorites in good repair; new heels and a shoe shine. What's the status of your everyday purse?

Start a list of things you not only want to sew next season but those you'll need to buy to pull your look together. Maybe you need a slip to go under that white skirt, or a new supply of color-matched hose—take the skirt and shoe along for a perfect match. Buy two or three pairs of hose in a favorite color. No khaki hose were available last season so I was grateful for an extra pair of two from a previous one.

If you plan to do some traveling, think through travel outfits carefully. Dark colored knits in cotton and wool conceal dirt and wrinkles better than their pastel counterparts. Lighten up the look with bright accessories. Sew both dressy and casual versions in the same fabric. A terrific top could have a straight mid-calf skirt, shorts, or a miniskirt, and a pant companion. Flat sandals could work with all three styles and get three very different looks. Travel light. Wear one and take two other favorite outfits at most. Let accessories give the outfit a different look; they are lighter to carry than everything needed for a whole new color scheme.

Wardrobe Gaps

If you are in a quandary about what garment to sew next, a good look at your wardrobe will reveal needed items that can put other pieces into service.

How about the beautiful blouse or sweater you bought last fall that never quite went with anything you own?

How about a replacement for those black suede pants you've worn three times a week for the lasts two years? Aren't the shiny knees beginning to bother you?

Once a season gets into full swing, we rarely find the time to pull the looks together.

Begin by buying two or three fashion magazines. Go through each magazine, taking notes on fashion trends. Notice skirt lengths and styles, amount or lack of hem fullness.

Observe shoulders. Are they getting bigger, smaller, rounder or squarer? Is the waist emphasized or de-emphasized? What style and width belts are featured?

Study the silhouette. Are the shapes close to the body or loose? What fabrics are featured? What colors are repeated magazine after magazine? Study the styling details carefully-many of these details can be incorporated into patterns you already own.

Once you are familiar with the coming trends, find a few that will work for you. Be realistic. If you are older than 40, the miniskirt is out. If your waist is larger than 30 inches, forget the wide belt.

To appear in fashion, one needs only to add a few new looks to update the existing wardrobe. Accessories may be all you need to give your favorites a contemporary look. Search through your personal stash of jewelry for a great item you may have forgotten about.

If you have already built a wardrobe in black, accessories may be the only thing you need to add this season. Accessories are what give the shot of color to simple, elegant styling. If you can afford a pair of gloves, buy them in suede in one of the season's hot colors. Team this up with a standard or oversized beret or matching scarf and you have created a look that makes you stand out from the crowd.

Scarves and shawls can be used to add character, color, and texture to an outfit.

If your hair is long enough, take advantage of beautiful bows, flowers and combs to pull the hair softly away from the face. Now armed with your new knowledge, go back into your closet. Look carefully at your wardrobe. Perhaps a longer, fuller skirt will bring that sweater up to date. Perhaps narrowing the legs on your pants will make them compatible with your long top. Maybe a larger pair of shoulderpads can give more emphasis to your softly tailored jacket. If you like belts, splurge on a new one. Go through your hose drawer.

Matching hose color with skirt and shoes is an easy trick to make you appear taller or slimmer.

Sewing Vacation

If you love to sew and would consider a week of uninterrupted sewing paradise, consider a sewing vacation. Since all of my four children and my husband love to ski, we spend one or two weeks a year at Squaw Valley in the Sierra. Not being a skier myself, my week is a genuine vacation: quiet—no telephone, no children or friends to distract, a blissful time indulging in my favorite hobby—sewing.

The secret to a successful sewing vacation is bringing everything you need. Since I have done this numerous times, here's my list of what to pack: shears, small scissors, seam ripper, tape measure, point turner, beeswax, clapper, zippers, hooks or buttons for closures, cording if you decorate seams, 2 to 3 hangers, an assortment of sewing machine needles, thread to match all projects, an assortment of shoulderpads, fleece for tailoring, waistband interfacing, and elastic.

Not knowing what type of cutting surface you will find, it is best to cut out, mark, interface, and overlock all projects at home. Overlocking at home eliminates one more piece of equipment. As you are doing this, think through the project and anticipate notions you might need. Even though garments are cut out, take along scrap fabric and extra interfacing in a separate bag. Every project seems to need more of one or the other before completion. Put each project with notions needed such as buttons or zippers in a plastic bag. Don't forget to include the pattern and instructions.

M. GRAYSMITH

Sewing Vacation

If you machine is big and bulky, perhaps you want to invest in a truly portable machine. Don't forget to take the instruction manual for whatever machine is accompanying you on your vacation (Most sewers need to refer to the manual whenever making buttonholes).

Since few vacation accommodations are equipped with a quality iron, take along a good steam iron like the Rowenta (model DA821 or 151) and a presscloth as well. A good pressing surface can be made with two towels on a table.

Now for one big question—how to transport these necessities to your destination? Crosby Creations manufactures a series of durable nylon foam padded bags designed for sewing machines and supplies at reasonable prices which are excellent for this purpose (see Sources).

If you are traveling by car and want to make the most of your sewing time, do a little cooking in advance. Take a big tin of cookies as well as spaghetti, pesto sauce, and homemade soup. Those won't get you out of all cooking chores, but they'll help!

■ Don't feel guilty when you sew. You could be up to much greater mischief.

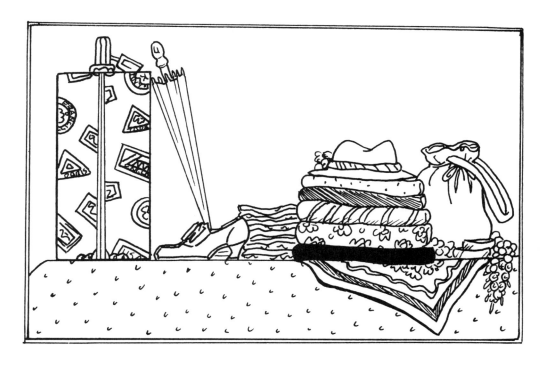

Project Burnout

"That's it! I am giving up sewing," Every sewer feels like this when a sewing project is not going well. The difference between a committed sewer and an occasional sewer is moving past the stumbling block.

Before motherhood taught me to control my temper, I used to stand up, throw the garment in the trash can, kick the trash can, and walk out of the room. Sometime during the night my subconscious would solve the problem. The next morning, I would take the garment out of the trash can and continue.

Usually one feels too much time or money or both is invested to abandon the project. Such is the case with my recent frustration making a white wool crepe suit. Once a year I take on a project that I label my epic piece. Last year was a rayon crepe hand beaded skirt. This took a week to make. This year it was the classic white dinner suit. Not only did this suit need to be lined but underlined as well. The fit was crucial since I wanted the suit to be sexy but not lewd when buttoned.

All was going well until the fourth day. To be honest, I was getting sick of working on this suit. Since the suit was white I had to remember to keep my hands and sewing area spotless. With four children, that task alone is nearly impossible, resulting in a jacket which needs to be dry cleaned even before the first wearing.

I also began to have serious doubts about how often I would really wear this suit. After all, if a white suit is such a classic, why hadn't I missed having one until now?

Well, to make a long story short, I got the sleeve lining twisted in the sleeve. Easy to fix—Yes. Willing to fix—No! I wadded up the perfectly steamed and pounded jacket, put it in a plastic bag and threw it in the closet. I would like to say that I woke up the next morning feeling refreshed and willing to put in another morning on the suit, but I didn't. I was mad—four full days wasted on a suit I will probably never wear and now don't even like. The next day I felt the same about the suit, but I did want to sew again so I tried an easy wrap skirt. I cut it out, sewed it and was wearing it within three hours. In short, the skirt looked terrific.

Later on that evening after the children were in bed, I sheepishly pulled the epic jacket out of the bag, fixed the twisted sleeve lining, re-pressed and pounded the entire jacket and tried it on. Although the jacket now looked fabulous, the entire look was tragic with no makeup and uncombed hair. A sexy white crepe dinner jacket over a flannel nightgown does not really make for a great first impression. But I knew, despite this, that this suit was not a wardrobe mistake and the time was well spent.

Project Burnout

M.GRAYSMITH ©

■ Take the phone off the hook when you sew. Peacefulness is healing.

■ Slow down. Trying to finish a garment by a deadline not only causes stress but errors as well.

Organize
Your Space

FUTURE
OF SEWING

Who Is Sewing Today?

"I don't have time to sew anymore," is no longer a valid excuse for leaving the sewing machine in the closet. Working women are the majority of the home sewing market today. The core of the market is made up of well-educated working women ages 25 to 44 who enjoy making high quality fashionable clothes in their limited leisure time. In 1973, 46% of American women sewed; in 1989, only a quarter. 85% of American households have a sewing machine. Are most in the closet?

What about our younger citizens? The average age of home sewers is now 42. The number of young people enrolled in the New York State's 4-H sewing programs has been declining—by about 56% between 1976 and 1986, for example, and sewing courses were phased out of American public schools in the late 1970s.

During the last ten years, many independent fabric stores and most fabric departments in department stores closed. Due to interest in crafts and home decorating, many of the chain fabric stores diversified and went heavily into crafts and home decorating, phasing out fine fabrics on the high end.

But because the sewer today sews for pleasure as well as love for high quality garments, the market for fine fabrics is still there, and perhaps even increased. According to Lucy Spector, owner of Britex Fabric in San Francisco: "The individual who is looking for quality fabric understands having to pay a higher price." Keeping in line with inflation, the cost of fabric has increased both for designers and home sewers.

Today, mail order may sometimes be the only option for the quality-minded sewer if she wants something unique or has a certain color in mind. Small fabric stores cannot afford to carry a large inventory.

For the woman who loves fine fabrics, many of them imported, sewing may be the answer. The rising costs of women's apparel coupled with the devaluation of the dollar is pricing many connoisseurs out of the market. Fashion savvy women are knowledgeable about the importance of accessories as well as the simplicity of the most wearable designs. The results: "Even I could make that," is often heard in better ready-to-wear departments. If, indeed, women don't have the time to sew, more and more are employing the services of a dressmaker.

According to Nancy Radelet, owner of Great Fit Patterns of Portland, Oregon, 30 million American women wear at least a size 16. Professional women want a coordinated career wardrobe. Since fitting is often a problem for the the large woman, Great Fit, supplier of patterns sizes 38 to 60, is much in demand (see Sources).

Petite women, as well, find sewing the answer to finding fashionable non-juvenile styles in small sizes, or patterns which can be scaled down to fit petite portions.

Sewing Instruction: Where/How

Help for the novice or the experienced sewer is available but needs to be sought out. Call local fabric stores and adult education sources to find out if there are sewing classes one might attend. For example, The Sewing Workshop in San Francisco addresses the needs of the novice who knows nothing as well as the advanced sewer who wants to polish skills or learn industry shortcuts to replace home sewing techniques. When making enquiries into sewing classes, be specific about your needs. Be certain the class offered covers these areas.

If sewing classes are not available in your area, inquire at the local fabric store about a dressmaker or home sewer who might agree to a few private lessons. Most home sewers would be flattered by such a proposal. Lessons from a dressmaker or tailor need not be limited to the novice. I once paid a tailor $10 to let me watch him put a zipper in a pair of men's pants. Dressmakers can also help the intermediate sewer who finds herself in a project over her head. Rather than abandon the project, seek help from a professional to move you past the hurdle.

If all else fails, take the button and the shirt to the fabric store and ask the clerk to sell you the correct needle and thread for the job. If she is not busy, perhaps she could teach you how to sew on a button. If the store is crowded, ask one of the customers. From my experience, home sewers are friendly people more than happy to share their knowledge.

Anyone who has an interest in sewing and would like to interact with others sharing this interest should consider joining The American Sewing Guild (ASG), a nonprofit national organization with a network of chapters throughout the United States. The purpose of the ASG is to provide guidance, encouragement and instruction on new techniques, trends and products. (see Sources).

Like it or not, learning to sew by video is definitely the wave of the future. Few fabric stores are able to afford the luxury of classroom space, and few cities can boast of a thriving sewing school such as The Sewing Workshop in San Francisco or G Street Fabrics in Rockville, Maryland. On the positive side, videos have the advantage of instant replay, which takes the pressure off the student to remember everything seen or said in class.

If you cringe at the thought of paying $30 or more for a sewing video, look at it this way: A good video is like sitting in the front row of a sewing class taught by an expert. You don't have to worry about scheduling conflicts or getting a babysitter—the video can be popped into the VCR at your convenience. What's more, you don't have to ask the speaker to repeat a sentence you missed while daydreaming; you can back the tape up, hear and see it again. Not only that, you have the best seat in the house with no one blocking your view.

Probably the biggest advantage to sewing videos is the opportunity to see national speakers demonstrate techniques upon which they speak with authority. An expert can visually simplify difficult concepts that are hard to clarify in print.

SEWING LIBRARY

Sewing Instruction: Where/How

Not every sewing video is a great one, but not every sewing class you take is a great one either. Fortunately, some excellent sewing videos have been produced that meet all of the above standards. Look for them in fabric stores, sewing machine shops, and sewing magazines.

Now for the $64,000 question—which videos are worth your time and your investment? By viewing a sewing video for 5 to 10 minutes, the answer will be clear. Can the speaker hold your interest? Does the delivery drag? If you are bored in five minutes, you will never sit through the whole video. What are the speaker's credentials? Does the video show the technique in process at the sewing machine with good close-up shots of the work? Does the stitching show up on the samples or are the close-ups a blur? If the cameraman was not a professional with adequate equipment, close-ups may be nonexistent, not focused on the step being discussed, or completely out of focus.

Never compare a video on price alone. Consider the running time and the expertise of the speaker. A 20 minute sewing video selling for $15.95 is a poor value compared to a 90 minute or 2 hour video selling for $34.95.

■ Incorporate sewing into your life-style, like a tennis game, lunch with a friend, reading a favorite magazine. You will be surprised at how much you accomplish.

■ Transparency of chiffon becomes less noticeable by cutting blouse fronts double or strategically placing pockets.

■ When using a fusible in jacket construction, cut fusible 1 inch longer than pattern. Fuse interfacing to fabric. Re-pin pattern and re-cut—eliminates preshrinking and interfacing.

Get Your Daughter Hooked on Sewing

a.maeda

Are you sick of allocating $150 a month for your teenager's wardrobe? Isn't it time your daughter started sewing? If she has just one or two successes with sewing, she will almost certainly be hooked, just as you are.

Take a deep breath and let your daughter really use the machine without you hovering over her shoulder. Take out the needle and let her experiment controlling speed with the foot or knee pedal. This way, the beginner quickly gains confidence without danger.

Draw circles and angles on several pieces of paper. Put the needle back in the machine. Let your novice practice control and accuracy following the markings on the paper. The reward for accuracy is threading the needle. Complete the same exercise with thread in the machine. After this has been successfully completed, insert two pieces of fabric and demonstrate sewing with a seam allowance. Leave the room and let the beginner experiment.

Now you are both ready for a trip to the fabric store. For the first garment, choose loose fitting patterns which do not require fitting skills. Good first projects are elasticized shorts and skirts and boxy T-shirts without set-in sleeves. Cotton knits and soft cottons such as Hawaiian prints are good first fabric choices. If you want interest, even enthusiasm, be sure to let the new sewer pick out the fabric, even if it is not your choice.

Give a mini lesson on layout and cutting. Sharp scissors are a must. Be available for consultation. Allow her to make her own first mistakes, stressing that ripping is a part of sewing. Don't stress perfectionism. Get caught up in the excitement. Sewing practice leads to professional results. An individual who loves sewing gets better naturally.

If you feel you do not have patience or the temperament for teaching your child to sew, find a sewing class with an enthusiastic teacher.

Don't overlook sewing video instruction. This is a video generation. Most teens would rather see it on video than hear it from you.

■ Consider putting your daughter on a clothing allowance. If she wishes to sew, credit the cost of the fabric to her clothing allowance when garment is completed.

First Aid for Stains: Act Quickly

Many a garment has been permanently stained because the owner didn't know about the first aid of stain removal and waited for the expertise of a dry cleaner.

Promptness is often the determining factor in stain removal.

Time, heat and laundering before treatment can permanently set some stains.

Do not expect instant miracles. Repeated treatment or, in some cases, soaking overnight is often necessary. It is best to use a weak solution initially, repeating several times. Rinse out cleaning solution between treatments, Test chemical solutions, bleach or solvent on a seam allowance before applying to the spot. Do not mix chemicals. Chlorine and ammonia form toxic gases when mixed.

Remember to work stain remover from the underside of a garment. Work the stain out through the direction it came. This comprehensive stain removal information was prepared by Jo Anne Ross from Washington State University.

For washable garments, try these remedies:

Coffee and tea stains: Soak in cool water, work in one teaspoon liquid detergent and one tablespoon of vinegar. If stain remains, try enzyme presoak or cleaning fluid.

Cosmetic stains and lipstick stains: Apply prewash soil remover and wash using regular detergent. Rinse thoroughly and air dry. Repeat if necessary.

Catsup and spaghetti stains: Soak in cool water for a half hour. Apply pre-wash soil remover. Rinse. Apply enzyme paste. Rinse. Add clear vinegar to last rinse.

Blood stains: Flush with cool tap water. Soak in solution of three tablespoons ammonia to one gallon cool water for about an hour. Rinse. If stain remains, try enzyme paste, soak and rinse.

Alcoholic beverages and perfume: Sponge with cool water. Soak in enzyme presoak. If stain remains, sponge with rubbing alcohol. Rinse well.

Milk and ice cream: Apply enzyme paste and soak for 30 minutes. Rinse. Saturate with prewashable soil remover. Let stand for a half hour. Wash. Rinse with a solution of 1/4 cup vinegar to one gallon water.

Shoe polish, candle wax and crayons: Remove waxed surface with a dull knife. Place the stain between two white paper towels or napkins. Press with a warm iron. If color traces remain, wash using soap (not detergent) and one cup baking soda in hottest water safe for fabric.

Vomit stains: Work in liquid detergent, soak for 30 minutes. Apply a few drops of ammonia. Flush with water. Sponge with a solution of 1/4 cup salt to two quarts water. Rinse again with water.

Some stains may be impossible to remove, but here are a few solutions to try:

Nail polish stains: Work in acetone from the underside, blotting with a white paper towel from right side. Be sure to test for fabric safeness on a seam allowance first.

Oil paints: Try to keep paint from drying by wrapping the item in plastic. Sponge with cleaning fluid, paint thinner or turpentine. Work in detergent. Rinse. Soak in hot detergent solution overnight. Wash. Air dry.

Water-based paint: Spot wash with cool water and detergent. Work in pre-wash soil remover. Rinse. Apply cleaning fluid on remaining stain. Soak spot in rubbing alcohol.

Cover with plastic for an hour. Scrub off. Repeat if necessary.

Rust spots are almost impossible. Try a product called WHINK, available in grocery stores. Works on many other spots as well. Use with rubber gloves. If this doesn't work try a solution of distilled water, lemon juice and salt for set-in stains.

■ To make an enzyme paste, combine BIZ or AXION plus enough water to make a paste. Rub into stain.

Metric Conversion Table

Metric Conversion Table

<u>mm = millimetres cm = centimetres m = metres</u>

Inches into Millimetres and Centimetres
(Slightly rounded for your convenience)

in.	mm		cm	in.	cm	in.	cm
				7	18	29	73.5
1/8	3mm			8	20.5	30	76
1/4	6mm		1 cm	9	23	31	78.5
3/8	10mm	or	1.3cm	10	25.5	32	81.5
1/2	13mm	or	1.5cm	11	28	33	84
5/8	15mm	or		12	30.5	34	86.5
3/4	20mm	or	2cm	13	33	35	89
7/8	22mm	or	2.2cm	14	35.5	36	91.5
1	25mm	or	2.5cm	15	38	37	94
1 1/4	32mm	or	3.2cm	16	40.5	38	96.5
1 1/2	38mm	or	3.8cm	17	43	39	99
1 3/4	45mm	or	4.5cm	18	46	40	102
2	50mm	or	5cm	19	48.5	41	104
2 1/2	63mm	or	6.3cm	20	51	42	107
3	75mm	or	7.5cm	21	53.5	43	109
3 1/2	90mm	or	9 cm	22	56	44	112
4	100mm	or	10cm	23	58.5	45	115
4 1/2	115mm	or	11cm	24	61	48	117
5	125mm	or	12.5cm	25	63.5	47	120
5 1/2	140mm	or	14cm	26	66	48	122
6	150mm	or	15cm	27	68.5	49	125
				28	71	50	127

Sources

American Sewing Guild, National Headquarters, PO Box 8476, Medford, OR 97504-0476; (503) 772-4059.

Bay Area Tailor Supply, 8000 Capwell Dr. #A, Oakland, CA 94621; 1-800-359-0400.

Beaded Clothing Techniques by Therese Spears (price: $6.75 ppd.), Promenade, Box 2092, Boulder, CO 80306. Fax 303-440-9116.

Bee Lee Company, Box 36108, Dallas TX 75235-1108; (214) 351-2091. Source for snaps and western trim; free catalog.

Burda Patterns: 1-800-241-6887 to find the nearest source.

Carr, Bobbie, PO Box 32120, San Jose, CA 95127; (408) 929-1651. Sewing tool and book catalogue as well as source for videos produced by Bobbie Carr.

Cinema Leathers, 1663 Blake Ave., Los Angeles, CA 90031; (213) 222-0073. Mail order leather and suede skins.

Clotilde, Inc., PO Box 22312, Ft. Lauderdale, FL 33335; 1-800-761-8655. Mail order notion supplies.

C.R. Crafts, Box 8, Dept. 12, Leland, IA 50453; (515) 567-3652. Bear and doll patterns, kits, and supplies. Catalogue: $2.

Crosby Creations, East 124 Sinto Ave., Spokane, WA 99202, 1-800-842-8445. Travel bags for sewing machines and supplies.

Daisy Kingdom, 134 NW 8th Ave., Portland, OR 97209. Mail order nursery ensembles, dress kits, craft kits, and outdoor fabrics. Catalogue $2 ppd.

Dharma Trading Co., 1-800-542-5227. Great source for fabric paints; free catalogue.

Donna Salyers' Fabulous Furs, 700 Madison Ave., Covington, KY 41011; 1-800-848-4650. Free brochure.

Erickson, Lois, PO Box 5222, Salem, OR 97304, Books on wearable art.

Fouché (Shermaine) Patterns, 2121 Bryant St., San Francisco, CA 94107. Free brochure.

Garden of Beadin, PO Box 1535, Redway, CA 95560; (707) 923-9120. Mail order beads and findings. Catalogue $2.

Geisreiter, Andrea/*Travel Handbook,* PO Box 22934, Sacramento, CA 95822.

Ghee's, 106 E. Kings Hwy., Suite 205, Shreveport, LA 71104. Handbag patterns and findings.

Great Fit Patterns, 2229 NE Burnside, Suite 305, Gresham, OR 97030; (503) 665-3125. Patterns for large sizes. Catalogue $1.

Green Pepper, Inc., 3918 W. 1st St., Eugene, OR 97402. Mail order outdoor fabrics. Catalogue $2 ppd.

Horizon Leather Corp., 38 W. 32nd St., New York, NY 10001; (212) 564-1886. Leather and suede skins.

Islander School of Fashion Arts, Inc., PO Box 66, Grants Pass, OR 97526. 1-800-944-0213. Distributor of Margaret Islander's sewing videos.

Kwik Sew Patterns, 3000 Washington Ave., N., Minneapolis, MN 55411-1699. Home catalogue $5 ppd.

Nancy's Notions, PO Box 683, 333 Beichl Ave., Beaver Dam, WI 83916. Mail order notions.

Neue Mode Patterns, 1-800-862-8586.

Ornament, PO Box 35029, Los Angeles, CA 90035. Magazine for jewelers or anyone interested in embellishment.

Paco Despacio, Buttonsmith, PO Box 261, Cave Junction, OR 97523. Write, sending fabric sample, for information.

Practicality Press, 95 Fifth Ave., San Francisco, CA 94118; 1-800-845-7474. *Power Sewing* books and videos.

Rain Shed, 707 NW 11th St., Corvallis, OR 97330. Mail order outdoor fabrics. Catalogue $1 ppd.

Ranita Corp./Sure Fit Designs, PO Box 5567, Eugene, OR 97405; (503) 344-0422. Free brochure.

Revelli Design, 1850 Union St., San Francisco, CA 94123; (415) 673-6313. Color, style and design books, videos, and kits. Free catalogue.

Ruddy, Kathy, 10207 Marine View Dr., Everett, WA 98204. Producers of *Generic Serger* Video.

San Francisco Pleating Co., 425 2nd. St., San Francisco, CA 94107; (415) 982-3003.

Sew News, Box 3134, Harlan, IA 51537; 1-800-289-6397. Monthly fashion and information sewing magazine. $23.98 for 12 issues ppd.

Sewing Machine Exchange, 1131 Mission St., San Francisco, CA 94103; (415) 621-9877. Source of Naimoto industrial iron, costs approx. $400.

Sewing Workshop, 2010 Balboa St., San Francisco, CA 94121; (415) 221-SEWS.

Shaeffer, Claire, PO Box 157, Palm Springs, CA 92263. Source for *Fabric Resource Guide.*

Stretch and Sew Patterns, 19725 40th Ave. West, Lynnwood, WA 98036; (206) 774-9678. Catalogue $3.50.

Tailor, June, Inc., PO Box 208, Richfield, WI 53076. Mail order pressing supply and information source.

Tandy Leather Co., Box 2934, Ft. Worth, TX 76113. Mail order leather and suede skins. Catalogue $2.

Tex-Mar Publications/*Silks and Satins, Couture Action Knits,* #57-10220 Dunoon Dr., Richmond, B.C. Canada V7A 1V6; (604) 277-3231.

Threads Magazine, Taunton Press, Box 355, Newton, CT 06470-9955; 1-800-283-7252

Tire Silk Thread/Things Japanese, 9805 NE 116th St., Suite 7160, Kirkland, WA 98033

Treadleart, 25834-1 Narbonne Ave., Lomita, CA 90717; 1-800-327-4222. Mail order thread and machine supplies.

Update Newsletters, PO Box 5026, Harlan, IA 51537; 1-800-444-0454. *Sewing Update* is published bimonthly for $24 per year; *Serger Update* is published monthly for $48 per year. Also in-depth booklets available by subject for $3.95 ppd. per booklet. Send for list of titles.

Worldly Goods, 848 Camino de Pueblo Bernalillo, NM 87004; (505) 867-1303. Catalogue available, please call.

Index

POWER SEWING PRODUCTS

☐ **POWER SEWING book: New Ways To Make Fine Clothes Fast**
A method which combines the step-by-step time saving techniques used in the ready-to-wear industry with the fitting and finishing techniques used in couture houses. For professional results found in ready-to-wear, you must use ready-to-wear techniques.
Hard cased, spiral bound   ISBN: 1-880630-13-3   **$29.95**

☐ **MORE POWER SEWING book: Masters' Techniques for the Sewing Connoisseur**
More Power Sewing is the second step in the Power Sewing formula, providing behind the scene tips on inner structure, pattern refinements, embellishment and finishing techniques used in better ready-to-wear or fine quality "made to measure."
Hard cased, spiral bound   ISBN: 1-880630-14-1   **$29.95**

☐ **FEAR OF SEWING book: For the Novice**
written for the non-sewer or would-be sewer intimidated by the sewing machine. Learn simple survival skills for hemming pants and skirts, fixing zippers and sewing on buttons, then see sewing as a hobby.
                ISBN: 1-880630-15-X   **$7.95**

Do you have difficulty either remembering what you saw in a demonstration or visualizing a technique you readabout? Sewing videos with camera close-ups and step by step instructions are the answer – instant replay – like sitting right next to the teacher. Available in VHS, BETA and PAL.

☐ **VIDEO #1 *FEAR OF SEWING***
How to thread and operate any sewing machine plus skirt and trouser hems, sewing on a button and much more.
82 minutes   ISBN: 1-880630-03-6   **$24.95**

☐ **VIDEO #2 PATTERN SIZING AND ALTERATION** *(formerly Pattern Smarts)*
End fitting frustration by getting the facts on which patterns run large, small, and true to size plus an easy method to determine pattern alterations.
63 minutes   ISBN: 1-880630-04-4   **$24.95**

☐ **VIDEO #3 FITTING SOLUTIONS**
See sixteen women representing a wide array of fitting challenges. See pattern alterations and final garments.
63 minutes   ISBN: 1-880630-05-2   **$24.95**

☐ **VIDEO #4 FOOLPROOF PANTS FITTING** *(formerly Class Act I)*
Secrets of European fit are revealed with this foolproof method for perfect fit, eliminating guesswork, altering the pattern before you cut.
75 minutes   ISBN: 1-880630-06-0   **$24.95**

☐ **VIDEO #5 CONSTRUCTION DIFFICULTIES** *(formerly Design Details)*
Perfect to overcome obstacles found in garment construction: fly fronts, difficult seams, sleeve vents, lapels, shoulder pads and grainline changes to flatter the figure.
120 minutes   ISBN: 1-880630-07-9   **$24.95**

☐ **VIDEO #6 EASY LININGS**
Learn lining shortcuts used in the industry which cut lining time by two thirds. Jacket, vest and pants are covered.
75 minutes   ISBN: 1-880630-08-7   **$24.95**

☐ **VIDEO #7 HASSLE-FREE DESIGNER JACKETS***(formerly Troubleshooting 1)*
Learn interfacing choices for a wide variety of fabrics as well as world-class welt pockets and handling difficult fabrics at the machine and press.
62 minutes   ISBN: 1-880630-09-5   **$24.95**

☐ **VIDEO #8 EMBELLISHMENT** *(formerly Troubleshooting 3)*
Learn embellishment techniques for multiple piping, braid application, layered trim plus hand and machine beading.
78 minutes   ISBN: 1-880630-10-9   **$24.95**

☐ **VIDEO #9 COMMERCIAL PATTERN REFINEMENTS***(formerly Troubleshooting 2)*
Refine the pattern to eliminate shoulders which ride to the back, sleeves which wrinkle, armhole stabilization for silk and tips for good looking buttonholes.
59 minutes   ISBN: 1-880630-11-7   **$24.95**

☐ **VIDEO #10 FEARLESS SERGING**
Learn to use your serger to its full potential, adjusting tension knobs and varying thread type to achieve a variety of decorative effects.
51 minutes   ISBN: 1-880630-12-5   **$24.95**

☐ **VIDEO #11 MARKETING WHAT YOU MAKE**
Get the nitty gritty on determining your market, pricing items, sewing contractors and making your first sales - from informative interviews with a designer, a sales rep and a dressmaker.
59 minutes   ISBN: 1-880630-16-8   **$24.95**

☐ **VIDEO #12 HANDWOVEN AND QUILTED GARMENTS**
Learn construction and finishing for garments in handwoven or quilted fabric. Learn suitable interfacings, seam treatments, neckline facing and hem finishes, as well as lining and closure tips.
128 minutes   ISBN: 1-880630-17-6   **$24.95**

PASS IT ON
Many of us have been sewing a long time. This hobby has brought us pleasure and satisfaction. Many schools have eliminated sewing from their curriculum. While few have time to teach someone to sew, you can turn someone on to this wonderful craft. Send them a *Fear of Sewing* book and video - only $27.95 for the combination.

☐ **COMBINATION *FEAR OF SEWING* BOOK AND VIDEO**   **$27.95**

Available in stores everywhere